FIVE PLAYS OF THE *STURM UND DRANG*

Translated from the German by

Betty Senk Waterhouse

UNIVERSITY
PRESS OF
AMERICA

LANHAM • NEW YORK • LONDON

Copyright © 1986 by

University Press of America,® Inc.

4720 Boston Way
Lanham, MD 20706

3 Henrietta Street
London WC2E 8LU England

Library of Congress Cataloging in Publication Data

Five plays of the Sturm und Drang.

   Contents: The tutor / by Jacob Michael Reinhold
Lenz — The soldiers / by Jacob Michael Reinhold Lenz —
the childmurderess / by Heinrich Leopold Wagner — [etc.]
   1. German drama—18th century—Translations into
English.   2. English drama—Translations from German.
3. Sturm und Drang movement.   I. Waterhouse, Betty
Senk, 1954-
PT1258.F56   1987   832'.6'08   86-23329
ISBN 0-8191-5671-X (alk. paper)
ISBN 0-8191-5672-8 (pbk. : alk. paper)

All University Press of America books are produced on acid-free
paper which exceeds the minimum standards set by the National
Historical Publications and Records Commission.

CONTENTS

PREFACE

The plays of the Storm and Stress movement (1771–78) in German literature have been oddly neglected by twentieth-century scholars. This inattention may be attributed, in large part, to the inaccessibility of the works to an English-speaking audience. Although "Sturm und Drang" has become a catchphrase in our language, only one monograph in English—Mark O. Kistler's *Drama of The Storm and Stress* (Twayne: New York, 1969)—deals with the subject, and not one play from the movement has ever been translated into English. It is to be hoped that this collection will rekindle interest in the "Age of Genius."

England and France were the primary sources of inspiration for the Storm and Stress dramatists. Shakespeare was their ideal for his shattering of the dramatic unities of time, place, and action; and his sharply individualized, emotionally complex characters. They considered *Hamlet* the epitome of drama, and rare is the Storm and Stress play that does not contain a contemplation of suicide by the leading man, or an Ophelia-like mad scene for the leading lady. The plays of Denis Diderot (1713–84) and those of Louis-Sébastien Mercier (1740–84) were a secondary influence because of their social realism. Diderot created and Mercier continued the *drame bourgeois*, whose themes tended to be serious rather than tragic, and which focused on the problems of the middle class.

Hallmarks of Storm and Stress drama include a bombastic, often wildly exaggerated, language; a multiplicity of scenes; the use of dialect, pantomime, and folk ballads; concentration on the problems of the middle and lower classes; anticlericalism and disdain for organized religion. Rebelling against the confinements of Aristotelian drama, the Storm and Stress playwrights demanded freedom of expression as they sought to glorify nature and individual genius. Tragedy and comedy are blended into a single genre. The unities are cast aside: the time can span three or four years, and one play is generally set in several cities. Frequently, no one character can be called the hero; rather, the audience must consider a panorama of characters ranging from the nobility to the peasantry. Many of these characters will merely be mouthpieces for the authors' ideas, having no bearing on the plot at all, yet they will receive at least as detailed a treatment as the central figures.

What distinguishes the Storm and Stress playwrights from the Romantics is their pervasive cynicism. Their characters denounce the evils of society brilliantly, yet are powerless to escape its strictures. A "happy ending" in these plays is granted only to those characters who accept their social circumstance. Even as Storm and Stress authors demand social reform, they doubt the efficacy of any solution. This "modern" perspective was to have great influence on the theatre of Grabbe, Büchner, Hebbel, Hauptmann, Wedekind, and Brecht.

THE TUTOR

OR

THE ADVANTAGES OF PRIVATE EDUCATION

A COMEDY

BY

JAKOB MICHAEL REINHOLD LENZ

1774

DRAMATIS PERSONAE

COUNCILLOR VON BERG
MAJOR VON BERG, *his brother*
MRS. VON BERG, *the* MAJOR's *wife*
GUSTCHEN, *their daughter*
FRITZ VON BERG
COUNT WERMUTH
LÄUFFER, *a tutor*
PÄTUS, *a student*
BOLLWERK, *a student*
MR. VON SEIFFENBLASE
His TUTOR
MRS. HAMSTER, *an alderman's wife*
MISS HAMSTER
MISS KNICKS
MRS. BLITZER
WENZESLAUS, *a schoolmaster*
MARTHA, *an old woman*
LISE
PÄTUS's FATHER
PASTOR LÄUFFER, LÄUFFER's *father*
LEOPOLD, *the* MAJOR's *son, a young boy*
MR. REHAAR, *a lutanist*
MISS REHAAR, *his daughter*

Act One
Scene One

Insterburg, in Prussia

LÄUFFER: My father says I am not qualified to be his assistant. I think the only inadequacy lies in his purse; he doesn't want to pay the salary. Besides, I'm too young to be a minister, too well educated, I've seen too much of the world. And I can't teach in the public schools because the councillor didn't want to hire me. So be it! He is a pedant; the devil himself wouldn't be educated enough for him. I could go back to school for six months and then apply again. Then of course I'd be much too educated to be a schoolteacher, but the councillor must know best. He keeps calling me *Monsieur* Läuffer, and when we talk of Leipzig, he asks about Händel's vegetable garden and Richter's coffeehouse and heaven knows what. I don't know if that's supposed to be satire or—now and then I've heard him talking thoughtfully enough with our assistant headmaster; presumably he doesn't take me seriously. There he comes with the major; I don't know why, I fear him more awfully than the devil. There's something in the fellow's face that I find absolutely intolerable. (*He passes by the* COUNCILLOR *and the* MAJOR *with many friendly, obsequious bows.*)

Scene Two

COUNCILLOR. MAJOR.

MAJOR: Well, what do you want then? Isn't he a pleasant enough young fellow?

COUNCILLOR: Pleasant enough, oh, only too pleasant. But what is he supposed to teach your son?

MAJOR: I don't know, Berg. You always ask such peculiar questions.

COUNCILLOR: No, honestly! You certainly must have had something in mind, to hire a private tutor, and open your purse so wide that three hundred ducats fall out. So tell me, how do you intend to justify the salary? What do you require of your tutor?

MAJOR: That he . . . well, I . . . that he teach my son all the sciences and arts and give him some polish and manners. I don't know why you keep asking me this. I'll tell him everything he needs to know in due time.

COUNCILLOR: That is to say, you want to be the tutor of your tutor. But have you considered what you're taking on? What's going to become of your son, tell me that!

MAJOR: What's going to—he's going to be a soldier, the same sort of fellow that I was.

COUNCILLOR: Put away that last thought, dear brother. Our children should not and must not become what we were. The times are changing: customs, conditions, everything, and if you had been nothing more and nothing less

3

than the exact replica of your father—

MAJOR: Good God! To become a major and as upstanding a fellow as I, and to serve the king as honorably as I!

COUNCILLOR: All well and good, but in another fifty years we'll probably have a different king and a different way to serve him. But I see already I can't get anywhere with you on this matter; I can keep asking, but I'll get no answers. You never see anything but the straight line your wife has laid down for you.

MAJOR: And what business is it of yours, Berg? Listen, stop mixing in the affairs of my family. I don't mix in yours, and—Ha! There goes your gracious young son, with two of his schoolmates. Splendid education, Mr. Philosophus! Who could possibly disagree with you? Who in the world would believe that that street urchin is the only son of His Excellency, the Privy Councillor?

COUNCILLOR: Let him be! His fun-loving friends are less corrupting than some liveried idler, supported by some vain patroness.

MAJOR: You're getting a little too free with your comments. Adieu!

COUNCILLOR: I'm sorry for you.

Scene Three

MRS. VON BERG's *room*
MRS. VON BERG *is seated on the settee.* LÄUFFER *sits next to her in a very submissive attitude.* LEOPOLD *stands.*

MRS. VON BERG: I have spoken with your father, and instead of that three hundred ducats salary we agreed on one hundred and fifty. For that, however, I require in addition, Mr.—What is your name?—Mr. Läuffer, that you always be presentable, in clean clothes, and that you bring no shame upon our house. I know that you have taste; I had already heard about you while you were still in Leipzig. You know that these days people notice nothing about a man so much as whether he knows how to conduct himself.

LÄUFFER: I hope madam will be satisfied with me. In Leipzig at least, I never missed a ball, and I've had well over fifteen dancing-masters in my life.

MRS. VON BERG: Oh? Let me see. (LÄUFFER *stands.*) Not so timidly, Mr.—er—Läuffer! Not so timidly! My son is bashful enough; if he's stuck with a bashful tutor, he's done for. Come on, try now, bow to me and dance a minuet, just a test, so I can see. Well, now, that's just fine! I won't have to hire a dancing-master for my son! And now a pace-step, if you would. That will do fine; it looks as if you'll be able to fit in at our soirees . . . are you musical?

LÄUFFER: I play the violin and, in a pinch, the piano.

MRS. VON BERG: So much the better for when we go to the country and Miss Milktooth visits us. Up to now I've always had to sing something for them, when the dear children felt like dancing, but this will be better .

LÄUFFER: I am beside myself, madam. Where is there a virtuoso on earth who

4

might hope to match the perfection of madam's voice on his instrument?

MRS. VON BERG: Ha, ha, ha! You haven't heard me yet . . . wait a minute, do you know the minuet? (*Sings.*)

LÄUFFER: Oh . . . oh . . . forgive the rapture, the enthusiasm that tears me apart. (*Kisses her hand.*)

MRS. VON BERG: I am catching cold; I must be cawing like a crow. *Vous parlez français, sans doute?*

LÄUFFER: *Un peu, Madame.*

MRS. VON BERG: *Avez-vous déjà fait votre tour de France?*

LÄUFFER: *Non, Madame . . . oui, Madame.*

MRS. VON BERG: *Vous devez donc savoir, qu'en France, on ne baise pas les mains, mon cher . . . .*[1]

SERVANT (*enters*): Count Wermuth . . . .

(COUNT WERMUTH *enters.*)

COUNT (*after a few stiff bows, sits next to* MRS. VON BERG *on the settee.* LÄUFFER, *self-consciously, remains standing*): Madam, have you already seen the new dancing-master, just arrived from Dresden? He is a marquis from Florence, and is called—frankly, I've only met two in my travels that I would prefer to him.

MRS. VON BERG: That astounds me, only two! You make me curious indeed; I know what extremely refined taste Count Wermuth has.

LÄUFFER: Pintinello, right? I've seen him dance in Leipzig at the theater; there's nothing remarkable about his dancing.

COUNT: His dancing—*on ne peut pas mieux*[2]—as I was saying, dear lady, in Petersburg I did see Beluzzi, and he *is* to be preferred, but this one has a lightness in his feet, something so free, so divinely negligent in his bearing, in his arms, in his turns—

LÄUFFER: The last time he appeared at Cook's Theater, he was booed off the stage.

MRS. VON BERG: See here, my lad, domestics do not engage in conversation with people of quality! Go to your room at once! Who asked you to speak?

(LÄUFFER *falls back several steps.*)

COUNT: Presumably the tutor that you employed for your young son?

MRS. VON BERG: And fresh out of the academy. Go at once! You hear that we are speaking of you, so it's all the less proper for you to remain. (LÄUFFER *exits, with a stiff bow.*) It's intolerable that we can't find a decent servant these days, considering all the money we pay. My husband wrote a good three times to that professor, and *this* was supposed to be the most genteel one in the whole academy. You can see it, of course, even from his clothes—trimmed on the left! Just imagine, two hundred ducats travelling expenses, from Leipzig to Insterburg, and a yearly salary of five hundred ducats! Isn't that terrible?

---

[1]MRS. VON BERG: You speak French, of course?

LÄUFFER: A little, Madame.

MRS. VON BERG: Have you made your tour of France?

LÄUFFER: No, Madame . . . yes, Madame.

MRS. VON BERG: You should know then that in France nobody kisses hands, my dear

[2]One could not do better.

COUNT: I believe his father is the parson here?

MRS. VON BERG: I don't know . . . it could be . . . I didn't ask about it . . . yes, certainly, I'm sure that's right, his name is Läuffer, too. Well, then, he certainly must be good enough, for that father of his is an absolute bear! At least he's thundered me out of the church once and for all.

COUNT: Is he a Catholic?

MRS. VON BERG: No, of course not. You know there isn't a Catholic church in Insterburg. He's a Lutheran, or Protestant, I should say. Yes, he's a Protestant.

COUNT: Pintinello dances . . . it's true, I've spent some thirty thousand guilders on my dancing already, but I would gladly spend as much again in order to . . .

Scene Four

LÄUFFER's room

LÄUFFER. LEOPOLD. MAJOR. LÄUFFER *and* LEOPOLD *are seated at a desk, a book in their hands. The* MAJOR *harangues them.*

MAJOR: Right, that's the way I like it, everybody hard at work. If the good-for-nothing won't learn, Mr. Läuffer, then smack him on the head with the book, hard enough that he can forget about getting up for a while. Or, I should say, you need only come to me with your complaint. I'll set your head on straight, you heathen! See, now, he's pouting again. Are your feelings hurt by what your father says? Well, who's supposed to say it to you then? You'll learn to treat me with more respect, or I'll beat you till your guts collapse, you spiteful little rat! And you, sir, be diligent with him, on that I insist, and no vacation or breaks or recreation. That I won't tolerate! It's all nonsense what they say, no man ever got *malum hydropisiacum* from work. That's just some excuse dreamed up by you intellectuals. How's it going, does he know his *Cornelio*? Idiot! I've told you a thousand times, for God's sake, hold your head up! Head high, boy! (*Firmly straightens him.*) Damn it all, get your head off your shoulder, or I'll break your backbone into a thousand million pieces!

LÄUFFER: Pardon me, Major, but he can hardly read Latin.

MAJOR: What? So the little scamp has forgotten. The tutor before you told me he was perfect in Latin, perfect . . . he sweated it out of him . . . well, for God's sake, I don't want to be blamed for not keeping a tight rein on you. I don't want you to turn into a good-for-nothing like young Hufeise, or your uncle Friedrich, such a good-for-nothing! I'll beat you to death first! (*Gives* LEOPOLD *a box on the ears.*) Again like a question mark? He never listens. Get out, get out of my sight! Get out! Do I have to get you moving? Get out, I say! (*Stamps his foot.* LEOPOLD *goes. The* MAJOR *sits in* LEOPOLD's *chair. To* LÄUFFER.) Keep your seat, Mr. Läuffer, I wanted to have a few words with you alone, that's why I sent the boy away. You can always

6

remain seated, always, always. Damn it, you could break the chair in two, for all the use you—that's why the chair is there, so you can sit on it. You've travelled so widely, but you never learned that. But listen now, I see you as a nice, decent sort of fellow, God-fearing and obedient, otherwise I would never do the things I do for you. I promised you a hundred and forty ducats a year, that makes three . . . wait . . . three times a hundred and forty: how much does that make?

LÄUFFER: Four hundred and twenty.

MAJOR: Right! Really, so much? Anyway, now that we have the same number, I've decided to pay you four hundred talers, Prussian currency. You see, that's more than the whole income of the estate.

LÄUFFER: But by your leave, sir, your wife promised me a hundred and fifty ducats. That makes four hundred and fifty talers and I agreed to those terms.

MAJOR: Eh, what do women know? Four hundred talers, Monsieur, you can't ask for more with a clear conscience. The man before you only got two hundred and fifty, and he was happy as a clam. And on my soul, he was certainly a learned man too, and a courtier, to boot. Everybody vouched for him, and you're going to have to go quite some way, sir, before you're anything like him. What I'm doing for you I do only out of friendship for your father, and also for your sake, if you are properly obedient. I know how to take care of you; you can be sure of that. Now just listen: I have a daughter who's the very image of me. Everybody will swear to you that her equal in beauty is not to be found in all of Prussia. The girl has quite a different temperament than my son—that cutpurse! She's the exact opposite: she knows her catechism through and through, but that's still not enough, because soon she's going to make her Communion and I know how parsons are. So every morning you should also teach her something about her catechism. One hour every morning, and for that you go to her room, *dressed*, it goes without saying, for God forbid you should be such a dirty pig as one that I had, who wanted to come to breakfast in his dressing-gown—can you also draw?

LÄUFFER: A little, Your Grace. I can show you some samples.

MAJOR (*examines them*): These are *charmants*! Well and good: you'll also teach my daughter to draw—but be careful, my fine Mr. Läuffer. Treat her gently, for God's sake, the girl has quite a different temperament from the boy. God knows, it's as if they weren't brother and sister. Day and night she's holed away with her books, her precious tragedies, and if someone says just one word to her—especially me, she can't take any criticism from me—her cheeks are on fire and tears run down her face like pearls. I just want to tell you: that girl is the only joy of my life. My wife has given me bitter-enough times; she always has to have her way and, Lord knows, she's got more tricks and strategems than I have. And our son, he's her favorite. She wants him educated according to *her* methods: right sweetly with young Absalom, and turn him into some kind of gallows-bird that isn't of any use to God or man. Well, I won't have it! As soon as he does something wrong, or looks wrong, or hasn't learned his lesson, you just tell me and I'll beat the living hell out of him. But with my daughter take care! My wife will try to persuade you to treat the girl sharply. My wife can't stand the girl, in fact, but that's of no importance whatsoever. Know this: *I* am the master of this house, and anyone who comes too close to my daughter—well, she is my one treasure,

7

and if the king would offer me his whole realm for her, I would send him away. Every day she is in my morning prayers and my evening prayers and my prayers at table and my everything in everything, and if God would grant that before I die I could see her married to a general or a minister of state—for no one else is worthy to share her life—I'd gladly die ten years earlier. Mark my words! Anyone who gets too close to my daughter, or causes her the slightest harm, gets my first, best bullet through his head. Mark my words! (*Leaves.*)

Scene Five

FRITZ VON BERG. GUSTCHEN.

FRITZ: You're not going to keep your word, Gustchen, you're not going to write to me while you're in Heidelbrunn, and so I shall grieve to death.

GUSTCHEN: Do you believe then that your Juliet is so inconstant? Now, now, I am a woman; only men are inconstant.

FRITZ: No, Gustchen, only women are. Yes, even if they all were Juliets! I know! When you write to me, call me your Romeo. Do me that favor, and I assure you I shall in every way be Romeo. I'll even carry a dagger. Oh, I can even stab myself, if it comes to that.

GUSTCHEN: Go on! Yes, you'll do it like in Gellert: he viewed the point and cutting-edge, and stuck it in again slowly.

FRITZ: You'll see. (*Takes her hand.*) Gustchen—Gustchen! If I should lose you, or if my uncle should give you to another! That ungodly Count Wermuth! I cannot tell you my thoughts, Gustchen, but you can read them in my eyes. He will be our Count Paris.

GUSTCHEN: Fritzchen! I shall be your Juliet.

FRITZ: Then what? So what? It's all make-believe. There isn't any sleeping-potion.

GUSTCHEN: True, but there are potions for eternal sleep.

FRITZ (*embraces her*): Cruel girl!

GUSTCHEN: I hear my father on the walk. Let's run to the garden. No, he's gone. We're leaving right after coffee, Fritzchen, and as soon as the carriage whisks me away, it'll be out of sight, out of mind for you.

FRITZ: May God never remember me if I forget you! But beware of the count; your mother highly approves of him, and you know she'd like to get you out of *her* sight. And do it before I finish school and—three years of the university, that is too long.

GUSTCHEN: What can we do, Fritzchen? I am still a child; I haven't even made my First Communion yet. Tell me—oh, who knows when I shall speak to you again! Wait, let's go into the garden!

FRITZ: No, no, Papa's just gone by. Damn it, he's in the garden. What did you want to say to me?

GUSTCHEN: Nothing . . .

FRITZ: Dear Gustchen . . .

GUSTCHEN: You must—no, I cannot demand that of you.

FRITZ: Demand my life, my last drops of blood!

GUSTCHEN: We should both swear a vow of fidelity.

FRITZ: Oh, yes! Marvelous! Let's kneel here on the settee. You raise your finger in the air like this, and I'll raise mine. But what should I swear?

GUSTCHEN: That in three years you will return from the university and make your Gustchen your wife, no matter what your father says.

FRITZ: And you will swear to wait for me, my angel. (*Kisses her.*)

GUSTCHEN: I swear that never in my life will I be any man's wife but yours, even if the Tsar of Russia himself asks me!

FRITZ: I swear to you a hundred thousand vows—

(*The* COUNCILLOR *enters.* GUSTCHEN *and* FRITZ *leap up with a loud cry.*)

Scene Six

COUNCILLOR. FRITZ VON BERG. GUSTCHEN.

COUNCILLOR: What's going on here? Foolish children! Why are you trembling? Right now, tell me everything! What have you been doing here? You're both on your knees. Fritz, I expect an answer this instant: what were you two doing?

FRITZ: I, Papa dearest?

COUNCILLOR: "I?" Such an innocent tone? I know what's going on: you'd like to tell me a lie right now, but you're either too stupid or too lily-livered, so you hope this "I?" will buy you time. And you, little lady? I know Gustchen would never keep anything from me.

GUSTCHEN (*falls at his feet*): Oh, my father—

COUNCILLOR (*lifts her up and kisses her*): Do you want me to be your father? Too soon, my child, too soon, Gustchen, my child. You haven't even made your First Communion yet—why should I hide that I eavesdropped on you? That was a very simpleminded little play you were putting on, especially on your part, big sensible Fritz. Soon you'll have a beard and put on a wig and wear a sword. Hmph, I thought I had a more reasonable son. But you're evidently a year younger than I thought you were; you'll have to stay at school longer. And you, Gustchen, I have to tell you as well that it isn't proper at your age to act so childishly. What kind of novels are you acting out? What kind of vows are you swearing to each other? Vows you're sure to break, as surely as I am speaking to you. Do you believe you are old enough to swear vows, or do you believe a vow is some sort of child's game, like hide-and-seek or blindman's bluff? Learn first what a vow is, learn first to tremble before it, and only then dare to swear it! You know that a perjurer is the most shameful and infamous creature that ever the sun shone upon. Such a man shall never see the Heaven to which he has lied. All men shall shun him forever and draw away from him as if he were a serpent or a vicious dog.

FRITZ: But I intend to keep my vow.

COUNCILLOR: Really, Romeo? Ha! You can even stab yourself if it comes to

9

that. Your vows make my hair stand on end. But you intend to keep your vow?

FRITZ: Yes, Papa, by God, I intend to keep it.

COUNCILLOR: A vow pledged by another vow! I shall speak to your headmaster. He should put you back in the second form for two weeks. Child, in the future learn to swear more cautiously. Why did you even try? Is it in your power to do what you have sworn? You want to marry Gustchen! Just think a minute! Do you have any idea what marriage is? Go on, marry her, take her with you to the academy! No? I don't mind that you like to see each other, that you love each other, or that you tell each other of your love. But you must give up this foolishness! No aping your elders till you've reached our ripe old age. No more living in novels, which are only hatched in the dissolute imagination of some starving poet, and which never bear any resemblance to the real world! Go! I won't tell anyone about this, so there'll be no need to go red when you see me. But from now on you two are not to see each other alone. Do you understand me? And you will not write to each other, except for general letters to the family, and even that only once a month, or at most every three weeks. As soon as a secret letter from Fritz or Gustchen is discovered, Fritz goes into the army and Gustchen into the convent until they become more reasonable. Do you understand me? Now say good-bye, here in my presence. The carriage is ready, the major is ready to leave, my sister-in-law has finished her coffee. Say good-bye, you don't need to be afraid of me. Hurry up, embrace! (FRITZ *and* GUSTCHEN *embrace each other, trembling.*) And now, my daughter, Gustchen, because you like to hear the word so much (*Raises her and kisses her.*) fare you well, a thousand times, fare you well, and treat your mother with respect, no matter what she says! Now go, go! (GUSTCHEN *takes a few steps, looks back;* FRITZ *flies to her; they embrace, crying.*) These little fools are breaking my heart! If only the major were more reasonable—and his wife less thirsty for power!

Act Two
Scene One

PASTOR LÄUFFER. COUNCILLOR.

COUNCILLOR: I feel sorry for him—and sorrier for you, Pastor, that you have a son like him.

PASTOR: Begging Your Excellency's pardon, I cannot complain about my son. He is a virtuous and well-mannered boy. The whole world and your brother and sister-in-law themselves would vouch for him.

COUNCILLOR: I don't deny any of that, but he's a fool nonetheless, and has himself to thank for all his dissatisfaction. He should thank his lucky stars that my brother is beginning to think that the money he pays his tutor is too dear.

PASTOR: But think of it: only a hundred ducats! One hundred measly ducats! When he had promised him three hundred for the first year alone! Now for the first year he'll only pay him one hundred and forty, and for the second year, even though my son's workload keeps increasing, only one hundred. And now at the start of the third year he thinks even *that* is too high. It's against all principles of justice! Forgive me!

COUNCILLOR: Quite all right. I could have told you this would happen. Your son should thank God if the major takes him by the scruff of the neck and throws him out of the house. What is he doing there, pray tell? How can you call yourself a father to your child, when you keep eyes, ears and mouth shut when his happiness is at stake? A wastrel and you let him get paid for it? To spend the noblest hours of the day with a young boy who doesn't want to learn anything, and with whom he doesn't dare quarrel. And the other hours, which should be held sacred for eating and sleeping—the maintenance of his life—to sigh on a slave chain, to hang on the slightest word of Mrs. von Berg, to read messages in the furrows of the major's brow, to eat when he's full, to fast when he's hungry, to sip punch when he'd like to piss, to sit and play cards when he'd like to run! Without freedom life runs downhill and backwards; freedom is the element of man as water is for fish, and a man who gives up his freedom poisons the noblest spirits of his blood, nips the sweetest joys of life in the bud, and destroys himself.

PASTOR: But—forgive me, but every tutor has to put up with that sort of thing. No one can have his own way all the time, and my son of course would gladly put up with that, only—

COUNCILLOR: So much the worse for him if he puts up with it, so much the worse. He's relinquished all the privileges of a man; if he can't live according to his principles he can't call himself a man. Those wretched people who don't know any higher happiness than eating and drinking may lock themselves in a cage of death, but an educated man, who is aware of the nobility of his soul, should be less afraid of death, than of acting against his principles.

PASTOR: But what in the world is he supposed to do? What would my son do if your brother withdrew the position?

COUNCILLOR: Let the boy learn something, so he can be of some use to the state.

11

Good God, Pastor, you certainly didn't raise him to be a servant. Well, what is he *but* a servant when he sells his freedom as a citizen for a handful of ducats? He's a slave and his masters have absolute power. The only difference is that he learned enough at the academy to anticipate from afar their every stupid demand, thus putting a fine veneer on his servitude. Oh, he's a nice sort of man, an incomparable man—an incomparable scoundrel! Instead of using his strength and reason for the general good, he supports the madness of a raging woman and a muzzled officer whose corruption spreads daily like a cancerous sore. Soon he'll be beyond cure, and where will it get him in the end? Bread every morning, punch every evening, and a large portion of gall rising in his throat all the day. He lies in bed at night, gulping it down—that makes for healthy blood, on my honor! And of course a splendid heart too, in the long run. You complain so much about the nobility and its pride, and that everybody treats tutors like servants. Fool! What else are they? Don't they work for their bread and board? But who orders you to nourish their pride? Who orders you to become servants, when you've learned something, to work for a pigheaded officer who was used to nothing from his men but slavish obsequiousness?

PASTOR: But, Your Excellency—merciful God! There isn't anything else. One *must* have a patron to obtain a suitable position after university; we need only then watch and await the divine call. And a patron is very often the source of our advancement. At least that's how it was for me.

COUNCILLOR: Hold your tongue, Pastor, I beg you, hold your tongue! Your opinions do you no honor. We all know that your late wife was your divine calling; otherwise you'd still be stuck at von Tiesen's, spreading dung on his fields. Ye gods! You can't take off your rose-colored glasses for an instant! Never once has a nobleman employed a tutor without painting some pretty picture of advancement. But after seven years of slavery, the tutor finds himself to be Jacob to another Laban and serves another seven. Fraud! Learn something and be honest! Honest people are needed everywhere, but the scoundrel who carries the name of scholar on a piece of paper, when his mind is a *tabula rasa . . .*

PASTOR: Those are broad statements, Your Excellency! There certainly have to be tutors in the world, for heaven's sake. Not everyone can become privy councillor, even if he be another Hugo Grotius. These days other things enter into it besides scholarship.

COUNCILLOR: You're getting excited, Pastor. Dear, esteemed Pastor, let us not lose the thread of our argument. I maintain: there must be no more tutors in the world! The vermin aren't fit for anything. Let them go to the devil!

PASTOR: I did not come here to be subjected to such rudeness. I have also been a tutor, and I have the honor—

COUNCILLOR: Wait, stay, Pastor! Heaven knows, I did not intend to insult you. If it happened accidentally, I beg of you a thousand pardons. It's a bad habit of mine to become overexcited when a conversation interests me. I lose track of everything else and see only the topic at hand.

PASTOR: But you're throwing out—forgive me, I am also a choleric man and like to raise my voice—you're throwing out the baby with the bathwater. "Tutors aren't fit for anything." How can you say that? Who should instruct your young men in reason and decent conduct? What would have become of you, Your Excellency, if you had not had a tutor?

12

COUNCILLOR: My father sent me to public schools. I bless his ashes for it as, I hope, my son will someday bless mine.

PASTOR: Yes, well—there's still more to say about this, sir! For my part, I don't share your opinion, not even if the public schools were what they should be. But the stultifying *subjecta* so often taught in those classes, the pedantic methods they use, the disgusting habits that prevail there—

COUNCILLOR: Whose fault is that? Who's responsible for that except you scoundrelly tutors? Aren't you just encouraging the nobleman to enjoy his own little whims, to have his own little court where he can be the monarch sitting on his throne, while his tutor, housekeeper, and a whole herd of idlers do him homage? Better he should send his children to public school, better he should spend the money he now wastes turning his son into an aristocratic idiot on the funding of public schools. Then educated people could be paid to teach there, and everything would proceed very nicely. The students would have to learn something in order to be of use at such an establishment. The young nobleman, instead of having to hide his uselessness artfully and genteelly from Papa and Auntie, who hardly have the hundred eyes of Argus, would have to exert his mind to stay ahead of the middle-class boys—if indeed he *wants* to be distinguished from them. You're right, manners *are* a problem. Our stupid aristocrat learns from earliest infancy to carry his nose high, and to speak nonsense loftily and carelessly, and to expect people to doff their hats to him, while he troubles himself only to make clear that he need not return the courtesy. The devil take his fine manners! Engage dancing-masters privately for the boy, if you want, and introduce him into good society, but he must not be removed from the sphere of his schoolmates, and reinforced in the opinion that he is a better creature than others.

PASTOR: I haven't time (*Takes out his watch.*) to argue with you further, sir, but I know that most of the nobility would not share your opinion.

COUNCILLOR: No, but the middle class should. Necessity would soon bring the nobility to a different opinion, and we could promise ourselves better times. Damn! What's going to become of us aristocrats, when one man is supposed to be our child's factotum? Even if you make the impossible assumption that he would be a polymath, where would he find the fire and valor needed for his profession if he has to concentrate all his powers on one sheep's-head? Especially when the father and mother keep mixing helter-skelter in the education time and again, knocking holes in the bucket he's trying to fill.

PASTOR: I have to be at a sickbed at ten. You will excuse me. (*As he leaves, he turns.*) But wouldn't it be possible, sir, that you could board out your son with the major? My son will be quite satisfied with eighty ducats, but with the sixty that your brother wants to pay him, he cannot survive.

COUNCILLOR: Let him quit! No, I won't do it, Pastor! From that I am not to be dissuaded. I would rather just send your son the thirty ducats than entrust my son to a tutor. (*The* PASTOR *hands him a letter.*) What am I supposed to do with this? It's no good arguing, I tell you.

PASTOR: Read it . . . just read it.

COUNCILLOR: Now, look, there's really nothing I can do. (*Reads.*) "Will you do everything in your power to get Councillor von Berg to . . . you cannot imagine how wretched things are for me here. Nothing that was promised to me has been given. I only eat with the adults when no friends are visiting.

The most galling of all is that I have been absolutely forbidden to leave here. In a whole year I have not been able to take one step out of Heidelbrunn. They had promised me a horse, and that I could travel every three months to Königsberg. When I reminded them of this, the dear lady asked me if I wouldn't prefer going to the carnival in Venice." (*Throws the letter to the ground.*) So then, let him quit. Why is he such a fool as to stay there?

PASTOR: Yes, yes, you're right, of course. (*Picks up the letter.*) Please, just read it to the end.

COUNCILLOR: What is there to read? (*Reads.*) "Nevertheless I cannot leave this house, though it should cost me my livelihood and my health. I write to you all the hardships of my present station in expectation of a more blessed future."—Yes, perhaps he has expectations of a blessed eternity; otherwise I know of no expectations my brother is planning to satisfy. He is deceiving himself, believe me. Write him back that he is a fool. I shall give him thirty ducats extra pay this year from my own purse, but I require for my money that I be spared all further attempts to recruit my son Karl. I shall not ruin my son in order to please yours.

Scene Two

Heidelbrunn
GUSTCHEN. LÄUFFER.

GUSTCHEN: What's the matter with you?

LÄUFFER: How is my portrait coming? You haven't thought about it, right? If I had chosen to dawdle so . . . if I had known, I would have withheld your letter just as long, but I was a fool.

GUSTCHEN: Ha, ha, ha! Dear tutor! I really have just not had time for it.

LÄUFFER: How horrible!

GUSTCHEN: But what's bothering you? Tell me! You're brooding all the time, your eyes are always brimming, and I've noticed you're not eating anything.

LÄUFFER: Have you then? Really? Ah, you're the very model of sympathy.

GUSTCHEN: Oh, sir . . .

LÄUFFER: Would you like a drawing-lesson this afternoon?

GUSTCHEN (*grasps his hand*): Dearest tutor! Forgive me for abandoning you yesterday. It was really impossible for me to draw; I had the sniffles to such an astonishing degree.

LÄUFFER: So you will probably have them as well today. I think we should stop drawing altogether. It no longer gives you any pleasure.

GUSTCHEN (*almost in tears*): How can you say that, Mr. Läuffer? It's the only thing I do with any pleasure.

LÄUFFER: So postpone it until this winter in the city and get a drawing-master. I must ask your father immediately to keep me, the object of your repugnance, your hate, your entire revulsion, away from you. I can see that in the long run it will become unendurable for you to take lessons from me.

14

GUSTCHEN: Mr. Läuffer—

LÄUFFER: Leave me alone! I must labor to see how I can drag this wretched life out to its end, as death is forbidden me.

GUSTCHEN: Mr. Läuffer—

LÄUFFER: You're torturing me! (*Pulls free and leaves.*)

GUSTCHEN: How sorry I am for him!

Scene Three

Halle, in Saxony. PÄTUS's *room.*
FRITZ VON BERG. PÄTUS *in a dressing-gown, seated at a table.*

PÄTUS: So what, Berg? You're not a child anymore that has to run home to Papa and Mama. Damn! All this time I thought you were a decent sort of fellow, but if you weren't an old school friend I'd be ashamed to be seen with you.

FRITZ: Pätus, on my honor, it's not homesickness. I'm angry you'd even think such a stupid thing. I want to have news from home, that I confess, but I have my reasons.

PÄTUS: Gustchen—right? Ah, think, you poor soul! One hundred and eighty hours from her. What sort of forests and streams lie between you? But wait, we also have girls here. If I were better-dressed, I'd take you out today to meet some. I don't know how you do it: one year in Halle and still you haven't spoken to a girl. That must be what's got you so melancholy; it can't be anything else. I've got it, you should move in with me here. Then you'll be able to enjoy yourself. How can you do that staying at the reverend's? That's no place for you.

FRITZ: What do you pay here?

PÄTUS: I pay—really, Brother, I don't know. The man is a good, decent Philistine. His wife is of course a little bit strange now and then, but that's her right. Why should I care? We quarrel a bit and then I let her go. They write down everything: rent, coffee, tobacco, everything I ask for. Then I pay the bill each year when my allowance comes.

FRITZ: Are you much in debt now?

PÄTUS: I paid the previous weeks. That's true. This time she's made me mad: she kept my whole allowance right down to the last penny. My coat, which I'd only pawned the day before, because I was in the most extreme need, is still at the shop. God only knows when I'll be able to get it back.

FRITZ: How are you doing otherwise?

PÄTUS: I? I'm sick. This morning the alderman's wife, Mrs. Hamster, invited me over. Right away I crawled into bed.

FRITZ: But to stay indoors all the time in such beautiful weather?

PÄTUS: What does that matter? Evenings I go walking in my dressing-gown; I couldn't stand to do that afternoons in these dog days. Good God! Where is my coffee? (*Stamps his foot.*) Mrs. Blitzer! Now you'll see how I deal with these people. Mrs. Blitzer! What in the world—Mrs. Blitzer! (*Rings and*

15

stamps.) I just paid her a little while ago; I should be able now to be a little more plain-spoken. Mrs.—

(MRS. BLITZER *enters with some coffee*.)

PÄTUS: What took you so long, old lady? Where were you? Are you ruled by the weather? I've been waiting here for over an hour.

MRS. BLITZER: What? You good-for-nothing trash, what are you complaining about? Are you down to your last dime again, you threadbare louse! One more word and I'll take my coffee back downstairs.

PÄTUS (*pours the coffee*): Now, now, don't get all worked up, Mother. The cookies! Where are the cookies?

MRS. BLITZER: Yes, precious gems to you! There's not a cooky in the house. Do you think that whether a lousy, threadbare good-for-nothing eats cookies every afternoon is—

PÄTUS: Damn it to hell! (*Stamps his foot*.) You know that I can't drink coffee without a cooky in my mouth. What am I getting for my money?

MRS. BLITZER (*gives him a cooky from her apron, and ruffles his hair*): There you are, there's a cooky, my little trombone! He has a voice like a regiment of soldiers. So, is the coffee good? Is it? So tell me already or I'll rip out every hair on your head.

PÄTUS (*drinks*): Incomparable! Ayee! I've never in my life drunk better.

MRS. BLITZER: You see, scamp! If you didn't have a mother who took care of you and gave you food and drink, you'd have to go hungry on the street. You see, Mr. von Berg, how he goes about, no coat on his back, and his dressing-gown looks as though he'd been hanged in it and fell off the gallows. You are certainly a good-looking fellow; I don't know why you bother with this lout, but I suppose among people from the same place there is always a little of the same blood. That's why I'm always saying, if only Mr. von Berg would come to live with us. I know that you have much power over him, and I'm sure he could become something quite respectable, but otherwise really— (*Leaves*.)

PÄTUS: You see, isn't that a good, jolly woman? I turn a blind eye to her somewhat, but good God, when I want to be serious sometimes, she's as cold as the wall. Won't you have a cup with me? (*Pours him one*.) You see, I'm well served here. I pay a good bit, that's true, but for that I do get something.

FRITZ (*drinks*): The coffee tastes like barley.

PÄTUS: What are you saying? (*Tries his at the same time*.) Yeah, you're right, with the cooky I couldn't tell. (*Looks in the pot*.) Oh, damn it all! (*Flings the coffeepot out the window*.) Barley coffee and five hundred guilders a year!

MRS. BLITZER (*Rushes in*): What's going on! What the devil, what is this? Sir, are you mad or possessed by the devil?

PÄTUS: Oh, be quiet, Mother!

MRS. BLITZER (*with a horrible cry*): Where is my coffeepot? Ay! Damn it! Out the window! I'll scratch your eyes out!

PÄTUS: There was a spider in it and I threw it out of fear. Is it my fault the window was open?

MRS. BLITZER: You were frightened by a spider! If I sold you outright you couldn't pay for my coffeepot, you good-for-nothing dog! You can't do anything but bring shame and misfortune! I'll sue you! I'll have you thrown in jail! (*Runs out.*)

PÄTUS (*laughing*): What can I do? You have to let her rant and rave.

FRITZ: But what about your money?

PÄTUS: Who knows? I may have to wait till Christmas, but who'll give me credit till then? Ah, well, it was only a woman who abused me, and a stupid housewife to boot, so I don't take it to heart. If her husband had said it to me, that would be something else. I'd tan his hide.

FRITZ: Do you have pen and ink?

PÄTUS: Over there, by the window.

FRITZ: I don't know, my heart is so heavy. I've never had anything to do with grudges.

PÄTUS: Yeah, me neither. The Döbblin company has arrived. I would really like to go to the theater, but I have no coat to wear. My landlord, the bugger, won't lend me one, and I am such a thick, great beast that none of your coats would fit me.

FRITZ: I must write home right away. (*Sits by the window and writes.*)

PÄTUS (*sits down, facing a wolf-pelt coat that hangs on the wall*): Hm! Nothing but the coat left of all my clothes, at least nothing else left that I'd want to have. But I can't possibly wear the fur in summer. The Jew wouldn't even let me pawn it because it was a little moth-eaten. Hanke! Hanke! It is inexcusable that you wouldn't make a coat for me! (*Rises and paces about.*) What did I ever do to you, Hanke, that even now you won't make a coat for me? Just me, because I need it the most, because I don't have one now, just me! The devil take you! He extends credit to every Tom, Dick, and Harry—just not me! (*Holds his head and stamps his foot.*) Just not me! Just not me!

BOLLWERK (*who meanwhile has entered silently and eavesdropped, grabs him. PÄTUS whirls round and stands dumb before him.*): Ha, ha, ha! Poor, poor Pätus! Ha, ha, ha! What a godless Hanke, not to trust you. But where is the red outfit with gold that you ordered from him, and the blue-silk one with silver buttons on the vest, and the red-velvet with black-velvet lining? Oh, that one would be splendid this season. Tell me! Tell me about that damned Hanke! Shall we go and pound his hide? Why is he taking so long with your work? Shall we go?

PÄTUS (*throws himself on a chair*): Leave me alone!

BOLLWERK: But listen, Pätus, Pätus, Pä, Pä, Pä, Pätus. (*Sits down next to him.*) The Döbblin company has arrived. Listen, Pä, Pä, Pä, Pä, Pätus, how should we handle this? I think you should wear the fur coat and go to the play tonight anyway. What can it hurt? You're a stranger here, and everybody knows that you've ordered four suits from Hanke. Whether he makes them for you is something else! Damned old fool! Let's break his windows if he doesn't make them for you!

PÄTUS: Leave me alone, I said!

BOLLWERK: But listen, Pätus, Pätus, Pä, Pä, Pä, Pätus. Listen, listen, just listen to me, Pätus. Take care, Pätus, that you don't run through the streets any more at night in your dressing-gown! I know that you're afraid of dogs. Well, it's been reported that ten rabid dogs are running about the city. They're supposed to have already bitten some children; two survived, but four died on the spot. You called these the dog days? Right, Pätus? It's good that you can't go out, isn't it? You'll take care not to go out now, won't you? Right, Pä, Pä, Pätus?

PÄTUS: Leave me alone . . . or we'll get angry.

BOLLWERK: Don't be a child. Berg, are you coming with us to the theater?

FRITZ (*distracted*): What? What kind of play?

BOLLWERK: It'll be quite a social gathering . Put all your lovesick drivel away for now. You can write more in the evening. Tonight it's *Minna von Barnhelm*.

FRITZ: Oh, that I must see. (*Puts his letter away.*) Poor Pätus, that you have no coat!

BOLLWERK: I'd be glad to lend him one, but this one on my back, may I be damned if I'm lying, is the only one I have. (*He and* FRITZ *leave.*)

PÄTUS (*alone*): The hell with your sympathy! That's worse than if he'd slapped me in the face! Damn! What am I going to do? (*Takes off his dressing-gown.*) *Let* everybody think I'm crazy! I'll see *Minna von Barnhelm,* even if I have to go naked! (*Throws on his wolf coat.*) Hanke! Hanke! If I ever get my hands on you! (*Stamps his foot.*) If I ever get my hands on you! (*Leaves.*)

Scene Four

MRS. HAMSTER. MISS HAMSTER. MISS KNICKS.

MISS KNICKS: I can't tell you for laughing, Mrs. Hamster, oh, I'm going to be sick from laughing. Just imagine: Miss Hamster and I were going down the lane here, and a man in a wolf coat ran by as if he were dodging spears. Three large dogs were chasing him. Miss Hamster got shoved so, her head hit the wall, and she cried out so loudly.

MRS. HAMSTER: Who was it?

MISS KNICKS: Can you imagine, after we got a look at him—it was Mr. Pätus! He must have been out of his mind.

MRS. HAMSTER: Wearing a wolf coat in this heat!

MISS HAMSTER (*holding her head*): I believe he must have been suffering from fever. He had sent word to us this morning that he was sick.

MISS KNICKS: And the three dogs behind him, that was the funniest. I thought I'd go to the comedy tonight, but now I think I won't. It couldn't be as funny as this. All my life I'll never forget it. His hair flew behind him like the tail of a comet, and the harder he ran, the harder the dogs chased him, and he didn't dare to look round. Oh, it was priceless!

MRS. HAMSTER: Didn't he scream? He must have thought the dogs were rabid.

MISS KNICKS: I think he didn't have time to scream; he was red as a crab, and his mouth hung open as the dogs closed in—oh, it was priceless! I would have given my string of real pearls, not to have missed it.

18

Scene Five

Heidelbrunn. GUSTCHEN's *room.*
GUSTCHEN *is lying on the bed.* LÄUFFER *is sitting on the bed.*

LÄUFFER: Try to understand, Gustchen, His Excellency won't. You see that your father is making my life more and more intolerable. He only wants to pay me forty ducats for next year. How can I put up with it? I have to quit.

GUSTCHEN: That's horrible. What would I do? (*They regard each other for several minutes, silently.*) You see, I am weak and sick, here in my loneliness, under the rule of a barbaric mother. Nobody asks about me, nobody cares about me, nobody in my family can stand me any longer, not even my father, and I don't know why.

LÄUFFER: Ask them to let you take catechism lessons from my father, in Insterburg.

GUSTCHEN: We'd never manage to see each other there. Besides, my uncle would never let my father board me out with your father.

LÄUFFER: That damn aristocratic conceit!

GUSTCHEN (*takes his hand*): Don't be malicious, little man! (*Kisses his hand.*) Oh, death! Death! Why do you not take pity on me?

LÄUFFER: You don't have to tell me about your family. Your brother is the most ill-bred, ill-mannered brat that I have ever seen. He recently gave me a box on the ears, and I couldn't take any action in return. I couldn't even complain about it. Your father would have broken all his arms and legs, and your most gracious mama would have blamed everything on me.

GUSTCHEN: But for my sake . . . I thought you loved me.

LÄUFFER (*pushes himself with his other hand off her bed.* GUSTCHEN *continues to bring the hand she holds to her lips from time to time.*): Let me think . . . (*Sits down again, lost in thought.*)

GUSTCHEN (*during the preceding action*): Oh, Romeo! If this were only your hand! But still you abandon me, ignoble Romeo! Don't you know that your Juliet is dying for you—hated, despised, cast out, by the whole world, by her whole family! (*Presses his hand to her eyes.*) Oh, inhuman Romeo!

LÄUFFER (*looking up*): What are you babbling about?

GUSTCHEN: It's a monologue from a tragedy that I like to recite when I am sad. (LÄUFFER *sinks back into thought. After a pause, she begins again.*) Perhaps you are not totally to blame. Your father forbade you to write to me, but love flies over seas and streams, over prohibitions and fear of death. You have forgotten me . . . perhaps you were concerned for me. Yes! Yes! Your tender heart saw me threatened by something far more frightful than what I currently suffer. (*Kisses* LÄUFFER's *hand ardently.*) Oh, divine Romeo!

LÄUFFER (*kisses her hand a long while, then regards her quietly*): I should do as Abelard—

GUSTCHEN (*sits up in bed*): You're wrong . . . my sickness lies in my soul . . . no one will suspect you. (*Falls back on the bed.*) Have you read *The New Heloise*?

19

LÄUFFER: I hear somebody outside, by the schoolroom.

GUSTCHEN: My father! Oh my God, you've been here three-quarters of an hour too long!

(LÄUFFER *dashes out*.)

Scene Six

MRS. VON BERG. COUNT WERMUTH.

COUNT: But dear lady! Can't I ever manage to see Miss Gustchen any more? How was she on the hunt two days ago?

MRS. VON BERG: If you please, she had a toothache all night long. That's why she doesn't want to be seen today. And how is your stomach, my lord, from all the oysters?

COUNT: Oh, I'm used to them. Just recently my brother and I alone ate six hundred of them and drank twenty bottles of champagne.

MRS. VON BERG: You mean Rhine wine.

COUNT: Champagne. It was a whim and it agreed with us both. That same evening there was a ball in Königsberg. My brother danced till the next afternoon, and I lost some money.

MRS. VON BERG: Shall we play a hand of piquet?

COUNT: If Miss Gustchen would come, I'd rather take a few turns of the garden with her. I would not presume to ask you, dear lady, because I know about that fontanel in your foot.

MRS. VON BERG: I really don't know what the major is up to. He's never acted so crazily before. He wastes every blessed day out in the fields, and when he comes home he just sits, as silent as a stick. You can believe that I'm beginning to worry.

COUNT: He seems melancholy.

MRS. VON BERG: Heaven only knows. Just the other night he had a notion to sleep with me. Then, in the middle of the night, he—heh, heh, I shouldn't be telling you this, but you already know about my husband's . . . laughable side.

COUNT: And he . . .

MRS. VON BERG: Threw himself on his knees and beat his breast and sobbed and howled so much I began to become frightened. But I haven't been able to find out from him how his foolishness concerns me. Maybe he's becoming a Pietist or a Quaker. As far as I'm concerned, fine! He will be neither more hateful nor more endearing. (*Looks at the* COUNT *roguishly*.)

COUNT (*chucks her under the chin*): Wicked woman! But where is Gustchen? I would be only too glad to go walking with her.

MRS. VON BERG: Be quiet, the major is coming. You can walk with him, my lord.

COUNT: Now, really, I would prefer to walk with your daughter.

MRS. VON BERG: She wouldn't be dressed yet; it's really insufferable how shoddily she behaves.

(*The* MAJOR *enters in a nightshirt and a straw hat.*)

MRS. VON BERG: Now then, how are you, husband? Why are you loitering about? We haven't seen you all day. Just look at him, my lord, doesn't he look like the Heautontimorumenos painted in my Madame Dacier? I swear, you've been out plowing. We *are* still in the dog days.

COUNT: Really, Major, you've never looked so ill, pale, haggard. You must have something weighing on your mind. Why is it when I look at you closely, I see tears in your eyes? I've known you for ten years and I've never seen you so, not even when your brother died.

MRS. VON BERG: Stinginess, nothing other than plain stinginess. He thinks we'll all go hungry if he doesn't root about in the field every day, like a mole. He digs, he plows, he harrows. You don't want to become a peasant, do you? Honestly, you're going to need a caretaker soon!

MAJOR: I must produce, I must scrimp and save, to get my daughter a place in the hospital.

MRS. VON BERG: What on earth kind of crazy talk is this? I really must summon Dr. Würz from Königsberg.

MAJOR: You never see anything, my high-class wife! That your child is declining day by day, that she's losing her beauty, her health, all her charms, and acts as if, damn it—God forgive me my mortal sin—as if she's trying to follow Lazarus. God, it gnaws at my liver!

MRS. VON BERG: Do you hear him? How he raves at me? Is it my fault? Have you gone completely mad?

MAJOR: Yes, of course it's your fault. Whose else could it be? I can't, may lightning strike me dead, figure it out. I always thought I'd make her the finest match in the empire, for there's nowhere in the world her equal in beauty. Now she looks like a milkmaid. *Your* cruelty, *your* jealousy. She took it all to heart. It shows in her face, but that is your joy, dear lady. Oh, you've been jealous of her a long, long time. You can't deny it, can you? You should be ashamed, truly ashamed! (*Leaves.*)

MRS. VON BERG: But . . . well, what do you say to that, my lord! Have you ever in your life heard a more infuriating collection of *sottises*?[3]

COUNT: Come, we shall play piquet, until Miss Gustchen is dressed.

Scene Seven

Halle

FRITZ VON BERG *in jail*. BOLLWERK, VON SEIFFENBLASE, *and* VON SEIFFENBLASE's TUTOR *stand around him*.

BOLLWERK: If I had him here, I'd fleece him good. Infamous business, to throw an honest lad like Berg in jail because nobody'd take responsibility for him.

---

[3]idiocies

21

And that's the God-honest truth, not one compatriot lifted a finger for him. If Berg hadn't pledged for him, he'd be rotting in prison. The money should be here in fourteen days. What a bastard, to place Berg in such a predicament! Oh, you damned Pä, Pä, Pä, Pä, Pätus! Just wait, you cursed Pätus, just wait!

TUTOR: I cannot begin to describe to you, my dear Mr. von Berg, how much it grieves me, considering your father and your family, to see you in such a position. And when it's not even your fault, but merely the imprudence of youth. As one of the seven wise men of Greece has said: beware of giving surety! Truly, there's nothing more shameless than that some young dissolute, through his own disgusting habits, has dragged others along into the mud with him. Presumably he had that in mind from the beginning when he sought out your friendship at the academy.

SEIFFENBLASE: Yes, yes, brother Berg! Don't take this the wrong way, but you've really botched things up. You're just as guilty; you should have seen that the fellow would betray you. He was at my place too, and told me about it: his creditors wanted to have him put away where neither sun nor moon would shine on him. Let them, I thought, it serves you right. Now I don't want you to scoff at this, but when you're in trouble, a nobleman is a good guarantor. He told me at great length how he had his pistols loaded in case his creditors attacked him. And now the miserable dog prostitutes you in his place. I tell you, if it had happened to me, I couldn't be so calm about it. Mr. von Berg between four walls, and all for the sake of some abominable student!

FRITZ: We were schoolmates. Leave him in peace! If I'm not complaining about him, why should it concern you? I've known him longer than you; I know that he isn't deliberately leaving me here.

TUTOR: But, Mr. von Berg, we must conduct ourselves in the world with reason. It doesn't bother him that you are here in his place. As far as he is concerned, you can stay here for a century.

FRITZ: I have known him since childhood; we've never refused each other anything. He loved me as his brother, and I loved him as mine. When he went to Halle he cried for the first time in his life, because he couldn't travel with me. He could have gone to the academy a whole year earlier, but in order to go with me he pretended before the preceptors to be more stupid than he was. Nonetheless, fate and our fathers decided that we would not travel together, and that was his misfortune. He never knew how to handle money, he gave anybody whatever he asked for. If a beggar had ripped the shirt off his back and said: "By your leave, Mr. Pätus," he'd have let him. His creditors went after him like highwaymen, and his father wasn't worthy of his prodigal son who, for all his misery, came home with such a good heart.

TUTOR: Oh, forgive me, but you are young and see everything from the most positive point of view. One must first have lived among men awhile, before being able to judge character. Mr. Pätus, or whatever he's called, has shown himself to you in a guise up to now. Only now is his true face revealed in the light of day; he must have been one of the most subtle and cunning swindlers, for inexperienced swindlers—

PÄTUS (*in travelling clothes, embraces* BERG): Brother Berg!

FRITZ: Brother Pätus!

PÄTUS: No . . . let me . . . I must prostrate myself at your feet. You here! Because of me! (*Tears his hair with both hands and stamps his feet.*) Oh, fate! Fate! Fate!

FRITZ: Now what's happening? Did you bring the money with you? Are you reconciled with your father? What does your return mean?

PÄTUS: Nothing, nothing. He refused to see me. To ride a hundred miles in vain! Your servant, gentlemen! Bollwerk, don't cry, you would humiliate me too deeply, if you should think well of me. Oh, Heaven! Heaven!

FRITZ: You are the most frustrating fool that ever wandered the earth. Why did you come back? Are you insane? Have you lost all your senses? Do you want your creditors to find out that you're here? Get out! Bollwerk, get him out of here; see that you get him out of the city! I hear the baliff! Pätus, you will be my enemy forever if you don't get out this—! (PÄTUS *throws himself at* BERG's *feet.*) I would like to go mad!

BOLLWERK: Don't be a fool, when Berg is magnanimous enough to take your place. His father will get him released soon, but if you stay here, there's no hope for you. You'll have to rot in jail.

PÄTUS: Give me a sword!

FRITZ: Get out!

BOLLWERK: Get out!

PÄTUS: You would show me great mercy if you would give me a sword!

SEIFFENBLASE: You can have mine!

BOLLWERK (*grabs* SEIFFENBLASE *by the arm*): Mr.—scoundrel! Don't—oh, don't put your sword away! You won't have drawn in vain. First I want to get Pätus safe, so you wait for me here. Outside, I mean, so for the time being—out! (*Throws* SEIFFENBLASE *out the door.*)

TUTOR: Mr. Bollwerk—

BOLLWERK: Not a word, sir! Go after your boy and teach him to behave better. I'll meet you wherever and however you wish. (*The* TUTOR *leaves.*)

PÄTUS: Bollwerk! I want to be your second!

BOLLWERK: Fool! You act as if—what do you want to do, hold my glove when I have to piss? What good is a second? Just come on and second yourself out of the city, rabbit-foot!

PÄTUS: But there are two of them.

BOLLWERK: I wish that there were ten of them and not a Seiffenblase in the lot! Come on! Don't cause any more trouble for yourself, you idiot!

PÄTUS: Berg!

(BOLLWERK *tears him away. They exit.*)

Act Three
Scene One

Heidelbrunn
MAJOR, *in a nightshirt.* COUNCILLOR.

MAJOR: Brother, I am the elder no longer. My heart is ten times more crazed than my face shows! It's very good that you visit me; who knows when we shall see each other again.

COUNCILLOR: You are always extravagant, in all your reactions. To let such a triviality wound you to the core! If your daughter loses her beauty, she'll still be the same good girl she was before. She can have a hundred other endearing attributes.

MAJOR: Her beauty—damn it, it's not just that that she's lost. I don't know, I shall soon go mad if I look at her much longer. Her bloom is gone, her cheerfulness, her sweetness—the devil only knows how I'm supposed to name all the things. But even though I can't name them, I can see them, I can feel them and understand them. You know that I have made the girl my idol. That I must see her dying under my care, rotting away. (*Cries.*) Brother, Excellency, you have no daughter; you don't know how much a father who has a daughter feels. I have fought in thirteen battles and received eighteen wounds and have looked death in the eye, and I am—oh, leave me in peace, clear out of my house, let the whole world clear out. I want to renounce the world, take the shovel in my hand and become a peasant.

COUNCILLOR: And your wife and children?

MAJOR: You're making a joke; I know of no wife and children. I am the blessed memory of Major Berg. I shall take the plow in hand and become Old Berg. Anyone who gets too close to me, I'll give him my pickax on his ears.

COUNCILLOR: I've never seen him so fanatical-melancholy.

(MRS. VON BERG *rushes in.*)

MRS. VON BERG: Help, husband! We are lost! Our family! Our family!

COUNCILLOR: God forbid, sister! What are you saying? Do you want to drive your husband mad?

MRS. VON BERG: He should go mad . . . our family . . . infamy! Oh, I can't go on any longer. (*Collapses on a chair.*)

MAJOR (*goes over to her*): Are you going to spit it out? Or do I have to wring your neck?

MRS. VON BERG: Your daughter . . . that tutor . . . gone! (*Faints.*)

MAJOR: Has he made her a whore? (*Shakes her.*) Why are you collapsing; now is not the time for collapsing. Out with it, all of it, or may you be struck dead. Is she a whore? Is that it? Now, then, let the whole world turn whore—and you, Berg, take up your dungfork. (*About to leave.*)

COUNCILLOR (*holds him back*): Brother, if you value your life, stay. I'm going to find out everything—your fury makes you unable. (*Leaves and closes the door.*)

MAJOR (*tries to open the door*): I am more able than you! (*To his wife.*) Come on, whore, you too. Look! (*Rips the door open.*) I want to establish examples for the world! God has kept me alive till now so that I can hold up my wife and children as examples for the world. Ashes! Ashes! Ashes! (*Carries his unconscious wife offstage.*)

Scene Two

A school in the village. It is a dark and gloomy night.
WENZESLAUS. LÄUFFER.

WENZESLAUS (*sits at a table, glasses on his nose, drawing lines*): Who's there? What is it?

LÄUFFER: Sanctuary! Sanctuary! Esteemed schoolmaster! They're trying to kill me!

WENZESLAUS: Who are you?

LÄUFFER: I am a tutor from the neighboring estate. Major Berg and all his servants are after me. They want to shoot me.

WENZESLAUS: God forbid! Sit yourself down by me here. Here is my hand: you shall be safe with me. Now tell me about it while I write out these lessons.

LÄUFFER: Let me just pull myself together.

WENZESLAUS: Right, catch your breath, and then I'll get you a glass of wine and we'll have a drink. In the meantime tell me . . . Tutor . . . (*Lays down his ruler, takes his glasses off, and studies him a while.*) Now then, to judge from your coat—yes, yes, I believe that you are a tutor. You've gone all red and white. But tell me, dear friend (*Puts his glasses back on.*) how have you arrived at this misfortune, that your patron is so filled with indignation at you? I cannot at all imagine that a man like Major von Berg—I know him well, I've heard enough said about him—he is supposed, I confess, to be of a rash temperament, much choler, much choler—You see, I even have to draw the lines for my lads, for the boys have more trouble with penmanship than anything else. A gentlemanly hand . . . not to write delicately, not to write quickly, I tell them again and again, but to write neatly, because that has a bearing on everything, on manners, on the sciences, on everything, Tutor. I always say, a man who can't write well, can't behave well—where were we?

LÄUFFER: Might I have a glass of water?

WENZESLAUS: Water? Of course? But—now what were we talking about? About penmanship . . . no, about the major. Heh, heh, heh. But you know, Mr.—what is your name?

LÄUFFER: My . . . it's . . . Almond.

WENZESLAUS: Mr. Almond—and you have trouble remembering it? Oh, well, people have memory lapses from time to time, especially you red and white young men. But you shouldn't be called Almond; you should be called Almondblossom, for you're as red and white as an almond blossom. Of course the position of tutor is one of those, *unus ex his,*[4] that is always strewn with roses and lilies, and where one is only rarely pricked by the thorns of life. For what does a man have to do? He eats, drinks, sleeps, has

---

[4]One of those

25

no cares, a good glass of wine, his daily bread, every morning his coffee, tea, chocolate, or whatever he drinks, and that's always the—now then, I wanted to say to you: do you know, Mr. Almond, that a glass of water is just as detrimental to health as excessive emotion or violent exercise? But, of course, what do you young men care about health? So tell me then (*Lays his glasses and ruler aside, and stands up.*) how in the world can health be maintained when all the nerves and arteries are jangled, and the blood is circulating most violently, and animal energy is in a . . . fever, in a—

LÄUFFER: For God's sake, Count Wermuth! (*Flees to the next room.*)

(COUNT WERMUTH *enters with several* SERVANTS, *all armed with pistols.*)

COUNT: Is there a fellow here called Läuffer? A student in a blue coat with braid?

WENZESLAUS: Here in our village it is the custom to take off one's hat when one enters a room and addresses the head of the house.

COUNT: The matter is urgent! Is he here or not?

WENZESLAUS: And what law is he supposed to have broken that you pursue him so heavily armed? (*The* COUNT *is about to check the next room;* WENZESLAUS *places himself before the door.*) Stop, sir! This room is mine, and if you don't clear out of my house this instant, I'll ring my bell and a half-dozen stalwart peasants will pulverize you. If you behave like highwaymen, you'll be treated like highwaymen. And so that you find your way out of the house as easily as you found your way in . . . (*Takes him by the hand, and leads him out the door. The* SERVANTS *follow.*)

LÄUFFER (*leaps out of the closet*): Blessed man! Heroic man!

WENZESLAUS (*back to his earlier mood*): In . . . your animal energy is in a . . . rapture, all passions are, as it were, in an uproar, in tumult. Now when you drink water, it's just like pouring water over a mighty flame. The strong motion of the air and the war between the two opposing elements makes an effervescence, a ferment, an unrest, a being in tumult—

LÄUFFER: I admire you.

WENZESLAUS: Gottlieb! Now you can drink a little—a little!—and then this evening you will perhaps have a taste for a salad and some knockwurst. Who was that uncouth lout that was here looking for you?

LÄUFFER: That was Count Wermuth, the future son-in-law of the major. He is jealous of me because the major's daughter can't stand him.

WENZESLAUS: What is that supposed to mean? What does the girl want with you, Monsieur Menial? Is she throwing away her good fortune for the sake of such a young Siegfried, who has neither hearth nor home? Put that out of your mind and follow me into the kitchen. I see my boy has gone to fetch the bratwurst. I'll get you the water myself, for I have no maid and I have not yet presumed even to think of a wife, because I know that I can't support one, to say nothing of actually looking for one, like you red and white young gentlemen. But I suppose it's true, the world is changing.

26

Scene Three

COUNCILLOR. SEIFFENBLASE. SEIFFENBLASE's TUTOR.

TUTOR: We only spent a year in Halle, and when we came from Göttingen, we made our return journey through all the famous universities in Germany. Naturally, then, we could not spend much time in Halle the second time. Just at that time your son was sitting in jail after that most unfortunate arrest, and I had the honor of speaking to him there only once; therefore frankly I can give you no detailed report on the conduct of your son.

COUNCILLOR: Heaven has laid a curse on our whole family. My brother—I can't hide it from you, the whole city and country are full of the news—his daughter is gone. She's disappeared without a trace. Now I hear that my son—if he has conducted himself well, how could it have been possible for him to be thrown into jail? Every six months, in addition to his extremely generous allowance, I sent him something extra—and, in any case—

TUTOR: The bad company and the overwhelming temptations outside the academy.

SEIFFENBLASE: The strangest thing is that he's sitting there for another, a paragon of depravity, a man I wouldn't give a groschen to if he were dying from hunger on my dunghill. He was here, you would have heard of him. He was looking for money from his father, on the pretext of setting your son free; presumably he would have gone to another academy and started up with his old tricks. I can imagine how the despicable student behaved, but his father smelled a rat and refused to see him.

COUNCILLOR: Certainly not young Pätus, the alderman's son?

SEIFFENBLASE: Yes, I believe so, the same one.

COUNCILLOR: Everybody thought the father was being unduly harsh.

TUTOR: Yes, but what else could he do, Your Excellency? If a son squanders his father's property, the father must turn away from him. The high priest Eli was not hard and broke his neck.

COUNCILLOR: One can never be too hard on the excesses of his children, but one can be too hard on their poverty. The young man supposedly had to beg around here. And my son is sitting in his place?

SEIFFENBLASE: Who else? He was his most intimate friend and found nobody more suited to act out Damon and Pythias. Granted, Mr. Pätus returned and wanted to take his place, but your son insisted on staying. You were expected to free him, so Pätus took off with some other archfiend and gambler, and they're looking out for themselves as well as they can. Perhaps they've put on masks and attacked some other poor student in his room, waving a pistol at his chest, taking his watch and purse, just as they already did to one in Halle.

COUNCILLOR: And my son is the third of this trio?

SEIFFENBLASE: I don't know, Your Excellency.

COUNCILLOR: Stay to dinner, gentlemen! I know too much already. God levies his judgment on certain families: in some, certain illnesses are inherited; in others, the children are degenerates, no matter what the parents do. Eat, eat. I shall fast and pray. Perhaps I have earned this evening by the excesses of my own youth.

Scene Four

The school
WENZESLAUS *and* LÄUFFER, *dining at a bare table.*

WENZESLAUS: Taste good? There's some difference between my table and the major's, right? But when schoolmaster Wenzeslaus eats his sausage, a clear conscience aids his digestion. When Mr. Almond ate roast capon with mushroom sauce, *his* conscience made every bite that he choked down stick in his craw. You are a—now, just tell me, Mr. Almond, and don't take offense that I tell you the truth, for truth seasons speech as peppers do a cucumber salad, but tell me: isn't it a vile thievery, if I am convinced that I am an ignoramus and can teach those in my charge nothing, to go on being of no use to them and let them be of no use, to steal their days from God and a hundred ducats to boot? Wasn't it that much? God have mercy, I've never in my life seen so much money together at once. A hundred and fifty ducats stuck in your sack for doing nothing!

LÄUFFER: Oh, and you don't know the half of it. You either aren't aware of your advantages, or only sense them without knowing them. Have you never seen a slave in a braided coat? Oh, freedom, golden freedom!

WENZESLAUS: Eh, what freedom? I am not so free; I'm bound to my school and must account to God and my conscience.

LÄUFFER: Granted. But how would you feel if you had to follow the whims of some eccentric who drove you a hundred times crazier than your schoolboys?

WENZESLAUS: Well, then, he must have raised his intellect above mine, as I have raised mine above my schoolboys', and *that* one finds seldom these days, especially among our nobility, *that* you can be sure of, at least for that lout who wanted to break into my room without asking permission. If I went to Mr. Count and wanted to visit his room, bold as brass—Good God! I've told you a million times already, eat, eat! You're making a face like you were taking a laxative. You'd like a glass of wine with your meal, right? I admit I promised you one earlier, but I haven't a drop in the house. Tomorrow I'll get some and then we'll drink Sundays and Thursdays and more if Franz the organist visits us. Water, water, my friend, *ariston men to hudôr,*[5] that I brought from the school, and a pipe to smoke after dinner in the moonlight, and a walk in the field. After that you'll sleep more soundly than the Grand Mogul. You *do* smoke, don't you?

LÄUFFER: I shall try; I never have.

WENZESLAUS: Right, of course not, not you red and white gentlemen. It'll rot your teeth, right? And make you go pale, right? I've smoked since I was weaned, just swapped the nipple for the pipe. Heh, heh, heh. It's good against bad air and bad inclinations as well. This is my daily regimen: cold water and a pipe every morning; school till eleven; then another pipe until the soup, which my Gottlieb can cook as well as a French chef, is ready; and then a piece of roast beef and some vegetables; then another pipe; then some more hours in school; then plan lessons till dinner—now there I usually eat something cold, a sausage with a salad, a piece of cheese, or whatever God

---

[5]for water is the best (Pindar, *Olympian Odes*, 1.1)

has provided—and then a pipe before going to bed.

LÄUFFER: God have mercy, I'm in a smoke-filled room.

WENZESLAUS: And so I grow fat and thick and live comfortably and never think about death.

LÄUFFER: It's inexcusable that the government doesn't see to it that your life is made more comfortable.

WENZESLAUS: Eh, what, that's the way it is, and so one must be content. I am after all my own man, and don't have to deal with some other man's goldbricking, because I know that every day I do more than I have to. I have to teach my boys to read and write; I teach them arithmetic and Latin as well, and to read with reason and to write good things.

LÄUFFER: And what sort of salary do you get for this?

WENZESLAUS: What kind of salary?—aren't you going to eat that little piece of sausage there? You'll get nothing better; if you're waiting for something better, you'll go to bed hungry. What sort of salary? That was a stupid thing to ask, Mr. Almond. Pardon me, but what sort of salary? I have God's salary for it, a clear conscience, and if I were anxious for a higher salary from the government, I'd lose my real reward. Do you want to let the cucumber salad go to waste? Eat, go on, eat already, don't be shy. At a skimpy meal, one can't afford to be shy, damn it. Here, I'll cut you another slice of bread.

LÄUFFER: I've eaten too much already.

WENZESLAUS: Well, then, let it go, but it's your own fault if it's not true. And if it is true, then you were wrong to have eaten too much, for that brings on evil inclinations and puts the intellect to sleep. You red and white gentlemen may believe that or not. Of course it's also been said of tobacco that it has a narcotic, sleep-inducing, stupefying oil, and I have now and then found that to be true, and have tried to throw the pipes and all the damned paraphernalia into the fireplace, but with the constant haze here and the humid winter and autumn air and then the splendid effect that I notice when it at the same time lulls all the evil inclinations to sleep—Holla! Where are you then, dear fellow? Even as I was speaking of going to sleep, you were nodding off. Well, that's the way it goes when the mind is empty and atrophied to boot, and never is exerted. *Allons!*[6] Quick, smoke a pipe with me. (*Fills his pipe and* LÄUFFER's.) Let's chew the fat a while. (*Smokes.*) I had wanted to say to you earlier in the kitchen: I see that you are weak in Latin, but you write a good hand. So you could, as you say, give me a hand evenings and write my students' lesson plans for me, because I have to start saving my eyes. I want to give you *Corderii Colloquia* and, if you are industrious, *Gürtleri Lexicon* as well. You'll have the whole day to yourself, so you can start improving your Latin and, who knows, if it pleases God to take me today or tomorrow from this earth—but you'll have to buckle down, that I tell you, for you are hardly yet fit to be my assistant, let alone my— (*Drinks.*)

LÄUFFER (*laying his pipe aside*): What a comedown!

WENZESLAUS: But . . . but . . . but (*Rips the toothpick out of* LÄUFFER's *mouth.*) What is all this? Haven't you even learned, great scholar, how to take care of your own body? Picking your teeth is suicide, yes, suicide, a

---

[6]Let's get started!

wanton destruction of Jerusalem, that one undertakes with his teeth. When you have something in your teeth (*Takes a swig of water and rinses his mouth out.*) there! Do like that if you want to keep your teeth healthy, and honor God and your fellow creatures, and not run about in your old age like an old watchdog, whose teeth were broken in youth and who drools from his jaw. It would be a fine sort of schoolmaster if, in his old age, the words fell unborn out of his mouth; if he has to snort out something between nose and overlip that neither dog nor cock could understand.

LÄUFFER: He'll control me to death. What's insufferable is that he's right.

WENZESLAUS: Now then, what's the matter? Don't you like the tobacco? I wager, only a few days with old Wenzeslaus and you'll be smoking like a sailor. I'll give you my hand on it: soon you won't know yourself.

Act Four
Scene One

Insterburg
COUNCILLOR. MAJOR.

MAJOR: You see, Brother, I'm wandering about like Cain here, restless and fugitive. Have you heard? The Russians are supposed to be at war with the Turks. I want to go to Königsberg for more details. I want to leave my wife and die in Turkey.

COUNCILLOR: Your extravagances will strike me dead. Oh, heaven, must it storm on all sides? There, read this letter from my son's professor.

MAJOR: I can't read any more; I've cried my eyes half blind.

COUNCILLOR: Then I'll read it to you, so you can see that you're not the only father who has something to bewail: "Your son was imprisoned some time ago as a guarantor. As he confessed to me through his tears the day before yesterday, after having written five letters to you and receiving no reply, he no longer has any hope of receiving forgiveness from Your Excellency. I tried to persuade him to put his mind at rest until I had interceded in this matter, and he promised me that he would. In spite of this, however, he escaped from the jail that very night. The creditors wanted to send out warrants of arrest and had intended to publish his name in all the newspapers; I have, however, prevented that and made good what was owed, because I am so much convinced that Your Excellency would not allow this offense to your family. In expectation of your resolving the matter—"

MAJOR: Write him back: Let them hang him!

COUNCILLOR: And the family . . .?

MAJOR: Ridiculous! There is no family, we have no family. Ludicrous thought! The Russians are my family; I want to become a Russian Orthodox.

COUNCILLOR: And still no trace of your daughter?

MAJOR: What are you talking about?

COUNCILLOR: Haven't you heard anything about your daughter?

MAJOR: Leave me in peace!

COUNCILLOR: You're not really serious about travelling to Königsberg?

MAJOR: When is the next mail from Königsberg to Warsaw?

COUNCILLOR: I will not let you go. It would all be for nothing. Do you think reasonable people are going to be carried away by your fantasies? I put you herewith under house arrest. Stern measures must be taken against people like you, otherwise their grief will turn to madness.

MAJOR (*crying*): A whole year, Brother, a whole year, and no one knows where she's flown?

COUNCILLOR: Perhaps dead.

MAJOR: Perhaps? Certainly dead! If I only had had the comfort of giving her a decent burial! But she must have killed herself, because nobody can tell me any news of her. A bullet through the brain, Berg, or a Turkish broadsword, that would be a victory.

COUNCILLOR: It is just as possible that she met Läuffer somewhere and left the country with him. Yesterday Count Wermuth visited me and told me he had

31

come that same night to a school where the schoolmaster would not let him into the room. He suspected then that the tutor was hidden in there, perhaps your daughter with him.

MAJOR: Where is this schoolmaster? Where is the village? And that scoundrel of a count didn't break the door down? Come on, where is Wermuth?

COUNCILLOR: Probably down at the "Dandy" as usual.

MAJOR: Oh, if I find her! If I could only hope to see her again! The hell with me, as old as I am, pining away and senseless, yes, the hell with me! All I want in my life is just once more to laugh, to laugh aloud for the last time and to lay my head on her dishonored bosom, then once again to cry and then—Adieu, Berg! That would be the way to die, that's what I would call sleeping safely and blessedly in Abraham's bosom. Come, Brother, your boy just got in a scrape. His is just a triviality. But my daughter is a streetwalker, which truly gives a father joy. Perhaps she already has three lilies on her back. *Vivat* the tutors and may they all go to hell! (*They leave.*)

Scene Two

A beggar's hut in the forest.
GUSTCHEN, *in a loose smock.* MARTHA, *an old blind woman.*

GUSTCHEN: Dear Martha, stay at home and look after the child. It's the first time I've left you alone in a whole year. Surely you can let me take one walk by myself. You have enough food for today and tomorrow, so you don't have to go out on the main road today.

MARTHA: But God help us, Greta, where will you go? You're still so sick and weak. I can tell you, I have had children and without much pain, like you, thank God! But just once I tried to go out the second day after delivery. Never again! I almost gave up the ghost then and there; believe me, I can tell you how it feels to be dead. So learn from me. If you have to get something from the next village, I'll find it for you even if I am blind. You just stay at home and get your strength back. I'll straighten out everything for you, whatever it is.

GUSTCHEN: Oh, please let me, Mother. I have the strength of a young bear. Just see to my child.

MARTHA: But holy mother of God, how am I supposed to see to the child when I am blind? If it wants to suck, am I supposed to give it my black, drooping tits? And you don't have the strength to take it along. Stay at home, Gretel dear, stay at home.

GUSTCHEN: I can't, dear mother, my conscience is driving me away from here. I have a father who loves me more than his body and soul. I saw him last night in a dream, with blood in his eyes and tearing his white hair out. He must think that I am dead. I must go into the village and ask someone to give him news of me.

MARTHA: God help us, who will push you? What would happen if you collapsed along the way? You *can't* go out.

32

GUSTCHEN: I must—my father stood there, wavering. Suddenly he threw himself to the ground and lay there as if dead. He will kill himself if he doesn't get any news of me.

MARTHA: Don't you know that dreams often mean just the opposite?

GUSTCHEN: Not mine. Let me go. God will be with me. (*Leaves.*)

Scene Three
The school.
WENZESLAUS, LÄUFFER, *sitting at a table. The* MAJOR, *the* COUNCILLOR, *and* COUNT WERMUTH *enter, with* SERVANTS.

WENZESLAUS (*as his glasses fall off*): Who are you?

MAJOR (*with pistol drawn*): Damn you to hell! There sits the pig in clover. (*Fires, and hits* LÄUFFER *in the arm.* LÄUFFER *falls from his chair.*)

COUNCILLOR (*who had tried to restrain the* MAJOR): Brother! (*Strikes him furiously.*) Now you've done it, madman!

MAJOR: What? Is he dead? (*Covers his face.*) What have I done? Can you give me any news of my daughter?

WENZESLAUS: Sirs! Is this the Day of Judgment or something? What is all this? (*Rings a bell.*) I shall teach you to attack an honest man in his own house!

LÄUFFER: I beg of you, don't ring! It's the major . . . I deserve it . . . his daughter. . .

COUNCILLOR: Good schoolmaster, is there a doctor in the village? He's only wounded in the arm; I want him taken care of.

WENZESLAUS: Oh, you want him taken care of! Highwaymen! Do you shoot people because you have so much money you can afford to have them taken care of? He is my assistant; he's been in my house a year. A quiet, peaceable, hardworking man, who never caused any trouble in his life, and you come in and shoot my assistant in my own house! I'm going to find out why, or be damned! You understand?

COUNCILLOR (*while bandaging* LÄUFFER's *arm*): Why all the blathering, sir? We're already sorry enough—this wound won't stop bleeding. Go get a doctor!

WENZESLAUS: Eh, what? You made the wound, you heal it, highwayman! Oh, I'll go get my neighbor Schöpsen. (*Leaves.*)

MAJOR (*to* LÄUFFER): Where is my daughter?

LÄUFFER: I don't know.

MAJOR: You don't know? (*Draws his pistol again.*)

COUNCILLOR (*tears the gun away from the* MAJOR, *and flings it out the window*): Do we have to put you in chains, you—

LÄUFFER: I haven't seen her since I fled your house, I swear to God, before Whose tribunal I may soon appear.

MAJOR: Then she didn't run away with you?

LÄUFFER: No.

MAJOR: Damn, a whole load of powder shot in vain. I wanted it to go through your brain so you'd never say another filthy word, you degenerate! Let him lie there, till the end of the world! I must have my daughter again! If not in this life, then in the next. Then my extremely wise brother and my even more extremely wise wife won't be able to hold me back. (*Runs away.*)

COUNCILLOR: I can't let him out of my sight. (*Throws a purse at* LÄUFFER.) Get yourself cared for, and remember that you have wounded my brother far more deeply than he has you. There's a bank note in there. Take care and do as much with it as you can. (ALL *except* LÄUFFER *leave.*)

(WENZESLAUS *returns with the barber* SCHÖPSEN *and some* PEASANTS.)

WENZESLAUS: Where are the hooligans? Tell me!

LÄUFFER: I beg of you, calm down. I have been treated far less harshly than I deserve. Master Schöpsen, is my wound fatal?

(SCHÖPSEN *examines him.*)

WENZESLAUS: Now what? Where are they? I won't stand for it! No, I won't stand for it, if it costs me my school, my position, every hair on my head. I'll beat them to a powder, the dogs! Imagine, neighbor, where in the world in *iure naturae* or in *iure civili* or in *iure canonico* or in *iure gentium*,[7] or wherever you want, was it ever heard of that somebody can attack a honest man in his house, and a school to boot, a sacred spot? Dangerous business, right? Have you examined him? Is it fatal?

SCHÖPSEN: A lot could be said about it . . . well, we shall see . . . we'll certainly know in the end.

WENZESLAUS: Oh, right, sir. Heh, heh, *in fine videbitur cuius toni.*[8] That means, only after he's dead or fully recovered will you tell us if the wound was dangerous or not. And of course, even that's not medically spoken, forgive me. A qualified doctor would know ahead of time. Otherwise I would tell him to his face that he has only half-learned his pathology or surgery, and that he's spent more time in brothels than in medical school. For *in amore omnia insunt vitia,*[9] and if I see an ignoramus, he can be from whatever university you like, I'll tell him to his face that he's a ladies' man and a whore's stud; I won't let myself be dissuaded.

SCHÖPSEN (*after he has examined the wound again*): Yes, the wound is as I see it. We shall see, we shall see.

LÄUFFER: Here, Schoolmaster, the major's brother left me a purse full of ducats, and a bank note besides. That should help us out for many years.

WENZESLAUS (*picks up the purse*): Well, that's something. But a man's house is still a man's house, and sacrilege is still sacrilege. I'm going to write him a letter, that major, one that he won't just stick in the window.

SCHÖPSEN (*who all this while has been glancing eagerly at the purse, pounces on the wound*): You will be cured eventually, but with great difficulty, I hope with very great difficulty.

WENZESLAUS: I hope not, neighbor Schöpsen, I hope not, I hope not. So I want to tell you in advance that if you take your time curing the wound, you'll also take your time about receiving your payment. If he, however, is recovered in

---

[7]natural law . . . civil law . . . canon law . . . international law
[8]It'll all be clear in the end.
[9]In love, all vices are contained. (Terence, *Eunuchus*, 1.59)

two days, then that's when you'll get your payment. Let this be your guide.
SCHÖPSEN: We shall see.

Scene Four

GUSTCHEN (*lying by a pond surrounded by bushes*): Am I to die here? Father! Father! It's not my fault that you've had no news of me. I've spent my last ounce of strength . . . I'm exhausted . . . your face, oh, your face, always before my eyes! You are dead, yes, dead . . . you died of grief. Your spirit appeared to me tonight to give me the news . . . to call me to account. I'm coming . . . I'm coming. (*Struggles to her feet and throws herself in the pond.*)

(*The* MAJOR *appears. The* COUNCILLOR *and* COUNT WERMUTH *follow him.*)

MAJOR: Hi! Ho! Somebody went into the pond. It was a girl. Not my daughter perhaps, but still some unfortunate girl. Come on, Berg! This is the way to Gustchen or to hell! (*Leaps in after her.*)

COUNCILLOR: God in heaven! Now what are we supposed to do?

COUNT: I can't swim.

COUNCILLOR: To the other side! I think he's caught the girl. There, there behind the bushes. Don't you see? Now he's gone to the bottom with her. After him!

Scene Five

The other side of the pond
Cries heard offstage: "Help! It's my daughter!" "Great God and all his mercies!"
"Count Wermuth, hand me that pole at once!"
The MAJOR *carries* GUSTCHEN *onstage. The* COUNCILLOR *and*
COUNT WERMUTH *follow.*

MAJOR: There! (*Lays her down. The* COUNCILLOR *and the* COUNT *try to bring her around.*) Accursed child! Did I bring you into the world for this? (*Kneels beside her.*) Gustel! What is it? Have you swallowed water? Aren't you still my Gustel?—godless blackguard! If you had said just one word earlier, I'd have bought the lout a patent of nobility. Then you could have crawled off together—God save us! Help her! Help her, she's fainted! (*Leaps up, wrings his hands, paces about.*) If I only knew where that cursed surgeon in the village was to be found!—isn't she awake yet?

GUSTCHEN (*weakly*): Father!

MAJOR: What do you want?

35

GUSTCHEN: Forgiveness.

MAJOR (*goes back to her*): Yes, let the devil forgive you, worthless child—No! (*Kneels again beside her.*) Don't die, my Gustel! My Gustel, I forgive you. All is forgiven and forgotten. God knows, I forgive you. Only you must forgive me! Nothing more can be done. I put a bullet through the dog's brain.

COUNCILLOR: I think we should carry her to shelter.

MAJOR: Let us alone! What concern is she of yours? She's not your daughter. You worry about your own flesh and blood at home! (*He takes her by the arms.*) There, Daughter—I should take you with me back into the pond. (*He swings her toward the pond.*) But we don't want to go swimming until we've learned to swim, I think. (*Clasps her to his bosom.*) Oh you, my only, my dearest treasure! That I can again carry you in my arms—that godless blackguard! (*Carries her away.*)

Scene Six

Leipzig
FRITZ VON BERG. PÄTUS.

FRITZ: There's just one thing that I hold against you, Pätus. I've wanted to tell you for a long time. Just examine your situation for a moment: what has been the source of all your misfortune? I don't blame a man if he falls in love. We're of age, we're at sea, the wind drives us—but reason must always rule the rudder. Else we'll run aground at the first obstacle. Miss Hamster was a coquette who did with you what she wanted. She took you for your last coat, your good name, and the good name of your friends. I thought that you would have been too clever for that. Miss Rehaar is an unsophisticated, innocent young lamb. When one uses all one's forces against a heart that will not and cannot defend itself, in order to—how should I say it?—to destroy it, reduce it to ashes. That is wrong, Pätus, that is wrong. Don't take this wrong, but as it is we cannot remain such good friends. A man who goes as far as he can with a woman is either a blockhead or a cad: a blockhead if he cannot master himself, master the reverence he should feel before innocence and virtue; a cad if he won't master himself, and like the devil in Paradise, finds his only pleasure in bringing a good woman to ruin.

PÄTUS: Don't preach at me, Brother! You are right, I regret it. But I swear to you, I can take an oath to you, I never touched the girl.

FRITZ: But you climbed out the window and the neighbors saw it. Do you think their tongues will be as modest as perhaps your hands were? I believe you, I know that even though you appear so bold, you are really very bashful around women. I like you for that, but even if nothing happened, the girl has lost her good name. A musician's daughter to boot, a girl whose only assets are those received from nature. She hasn't a penny to her name, and you robbed her of her only dowry, her good name. You've ruined her, Pätus.

MR. REHAAR (*enters, a lute under his arm*): Your devoted servant, your devoted servant, Mr. von Berg. I wish you a sincere good morning. Did you sleep well and how did you find the concerto? (*Sits and tunes his lute.*) Did you play it through? (*Tunes some more.*) I had a nasty scare during the night. I'll try to remember it. You probably know the fellow, he's from your area. Twing, twing. That damned E-string! I'll never get it tuned right. I'll bring you another one this afternoon.

FRITZ (*sits down with his lute*): I didn't get to the concerto.

REHAAR: Hee, hee, naughty little Mr. von Berg, didn't get to it, eh? Twing! I'll bring you another this afternoon. (*Lays his lute aside and takes a pinch of snuff.*) They say the Turks have crossed the Danube and have soundly whipped the Russians back, back to—what *is* that place called? Otschakof, I believe. But what do I know? I can tell you this, if I'd been among them, I'd have run back even further. Ha, ha, ha! (*Picks up his lute again.*) I tell you, Mr. von Berg, I have no greater joy than when I read in the newspaper that an army has retreated. The Russians are honest people to have run away. Rehaar would have run too, like any good coward. What good is staying and letting yourself be killed? Ha, ha, ha!

FRITZ: This is the first position, right?

REHAAR: Quite right, up with the second finger a bit, and down with the little one so—round, round the trill, round, Mr. von Berg. My sainted father always said a musician must have no courage, and a musician who has a heart is a swine. As long as he can play his concertos and his marches—. I also told this to the duke when I was going to Petersburg the first time, in the suite of Prince Czartorinsky, and had to play before him. I still have to laugh about it. When I came into the room and was about to make my deep bow, I didn't see that the floor was all mirrors, and the walls were all mirrors. I fell down like a log and got an immense hole in my head. Then the courtiers arrived and started laughing. "Don't take that, Rehaar," said the duke, "You've got a sword at your side. Don't take that." "Yes, Your Grace," I said, "I have a sword and it hasn't been out of its sheath for thirty years. A musician doesn't need to draw his sword, and any musician who has courage and draws his sword is a swine who can never in his life bring forth anything from any instrument"—no, no, the third chord, *k, k,* pure, pure, the trills round, the thumb still, and—

PÄTUS (*who has been off to the side during this, enters and offers* REHAAR *his hand*): Your servant, Mr. Rehaar. How are you?

REHAAR (*stands, holding his lute*): Your devoted ser—how are you, Mr. Pätus? *Toujours content, jamais d'argent,*[10] as my father always said. My students all know it, that's why they don't feel any need to pay me. Mr. Pätus also owes me for the last serenade, but he doesn't think about that.

PÄTUS: You'll be paid, esteemed Rehaar. I expect my allowance in a week, without fail.

REHAAR: Yes, you've been expecting it for quite some time now, Mr. Pätus, but the allowance still hasn't arrived. Ah, well, what can I do? One must have patience. I always say, treat no man with so much respect as a student. Granted, a student is nothing, but he can become anything. (*Lays his lute on the table and takes a pinch of snuff.*) But what else have you done for me,

---

[10]Always content, never any money.

Mr. Pätus? Was it right, was it honest business? Didn't you crawl out my daughter's bedroom window yesterday?

PÄTUS: What, Father, I?

REHAAR (*lets the snuffbox fall*): I'll father you, I'll let it be known in the right places, sir, you can be sure of that. My daughter's honor is dear to me, and she is a honest girl, damn it! If I had only seen you yesterday or had been awake, I'd have helped you out that window, head over heels! Was that honest, was that honorable? Damn, when I was a student, I behaved like a student, not a reprobate. When the neighbors told me the news, I thought I'd been struck dead. I sent the girl off on the next coach to Königsberg, to her aunt, for she has no more honor here. And who's going to pay me for her travelling costs? Truly the whole day I haven't been able to touch my lute, and I've broken over fifteen E-strings. Yes, sir, I tremble throughout my whole body, but Mr. Pätus, I have a bone to pick with you. It must not remain so, I must teach you, you young brat, not to lead the children of honest people astray.

PÄTUS: Sir, do not insult me, or—

REHAAR: You understand, Mr. von Berg. You understand, if I only had the courage I'd demand he give me satisfaction here and now. See, he stands there and laughs in my face. Are we among the Turks and heathens then, so that a father and his daughter may no longer be safe? Mr. Pätus, you shall not get away with this. I'm going to tell His Majesty on you! Into the army with such a despicable dog! Into the army, that's the place for you! You're a scoundrel, not a student.

PÄTUS (*gives him a box on the ears*): Enough of your insults! I've told you five times already!

REHAAR (*leaps up, a handkerchief before his face*): So? You'll see! If I can just keep this bruise until I see His Majesty! If it'll just last a week, I can travel to Dresden and show him. You just wait, you'll find out if that's allowed. (*Cries.*) To strike a lutanist? Because he won't give you his daughter so you can play with her instead? You just wait, I'm going to tell His Majesty that you struck me in the face. You should have your hand cut off—scoundrel! (*Runs off.* PÄTUS *is about to follow him;* FRITZ *holds him back.*)

FRITZ: Pätus! You've handled this very badly. He was an offended father; you should have treated him with respect.

PÄTUS: What did the villain have to start insulting me for?

FRITZ: Insulting actions deserve insults. He can't avenge the honor of his daughter any other way, but there are people who would.

PÄTUS: Who? What kind of people?

FRITZ: You have dishonored her, you have dishonored her father. A bad lot, who'd act bold with women and musicians who are even less than the women.

PÄTUS: You're calling me a bad lot?

FRITZ: You should publicly apologize.

PÄTUS: With my walking-stick.

FRITZ: Then I shall answer you in his name.

PÄTUS (*cries out*): What do you want from me?

FRITZ: Satisfaction for Mr. Rehaar.

PÄTUS: You don't want to force me, my naive little man, to—

FRITZ: Yes, I want to force you not to be a scoundrel.

PÄTUS: You are a—you'll have to come to blows with me.

FRITZ: Gladly—if you won't give Mr. Rehaar satisfaction yourself.

PÄTUS: Never!

FRITZ: We shall see.

Act Five
Scene One

The school
LÄUFFER. MARTHA, *holding the* CHILD *in her arms.*

MARTHA: For the love of God! Help a poor blind woman and an innocent child who's lost its mother!

LÄUFFER (*gives her some money*): How did you get here if you can't see?

MARTHA: With great difficulty. The mother of this child was my guide, but she left some days ago, two days after giving birth. She left in the afternoon and was supposed to come back in the evening, but she still hasn't returned. May God send her eternal peace and glory!

LÄUFFER: Why such a wish?

MARTHA: Because she is dead, poor girl, otherwise she would not have broken her word. A workman from the hill visited me; he saw her throw herself in the pond. An old man was behind her and threw himself in after her; that must have been her father.

LÄUFFER: Oh, heaven! What a trembling! Is that her child?

MARTHA: That it is, just see how round it is, fattened on good carrots and turnips. What am I, a poor woman, to do? I couldn't keep it quiet and, since my reserves are gone, I made like Hagar, took the child on my shoulder and left, trusting to God's mercy.

LÄUFFER: Let me hold it. Oh, my heart! That I can press it to my heart! I am possessed by you, most frightening enigma! (*Holds the* CHILD *in his arms and stands before the mirror.*) Eh? Isn't this my likeness? (*Faints. The* CHILD *begins to cry.*)

MARTHA: Did you fall? (*Picks up the* CHILD *from the ground.*) Sweetie, my dear little Sweetie. (*The* CHILD *quiets down.*) Here! What have you done?—he doesn't answer. I must call for help; I think he's hurt himself. (*Leaves.*)

Scene Two

A small forest outside of Leipzig
FRITZ VON BERG *and* PÄTUS *stand with crossed swords.* REHAAR.

FRITZ: Are you ready?

PÄTUS: Do you wish to begin?

FRITZ: You first!

PÄTUS (*flings his sword away*): I can't fight with you.

FRITZ: Why not? Pick it up! I have insulted you, so I must offer you satisfaction.

PÄTUS: You may insult me as you wish. I need no satisfaction from you.

FRITZ: Now you insult me.

PÄTUS (*dashes up to him and embraces him*): Dearest Berg! Don't take it as an insult if I tell you that you are not capable of insulting me. I know your heart, and the thought of it makes me the most lily-livered coward on earth. Let us remain the best of friends! I would duel the devil himself, but not you.

FRITZ: You'll give Rehaar satisfaction, or I shall not leave here.

PÄTUS: Gladly, if he asks for it.

FRITZ: He is as deserving as you; you slapped him in the face. Quick, Rehaar, draw!

REHAAR (*draws*): All right, but he mustn't pick his up.

FRITZ: You can't be serious. Would you draw against a man who can't defend himself?

REHAAR: Eh, let those who have courage draw against armed men. A musician must have no courage. But, Mr. Pätus, you must give me satisfaction. (*Thrusts at him.* PÄTUS *falls back.*) Give me satisfaction! (*Stabs* PÄTUS *in the arm.* FRITZ *knocks away his sword.*)

FRITZ: Now I see that you deserved that box on the ear, you swine!

REHAAR: Well, what else am I supposed to do when I have no courage?

FRITZ: You should get another box on the ears and keep your mouth shut.

PÄTUS: Quiet, Berg! I'm only scratched. Mr. Rehaar, I beg your pardon. I should not have struck you since I knew that you were not capable of defending yourself. Even less should I have given you cause to insult me. I admit this satisfaction does not nearly atone for the insult I have given your house. If fate will aid my good intentions, I shall offer a better resolution. I shall ride after your daughter and marry her. There will be a position for me in my fatherland. Even if my father and I are never reconciled, nonetheless there is an inheritance of fifteen thousand guilders assured. (*Embraces him.*) Will you grant me your daughter?

REHAAR: Why not? I have nothing against it, so long as you treat her properly and honorably, and can provide for her. Ha, ha, ha! All my life I've said: good always comes from students. They have integrity in their souls. But soldiers!—they get a girl pregnant and nobody bothers about it; that's because they're all dragoons and must let themselves be killed. A man who has courage is capable of any depravity.

FRITZ: You are also a student. Come, it's been a long time since we've had a drink together. Let's drink to the health of your daughter.

REHAAR: Certainly, and then your lute concertos, Mr. von Berg. I have already cut three hours of your lessons in a row, and because I am also an honest man, I'll stay three hours later today and play my lute until it grows dark.

PÄTUS: And I'll play the violin.

Scene Three

The school
LÄUFFER, *lying in bed.* WENZESLAUS.

WENZESLAUS: My God! What's going on that you called me from my work? Are you sick again? I think that old woman must have been a witch. Ever since she left, you haven't had a healthy hour.

LÄUFFER: I'm not going to be here much longer.

WENZESLAUS: Should I call Schöpsen?

LÄUFFER: No.

WENZESLAUS: Is something weighing on your conscience? Tell me, confess, out with it! You look so terrified, it gives me a fright: *frigidus per ossa.*[11] Tell me, what is it?—as if he'd killed somebody. Why is your face so twisted? God have mercy, I'd better get Schöpsen.

LÄUFFER: Stay! I don't know if I've done the right thing—I've castrated myself.

WENZESLAUS: What!—castrat—my heartiest congratulations! You splendid young man! A second Origen! Let me embrace you! What a precious stroke of genius! I cannot hide it from you, I almost cannot resist the heroic impulse to imitate you. So right a deed, valued friend! This is the path you can follow to become a shining light of the church, a star of the first magnitude, a father of the church. I congratulate you, I shout to you a *Jubilate* and *Evoë*, my spiritual son. If I weren't past those years where the devil casts his sly nets for our best forces, I would not hesitate for a moment to—

LÄUFFER: Nonetheless, Schoolmaster, I'm sorry I did it.

WENZESLAUS: What, you're sorry? Put such thoughts out of your mind, esteemed Brother! You would not debase such a noble deed with foolish remorse and befoul it with sinful tears? I already see some welling up around your eyelids. Blink them back again, and sing with joyfulness: "I have been set free from nothingness, give me only wings, wings, wings!" You will not be like Lot's wife and look back at Sodom now that you have achieved the tranquility of Zoar. No, colleague, I must tell you that you are not the only person to have thought this way. Even among the benighted Jews there was a sect whom I would gladly acknowledge publicly, were I not afraid of disturbing my neighbors and the poor little lambs in my school. To be sure the sect also had some garbage and foolishness that I wouldn't exactly want to go along with; for example, on Sundays they wouldn't once answer nature's call, which is against all the rules of a reasonable regimen. I prefer that of our blessed Dr. Luther: what elevates is for God, and what goes down is for you, Mr. Devil!—Where was I?

LÄUFFER: I'm afraid that my motives were of another sort . . . repentance, despair . . .

WENZESLAUS: Yes, now I have it—the Essenes! As I was saying, they also never married. It was one of their basic rules and thus they lived to a ripe old age, as you can read in Josephus. It doesn't matter how they managed to subdue the drives of the flesh, whether they did as I, living soberly and frugally and smoking honest tobacco, or whether they followed your way.

---

[11]chilled to the bone

42

This much is certain: *in amore, in amore omnia insunt vitia*, and I crown with laurels the youth who sails past these obstacles, *lauro tempora cingam et sublimi fronte sidera pulsabit.*[12]

LÄUFFER: I'm afraid I'm going to die from my wound.

WENZESLAUS: Not at all, God be with you! I'll go straight over to Schöpsen's. I admit, he'll never have seen a case like this before, but he cured your arm all right, and that was a wound that did not serve your welfare; so God will grant him the grace of a cure to aid the eternal health of your soul. (*Leaves.*)

LÄUFFER: His jubilation has wounded me more than my knife. Oh, chastity, what a pearl you are! Since I lost you, I have taken step after step in passion, and now I end in despair. If this last step does not bring me to death, perhaps I can begin a new life and be reborn as Wenzeslaus.

Scene Four

Leipzig
FRITZ VON BERG *and* REHAAR *meet on the street.*

REHAAR: Mr. von Berg, a little note just arrived, addressed in care of me. It's from Mr. von Seiffenblase; he also studied the lute a little with me once. He told me to give this letter to a certain Mr. von Berg in Leipzig, if the fellow was still around. How I've been dashing about!

FRITZ: Where is Seiffenblase staying now?

REHAAR: I should give this to Mr. von Berg, he writes, if you happen to know this esteemed man. Oh, how I've been dashing about! He is in Königsberg, Mr. von Seiffenblase is. Just think of it, and my daughter is there too, and lives right across the street from him! She writes me, Katrinka does, that she cannot praise his courtesy enough—and all for my sake, I'm sure, he studied seven months with me.

FRITZ (*taking his watch out*): Esteemed Rehaar, I must get to class—don't say anything about this to Pätus, I beg of you. (*Leaves.*)

REHAAR (*calling after him*): Until this afternoon—the concerto!

---

[12]I shall wreathe his temples with laurel, and he will strike the heavens with his high forehead. (A blend of lines from two odes of Horace, I. 1 and III. 30)

Scene Five

Königsberg, in Prussia
COUNCILLOR, GUSTCHEN, *and the* MAJOR *in their house, at the window.*

COUNCILLOR: Is he the one?

GUSTCHEN: Yes, he is.

COUNCILLOR: I say, the aunt must be an abominable creature, or else she has an incredible hatred of her niece and is trying to have her ruined.

GUSTCHEN: But, Uncle, she can't ban him from the house.

COUNCILLOR: After what I told her? Who would think bad of her if she said to him: "Mr. von Seiffenblase, you have let it be known at the coffeehouse that you want my niece for your mistress; go find some other friends in the city. You'll get a fight from me. My niece is not from these parts, she is under my supervision, and has no one else to support her. If she is led astray, I'm the one who'll have to answer for it. God and all mankind would have to condemn me."

MAJOR: Be quiet, Brother! He's coming out now, and his head is hanging pitifully. Ho, ho, ho, may you burst! How pale he is!

COUNCILLOR: I shall go over and see what's wrong with him.

Scene Six

Leipzig
PÄTUS, *at a table, writing.* FRITZ *enters, a letter in his hand.*
PÄTUS *looks up and continues writing.*

FRITZ: Pätus! Are you busy?

PÄTUS: Just a second. (FRITZ *paces up and down.*) All right, then. (*Lays his pen aside.*)

FRITZ: Pätus! I got a letter . . . but I didn't have the courage to open it.

PÄTUS: Who's it from? Is it your father's writing?

FRITZ: No, von Seiffenblase's. My hand is trembling so, I can't open it. Open it, Brother, read it to me. (*Throws the letter onto an easychair.*)

PÄTUS (*reads*): "The memory of so many pleasant hours, which I still remember having enjoyed so pleasantly with you, obliges me to write to you and remind you of those pleasant hours."—What drivel!

FRITZ: Just read it.

PÄTUS: "And, because I consider myself obliged to report to you of my arrival and the pieces of news that have occurred here, so I must report to you the news of your most esteemed family who, unfortunately, have experienced a great many misfortunes during this past year. And, because of the courtesies I received in your parents' house, I consider myself obliged, because I know that you and your father are estranged and that he has not written to you in a long time, and that therefore you would not have heard, to report the

44

catastrophe with the tutor who was thrown out of your gracious uncle's house, because he violated your cousin, whereby she took it so to heart that she leaped into a pond, because of which tragedy your family is in the direst"—Berg! What's the matter with you? (*Pours lavender water on him.*) Come on, Berg! Speak to me! Are you ill? I shouldn't have read you the damned letter! It has to be a fabrication, it has to! Berg! Berg!

FRITZ: Let me . . . it will pass.

PÄTUS: Should I get somebody to bleed you?

FRITZ: Oh, bosh! Don't be such a fop! Read me the rest!

PÄTUS: Right, I'll—I'll take care of the vile, malicious letter this instant! (*Shreds it.*)

FRITZ: Violated . . . drowned . . . (*Smites his forehead.*) My fault! (*Rises.*) My fault and mine alone!

PÄTUS: You're being stupid. Is it your fault she let herself be seduced by the tutor?

FRITZ: Pätus, I swore to her I'd return, I swore to her! The three years have flown by, I have not returned, I have left Halle, my father has had no news of me, she has discovered it. The pain of it for her! You know her tendency to melancholy. Her mother's harshness, the loneliness in the country—and then her love betrays her! Can't you see, Pätus, can't you see? Oh, I am a cad. I am responsible for her death. (*Throws himself in the chair and covers his face.*)

PÄTUS: Fabrication! It's not true, that's not how it was at all. (*Stamps his foot.*) Damn it all, that you are so stupid and believe anything you're told. That louse, that lowlife, that layabout, that Seiffenblase is playing a dirty trick on you. Let me just get my hands on him! It's not true, she's not dead, and even if she is dead, she didn't kill herself.

FRITZ: He can't just be making it up—Kill herself! (*Leaps up.*) Oh, that's horrible!

PÄTUS (*Stamps his foot again*): No, she has not killed herself. Seiffenblase is lying; we must have more corroboration. You know you told him once when you were drinking that you were in love with your cousin. You see, that set the malicious blackguard off. I know! You know what you can do? Show him you don't give a damn! Let him whistle for a response! Shame the lowlife, write him: "Your Noblesse, I thank you most heartily for your news and ask that you"—no, here's the best. Write him back: "You're a louse." That's the most reasonable thing you can do.

FRITZ: I want to go home.

PÄTUS: I'll go with you, Berg. I'm not letting you alone for a minute.

FRITZ: But how can I get there? If I weren't afraid of a negative answer, I'd seek out Lightfoot *et compagnie,*[13] but I already owe him a hundred and fifty ducats.

PÄTUS: We should go together. Wait, let's stop by the lottery office. The mail from Hamburg arrived today. I'll ask when we stop by just for the fun of it.

---

[13]and company

Scene Seven

Königsberg
COUNCILLOR *leads* MISS REHAAR *by the hand* . GUSTCHEN. MAJOR.

COUNCILLOR: Here, Gustchen, I've brought you a companion. You are the same age and of the same position. Give her your hand and be friends!

GUSTCHEN: That I have been for a long time, dear Mamsell. I do not know what it was that rose and fell in my bosom when I saw you at the window, but you were involved in so many goings-on, so busy with visits from carriages and serenades, that I feared a visit from me would come at an inopportune time.

MISS REHAAR: I would have come to you, Miss, if I had had the courage. To intrude, by myself, on such a grand house I thought ill-bred, so I always had to force myself to withstand the urging of my heart that has often led me to your door.

COUNCILLOR: You can imagine, Major, how Seiffenblase responded to the warning I gave to Mrs. Dutzend, using my name, as I asked. He said he would soon be revenged on me. He saw how to get the responsibility off himself and he arrived at the house the next day with Minister Deichsel, so that the poor woman didn't have the courage then to forbid his visits. Two nights ago he placed two carriages on this street and one at the Brandenburg gate, which was left open because of the fireworks. But Mrs. Dutzend found out his plans, so when he showed up yesterday afternoon to try to persuade the mamsell to go with him and the minister to the assemblage, Mrs. Dutzend didn't trust the overtures of peace and flatly refused. Twice he drove past the door and twice he had to turn around and drive back. Since his cards were thus on the table, he tried again today. This time Mrs. Dutzend not only forbade him to visit the house, but let him know she was going to request a police watch around her house. Then he spat flames, threatened her with the minister—well, to put her at ease, I offered to take the mamsell into our house. We will have her with us in Insterburg for six months, until Seiffenblase has forgotten her, or so long as it pleases her to—

MAJOR: I've already had the horses hitched up. When we travel to Heidelbrunn, Mamsell, you shall come with us, or else my daughter will stay with you in Insterburg.

COUNCILLOR: That would be best, certainly. Besides, the country doesn't suit Gustchen, and I don't intend to leave Mamsell Rehaar alone.

MAJOR: Good thing your wife can't hear you—or are you making plans for your son?

COUNCILLOR: Don't make the good child blush. She would have seen him often enough in Leipzig, the wicked boy! Gustchen, you go red at his name? He doesn't deserve it.

GUSTCHEN: My father has forgiven me. Should your son find a less benevolent heart in you?

COUNCILLOR: He hasn't jumped in a pond yet.

MAJOR: If only we had found the blind woman with the child that the schoolmaster wrote me about. Until then, I cannot rest. Come! I must start out today and retrieve what is mine!

COUNCILLOR: You can do nothing now. You must spend the night in Insterburg.

Scene Eight

Leipzig. FRITZ VON BERG's *room.*
FRITZ VON BERG *sits, chin in hand.* PÄTUS *bursts in.*

PÄTUS: Triumph, Berg! Why are you moping about? God! God! (*Grabs his head and falls to his knees.*) Fate! Fate! Lightfoot didn't want to lend you anything, right? Forget him! I have money, I have everything—three hundred and eighty pieces of gold won in a stroke! (*Leaps up, shouting.*) Hi-dee-di-dee-dum, to Insterburg! Get packed!

FRITZ: Have you gone mad?

PÄTUS (*pulls out a purse filled with gold, and empties it on the floor*): There is my madness! Oh, ye of little faith! Now help me pick them up. Come on, bend a little. Today to Insterburg! Hurray! (*They pick up the pieces.*) I want to give eighty pieces to my father—that's what my last allowance came to—and ask him: "Well, Father, how do you like this?" We can pay off all your debts and mine as well, and then we can travel like princes. Hurray!

Scene Nine

The school
WENZESLAUS. LÄUFFER. *Both in black clothes.*

WENZESLAUS: How did you like the sermon, colleague? Did it edify you?

LÄUFFER: Good, very good. (*Sighs.*)

WENZESLAUS (*takes off his wig and puts on a nightcap*): Well, that doesn't tell me much. You should tell me which parts of the sermon especially touched and blessed you. Listen—sit down! I noticed something in church today that staggered me. You were so obviously distracted that, to tell you the truth, I was embarrassed before the whole congregation and almost lost the thread of my argument. How, I thought, could this young warrior, who has already so gallantly triumphed over the most treacherous enemy, so to speak—I must confess, you have vexed me, *skandalon edidous, hetaire!*[14] I saw how it went, I saw you always looking toward the middle door by the organ.

LÄUFFER: I confess, a painting was hanging there that distressed me terribly. The evangelist Mark with a face that looked not a bit more human than the lion that sat beside him, and the angel by the evangelist Matthew looked like a winged serpent.

WENZESLAUS: It wasn't that, my friend! Don't tell me tales; it wasn't that. A man looks at a picture, looks away, and that is all. Did you hear what I said? Can you quote one word from my sermon? And it was meant for you: quite casuistic. Oh! Oh! Oh!

LÄUFFER: I was exceptionally taken by the idea that between our souls and their

---

[14]You have given scandal, my companion!

47

rebirth and between flax-growing and hemp-growing a great similarity prevails; as the hemp must be freed from its old husk through violent pounding and knocking, so must our souls suffer all kinds of crosses and sufferings and mortifications of sensuality to be prepared for heaven.

WENZESLAUS: It was casuistic, my friend.

LÄUFFER: Nonetheless I should tell you that your list of devils that were thrown out of heaven, and the history of the whole revolution there, that Lucifer considered himself to be the best—the modern world has long given up such superstition. Why would you want to drag it up again? In the entire, modern, rational world, there is no belief in devils.

WENZESLAUS: Then the entire, modern, rational world will go to the devil. I am not condemning them, Mr. Almond, but it is true that we are living in the times that destroy men's souls. This is the final, evil time. But I shall not express my opinion further; I see that you are a skeptic, and one must also endure such people. But even if I grant, *posito*,[15] though I do not concede, that our religious doctrines are all superstition, about spirits, about hell, about devils—well, why should it bother you? What's eating you that you have to fight it tooth and nail? Do nothing wrong, only do right, and then you have no need to fear devils, even if there be more of them, as our blessed Luther says, than tiles on the roof. And as for superstition—oh, hush, hush, dear fellow. Consider first with mature reflection what advantages there are to superstition, and then have the courage to stab at me with your dry-as-dust gibes. Stamp out the superstition in me, and the true belief will be expunged with it, and only a naked field remain. But I know someone who said that both should be allowed to grow: the time will come when the wheat shall be separated from the tares. Superstition! Take superstition away from the rabble and they'll become freethinkers like you, and bang you over the head. Take the devil away from the peasant, and he'll become a devil to his masters and prove to them that there is such a thing. But putting all that aside—what were we talking about? Right, you were telling me whom you were staring at all during the sermon. Don't hold back! And don't tell me it was me, unless you are pitifully cross-eyed .

LÄUFFER: The painting.

WENZESLAUS: It was not the painting! It was where the girls who take catechism lessons from you sit. Friend! Surely there was nothing of the old leaven in your heart then! Oh, oh, who has once tasted the power of the next world—I tell you my hair stood on end. The one with the yellow hair so carelessly pushed up under her bonnet, right? With the light-brown eyes that always winked so coquettishly under her black eyebrows, like the stars behind a raincloud. It's true, I tell you, the girl is dangerous. I only saw her once from the pulpit, but thereafter had to shut my eyes tightly when they fell on her, otherwise it would have happened to me as to the wise men, on the Areopagus, who forgot justice and righteousness for the sake of vile Phryne. But tell me, what are you trying to do, abandoning yourself to licentious yearnings when you lack the means to satisfy them? Do you want to give yourself over to the devil for nothing? Is that the vow that you made to the Lord? I speak to you now as your spiritual father. To you who with so little effort now could triumph over all carnality, soar over the earth, and fly to

---

[15]postulate

48

better lands! (*Embraces him.*) Ah, my dear son, I beg you by these tears that I pour out in true affection for you. Don't turn back to the fleshpots of Egypt, when you are so near Canaan! Hurry! Hurry! Save your immortal soul! There is nothing in the world to hold you back any longer. The world has nothing to give you as reward for your faithlessness, not even carnal pleasure, not to mention the tranquility of your soul—I'll leave you now to your resolutions. (*Leaves.*)

(LÄUFFER *remains seated, lost in thought.*)

Scene Ten

LISE (*enters, a hymnal in her hand, without* LÄUFFER'*s being aware of her. She observes him a long time, silently. He leaps up, is about to kneel, becomes aware of her, and stares at her a long while, confusedly.*)

LÄUFFER (*drawing close to her*): You have stolen a soul from heaven. (*Grasps her hand.*) What brings you here, Lise?

LISE: I came, Mr. Almond . . . I came, because you said that tomorrow there would be no catechism lesson . . . because you . . . so I came . . . you said . . . so I came to ask if tomorrow there would be a catechism lesson.

LÄUFFER: Ah! Look at those cheeks, you angel! How they burn in innocent fire, but would damn me if they could—Lise, why does your hand tremble? Why are your lips so pale and your cheeks so red? What do you want?

LISE: To know if there will be a catechism lesson tomorrow.

LÄUFFER: Sit down, next to me—put your hymnal aside. Who fixes your hair when you go to church? (*Sits her down on a chair next to his.*)

LISE (*about to rise*): Forgive me if the bonnet wasn't put on well. There was such a terrible wind when I was coming to church.

LÄUFFER (*takes both her hands in his hand*): Oh, you are—how old are you, Lise? Have you ever . . . what I wish to ask is . . . have you ever had a suitor?

LISE (*brightly*): Oh, yes, one just these past weeks. The shepherd's Greta was so jealous of me. She kept saying: "I don't know why he spends so much time on that simple girl." And then I had an officer, not three months ago.

LÄUFFER: An officer?

LISE: Oh yes, and one of the most distinguished, I can tell you that. He had three braids on his arm, but I was still too young, and my father didn't want to give me to him, because of a soldier's ways and rearing.

LÄUFFER: Would you . . . oh, I don't know what I'm saying! Would you . . . I am so unworthy!

LISE: Oh yes, with all my heart!

LÄUFFER: Enchanting girl! (*About to kiss her hand.*) You don't know yet, what I wanted to ask.

LISE (*pulls her hand away*): Oh stop! My hand is turning black! Fie! What are you doing? You see, I have always wanted a clerical man. For as long as I

49

can remember, I have always liked learned men; they are always so courteous, so mannerly, not so wham-bam-thank-you-ma'am as the soldiers—although I also like them too, for other reasons, that I don't deny. It's those lovely bright uniforms. If clerics would only dress the way soldiers do—oh, I'd just die!

LÄUFFER: Let me seal your impudent lips with a kiss. (*Kisses her.*) Oh, Lise! If you only knew how miserable I am!

LISE: Oh fie, sir, what are you doing?

LÄUFFER: Once more and then never again for all eternity! (*Kisses her. WENZESLAUS enters.*)

WENZESLAUS: What is this? *Proh deum atque hominum fidem!*[16] What now, false prophet! Rapacious wolf in sheep's clothing! Is that the sort of attention you give to your flock? Leading the innocent girl astray when you're supposed to protect her from temptation? Scandal will come, and woe to the man through whom such scandal comes!

LÄUFFER: Mr. Wenzeslaus!

WENZESLAUS: Not a word! Not a word! You have shown yourself in your true colors. Out of my house, seducer!

LISE (*kneels before WENZESLAUS*): Dear schoolmaster, he has done me no harm.

WENZESLAUS: He has done you a greater harm than your worst enemy could. He has led your innocent heart astray.

LÄUFFER: I proclaim myself guilty. But how can one withstand so much enticement? If you were to tear my heart from my body and rip me limb from limb, so that I had only one veinful of blood left, that perfidious vein would throb for Lise.

LISE: He has done me no harm.

WENZESLAUS: Hasn't done any harm! Merciful Father!

LÄUFFER: I told her that she was the most charming creature that ever Creation has blessed. I have pressed that on her lips. I have sealed with my kisses her innocent mouth that otherwise, with its magic tongue, would have enticed me to a far greater crime.

WENZESLAUS: Is that no crime? What do you young men call a crime nowadays? *O tempora, o mores!* Have you read Valerius Maximus? Have you read the section *De pudicitia*? He tells of Maenius, who killed his freedman, because the man once kissed his daughter. And the principle: *ut etiam oscula ad maritum sincera perferret.*[17] How do you like that? Is that to your taste? *Etiam oscula, non solum virginitatem, etiam oscula.*[18] And Maenius was a heathen, so what should a Christian do, who knows that matrimony was instituted by God, and that the happiness of such a condition can be poisoned at the roots, that a future husband destroys his trust and comfort, and profanes his heaven when—out of my sight, evildoer! I must have nothing to do with you! Go to a sultan and get yourself hired as overseer of his seraglio, but not as the shepherd of my sheep. You mercenary! You rapacious wolf in sheep's clothing!

---

[16] By the faithfulness of men and gods! (Cicero, *Tusculan Disputations*, V, 48)

[17] that she may also offer pure kisses to her husband

[18] Kisses as well, not just virginity, but kisses as well.

LÄUFFER: I want to marry Lise.

WENZESLAUS: Marry! Oh, yes, of course! As if she could be happy with a eunuch!

LISE: Oh, I could be most sincerely happy, Schoolmaster.

LÄUFFER: How miserable I am!

LISE: Believe me, Schoolmaster, I shall not abandon him. Take my life from me, I shall not abandon him. I like him and my heart tells me that I shall never like anybody else in the world so much as him.

WENZESLAUS: But . . . that notwithstanding . . . Lise, you don't understand the situation. I can't tell you why, Lise, but you cannot marry him. It's impossible.

LISE: Why should it be impossible, Schoolmaster? How can it be impossible if I want to, and if he wants to, and if my father also wants us to? And my father always told me that if I could marry a cleric—

WENZESLAUS: But damn it, he can't—God forgive me my sin—*you* tell her!

LÄUFFER: Perhaps she doesn't require that. Lise, I can't sleep with you.

LISE: So you can wake up with me. As long as we can spend the day together and laugh and kiss hands. By God, I like him! God knows, I like him!

LÄUFFER: You see, Mr. Wenzeslaus! She demands only love from me. Is it necessary for the happiness of the marriage that one satisfies his bestial instincts?

WENZESLAUS: Yes, but . . . *connubium sine prole est quasi dies sine sole.*[19] Be fruitful and multiply. It says so in the Bible. Where there is marriage, there must also be children.

LISE: No, Schoolmaster, I swear to you on my life I don't want to have any children. Oh, sure, children! You can't mean it. Oh, some favor I'd be doing myself to have children! My father has chicks and ducks enough that I have to feed. If I had to feed children as well!

LÄUFFER (*kisses her*): Divine Lise!

WENZESLAUS (*pulls them apart*): What! What! Before my eyes? Go, slink off together, it's all right with me. It is certainly better to marry than to burn. But it's all over with us, Mr. Almond! All the great hopes that I had for you, all the great plans that your heroism inspired in me—merciful heaven! How wide is the abyss between a father of the church and a capon! I thought you would be Origen the second. *O homuncio, homuncio!*[20] That will have to be a very different man, one who follows the path of purpose and principles to become a pillar of our sinking church! A very different man! Who knows when such a man will be seen again! (*Leaves.*)

LÄUFFER: Go to your father, Lise! Only his consent, and then I shall be the most fortunate man on earth!

---

[19]A marriage without offspring is like a day without sunshine.

[20]Oh, little man, little man!

Scene Eleven

Insterburg
COUNCILLOR. FRITZ. PÄTUS. GUSTCHEN. MISS REHAAR.
GUSTCHEN *and* MISS REHAAR *are hidden in an adjoining room,*
at the COUNCILLOR's *request. The* COUNCILLOR *and* FRITZ
rush to meet each other.

FRITZ (*falls to his knees*): My father!

COUNCILLOR (*lifts him to his feet and embraces him*): My son!

FRITZ: Have you forgiven me?

COUNCILLOR: My son!

FRITZ: I am no longer worthy to be called your son.

COUNCILLOR: Sit, sit. Don't think about it any longer. How did you support yourself in Leipzig? Did you run up debts and put them on my account? No? So how did you manage?

FRITZ: This magnanimous fellow paid off everything for me.

COUNCILLOR: How?

PÄTUS: This even more magnanimous fellow—oh, I can't go on.

COUNCILLOR: Sit down, children, and speak more clearly. Have you reconciled with your father, Mr. Pätus?

PÄTUS: I haven't heard a word from him.

COUNCILLOR: Then how have you both managed?

PÄTUS: I won the lottery. Chickenfeed, really, just a trifle. But it came in handy when we needed to come here.

COUNCILLOR: I see you wild students think more clearly than your fathers. What must you have thought of me, Fritz? But someone defamed you horribly.

PÄTUS: Seiffenblase, right?

COUNCILLOR: I should not name him. That could lead to brawling, and now is not the time or place.

PÄTUS: Seiffenblase! Well, I'll be hanged!

COUNCILLOR: But why have you returned just now?

FRITZ: Oh, that "just now," father! That "just now." Does it mean what I think?

COUNCILLOR: What do you mean?

FRITZ: Is Gustchen dead?

COUNCILLOR: Halloo, the gallant! What would make you ask such a question?

FRITZ: A letter from Seiffenblase.

COUNCILLOR: He wrote you that she was dead?

FRITZ: And dishonored as well.

PÄTUS: He's a slanderous villain!

COUNCILLOR: Do you know a Miss Rehaar in Leipzig?

FRITZ: Oh yes, her father was my lute instructor.

COUNCILLOR: Seiffenblase wanted to dishonor her. I saved her from his trap. Now he and I are sworn enemies.

PÄTUS (*rises*): Miss Rehaar! May he rot in hell!

52

COUNCILLOR: Where are you going?

PÄTUS: Is he in Insterburg?

COUNCILLOR: No, no. Don't be so eager to save the princess, Mr. Knight of the Round Table! Did you also know Miss Rehaar?

PÄTUS: I? No, I don't know her—yes, I know her.

COUNCILLOR: So I see. Wouldn't you like to step into the next room for a moment? (*Leads him to the door.*)

PÄTUS (*opens the door and falls back, clutching his head with both hands*): Miss Rehaar! Let me kneel! (*Offstage.*) Am I so fortunate? Or is this only a dream? An intoxication? An enchantment?

COUNCILLOR: Let's let him be! (*Turns to* FRITZ.) So you still think of Gustchen?

FRITZ: You still haven't resolved the terrible mystery. Did Seiffenblase lie?

COUNCILLOR: I think we should talk about it later. We don't want to spoil their present joy.

FRITZ (*kneeling*): Oh, my Father, if you have any remaining affection for me, do not let me hover between heaven and earth, between hope and doubt. That is why I came here: I couldn't stand the uncertainty any longer. Is Gustchen alive? Is it true that she was dishonored?

COUNCILLOR: That last is unfortunately only too tragically true.

FRITZ: And has she thrown herself in a pond?

COUNCILLOR: Yes, and her father plunged in after her.

FRITZ: Let the executioner's axe fall! I am the most miserable man among men!

COUNCILLOR: Get up. It wasn't your fault.

FRITZ: I shall never get up. (*Strikes his breast.*) I was guilty, I and only I. Gustchen, blessed saint, forgive me!

COUNCILLOR: And what are you blaming yourself for?

FRITZ: I swore to her, falsely swore. Gustchen! Would that it were possible for me to leap in after you! (*Leaps up excitedly.*) Where is the pond?

COUNCILLOR: Here! (*Leads him to the adjoining room.*)

FRITZ (*offstage, shouts*): Gustchen! Am I seeing a ghost? Heaven! What joy! Let me die! Let me die in your arms!

COUNCILLOR (*wiping away his own tears*): A tender reunion! If only the major were here! (*Joins the others.*)

Scene Twelve

MAJOR, *a* CHILD *in his arms.* PÄTUS's FATHER.

MAJOR: Come in, Mr. Pätus. You have restored me to life. That was the only maggot still gnawing at me. I must introduce you to my brother. And I want to encircle your old blind mother with gold!

FATHER: My mother has made me far happier by her unexpected visit than she has you. You only got back a grandson, who will be a reminder of sadder times. I got back a mother who brings back memories of the happiest times of my life, and whose maternal tenderness I have up to now only repaid with hate and ingratitude. I threw her out of the house, after she had given me the entire estate of my father and all her personal wealth too! I treated her as barbarically as a tiger. What a blessing from God it is that she is still alive, that she can still forgive me. The magnanimous saint! That it is still in my power to put right my accursed crime!

MAJOR: Brother Berg! Where are you? Hey! (COUNCILLOR *enters.*) Here is my child, my grandson. Where is Gustchen? My dearest little grandson! (*Caresses him.*) My dearest funny little doll!

COUNCILLOR: This is splendid! And you, Mr. Pätus?

MAJOR: Mr. Pätus found him for me. His mother was the old blind woman, the beggar Gustchen told us so much about!

FATHER: And a beggar because of me. Oh, the shame binds my tongue! But I shall tell the whole world what a monster I was.

COUNCILLOR: Have you heard the news, Major? A suitor has been found for your daughter. But don't try to make me tell you his name!

MAJOR: A suitor for my daughter? (*Throws the* CHILD *on the sofa.*) Where is she?

COUNCILLOR: Take it easy! Her suitor is with her. Do you give your consent?

MAJOR: Is he from a good family? Is he of the aristocracy?

COUNCILLOR: I doubt it.

MAJOR: But surely not too far beneath her station? She should marry into one of the first families of the kingdom. Cursed thought! I shouldn't have thought it; it could still send me to an asylum.

COUNCILLOR (*opens the door; at his wink,* FRITZ *and* GUSTCHEN *emerge.*)

MAJOR (*embraces* FRITZ): Fritz! (*To the* COUNCILLOR): Your Fritz is the suitor? You want to marry my daughter? God bless you! Do you not know then, or do you know everything? You see how gray my hair has become since that time! (*Leads him to the sofa.*) You see? There is her child. Are you a philosopher? Can you forget everything? Is Gustchen still good enough for you? Oh, she has repented. Lad, I swear to you she has repented as no nun or saint has ever done before. What else is there to say? Even the angels fell from heaven. But Gustchen has picked herself up.

FRITZ: Let me get a word in edgewise!

MAJOR (*continues to embrace him*): No, Son! I want to squeeze you to death. That you are so magnanimous, that you think so nobly, that you . . . are my son.

FRITZ: When I am in Gustchen's arms, I envy no king.

MAJOR: So right! That is right. She has confessed everything then, she has told you everything?

FRITZ: This false step only makes her more dear to me . . . makes her more angelic. She need only look in the mirror to be assured that she is the source of all my happiness. But she continues to tremble before her—what she calls—unbearable thought that she will make me wretched again. What have I to expect of such a woman other than a heaven!

MAJOR: Yes, a heaven, if it is true that not only the righteous enter there but also the sinners who repent. My daughter has done penance, as have I for my folly in not listening to a brother who understood things better, and God has welcomed us both back into the fold.

COUNCILLOR (*Calls into the room*): Mr. Pätus, come here at once! Your father is here.

FATHER: What do I hear? My son?

PÄTUS (*embraces him*): Your miserable, outcast son. But God has adopted this poor orphan. Here, Papa, is the money that you spent on my education. Here it is, all back, and my thanks with it. It returns with double interest: the capital has multiplied, and your son has become a righteous fellow.

FATHER: Must all today then vie to shame me through magnanimity? My son, accept again your father, who set aside his humanity for a while and degenerated into a wild animal. I treated your grandmother as I treated you. She has also returned and forgiven me and made me her son again. So shall you make me your father again. Take all my money, Gustav! Spend it as you wish, only never let me suffer the penalty for the ingratitude that I showed your grandmother for a similar gift.

PÄTUS: Permit me to make happy with it the most virtuous, sweetest girl—

FATHER: What? You are also in love? I permit everything with joy. I am old and would like to see grandchildren before I die, to whom I could prove as devoted as your grandmother proved to you.

FRITZ (*embraces the child on the sofa, kisses it, and carries it to* GUSTCHEN): This child is now mine too, a sad testimony to the weakness of your sex and the foolishness of mine. But most of all to the great advantages of a young girl's being educated by a tutor.

MAJOR: But dear son, how should they be educated then?

COUNCILLOR: Are there no institutes, no sewing-schools, no convent schools, no boarding-schools?—but we shall talk of this another time.

FRITZ (*kisses the child again*): And nonetheless infinitely precious to me because he's the image of his mother. At least, my dear boy, I shall never let you be educated by a tutor!

THE SOLDIERS

BY

JAKOB MICHAEL REINHOLD LENZ

1774

DRAMATIS PERSONAE

WESENER, *a jeweler in Lille*
MRS. WESENER, *his wife*
MARIE, *their daughter*
CHARLOTTE, *their daughter*
STOLZIUS, *a draper in Armentières*
His MOTHER
DESPORTES, *a baron from Hennegau, France, and an officer in the French army*
COUNT VON SPANNHEIM, *his colonel*
PIRZEL, *a captain*
EISENHARDT, *an army chaplain*
HAUDY, *an officer*
RAMMLER, *an officer*
MARY, *an officer*
COUNTESS DE LA ROCHE
Her SON, the YOUNG COUNT
His COUSIN
The COUSIN's TUTOR
MISS ZIPFERSAAT
AARON
MRS. BISHOP
Her COUSIN *and others*

The play is set in French Flanders.

58

Act One
Scene One

Lille
MARIE. CHARLOTTE.

MARIE (*head resting on one hand, writing a letter*): Sister, do you know how to spell Madame? *Ma, ma, tamm, tamm, me, me.*

CHARLOTTE (*sits and spins*): That's right.

MARIE: Listen, I want to read this to you. Does this sound right, what I've written? "My dear Matamm! Happily we have arrivé in Lille." Is *arrivé* right? Ar, ar, ree, vay?

CHARLOTTE: That's right.

MARIE: "We do not know how we deserved the kindnesses which you showered upon us, we wish only to be a position—" Is that all right?

CHARLOTTE: I won't know till you finish the sentence.

MARIE: "To repay all the politenesses and courtesies. Because, however, such is not yet in our power, beg of you to allow a delay in reciprocation."

CHARLOTTE: *We* beg of you.

MARIE: Let it go, don't interrupt me.

CHARLOTTE: *We* beg of you.

MARIE: Oh, what do you know? This is how Papa writes. (*Puts all the writing equipment away quickly, and is about to seal the letter.*)

CHARLOTTE: Well, go on. Read the rest.

MARIE: The rest doesn't concern you. She is certainly more educated than Papa, and even he said the other day, it wasn't courteous always to write *I* and *we* like that. (*Seals the letter.*) Here, Stefan. (*Gives him a coin.*) Take the letter to the post office.

CHARLOTTE: If you won't read me the last part, you must have written something really good about Mr. Stolzius.

MARIE: That's none of your business.

CHARLOTTE: Oh, I see, and I'm supposed to be jealous or something? I could have written just as well as you, but I didn't want to rob you of the pleasure of putting your fine hand on display.

MARIE: Listen, Lottie, don't tease me about Stolzius! Or I'll run right downstairs and tell Papa.

CHARLOTTE: What do I care? He certainly knows by now that you are in love with him, and that you just can't stand it when somebody else mentions his name.

MARIE: Lottie! (*Starts to cry, and runs downstairs.*)

Scene Two

STOLZIUS (*with bandaged head*): Mother, I don't feel well.

MOTHER (*standing, regards him a while*): Mm, I think that desperate girl's still on your mind, and that's what given you such a headache. Ever since she left, you haven't had a peaceful hour.

STOLZIUS: No, really, Mother, something's wrong with me.

MOTHER: Mm, if you'll let me speak, I'll make your heart a bit lighter. (*Pulls out a letter.*)

STOLZIUS (*leaping up*): She wrote to you?

MOTHER: Here, you can read it. (STOLZIUS *tears the letter from her hand and devours it with his eyes.*) But listen, the colonel wants to have some material measured for the regiment.

STOLZIUS: Let me answer the letter, Mother.

MOTHER: *Now,* dopey, the colonel needs some material measured for his regiment. Come along, then.

Scene Three

Lille
MARIE. DESPORTES.

DESPORTES: What are you doing there, my divine Mademoiselle?

MARIE (*who has been scribbling on a tablet of white paper, quickly sticks the quill behind her ear*): Oh, nothing, nothing, kind sir. (*Smiling.*) I'm just too fond of writing.

DESPORTES: If only I were so fortunate as to see one of your letters, to see only one line of your beautiful hand.

MARIE: Oh, forgive me, but I don't write beautifully at all. I'm ashamed to let my writing be seen.

DESPORTES: Anything that comes from your hand must be beautiful.

MARIE: Oh, sir, stop. I know all that is just flattery.

DESPORTES (*kneeling*): I swear to you that never in my entire life have I ever seen anything more perfect than you.

MARIE (*knitting, eyes cast down on her work*): My mother told me, yes, she did, about how untrue you were.

DESPORTES: I untrue? Can you believe that of me, divine Mademoiselle? Is it being untrue when I steal away from my regiment, that I have sold six months service, and risk that when they discover that I have not been at my parents' as I reported they will throw me in prison? Is it being untrue when I return here only to have the good fortune of seeing you again, most perfect one?

MARIE (*looking down at her work again*): My mother has told me, over and over,

60

I am not yet fully grown, I am at the age when we're neither pretty nor ugly.

(WESENER *enters*.)

WESENER: Eh, what do we have here? Your obedient servant, sir. To what do we owe the honor of your presence?

DESPORTES: I'm only here for a few weeks. I'm visiting one of my relatives who just arrived from Brussels.

WESENER: You will forgive me, I wasn't at home. My Marieel must have bored you terribly. And how are your esteemed parents? I assume they have received the snuffboxes?

DESPORTES: Believe it or not, I haven't been to see them yet. We still have an account to settle, little father.

WESENER: Oh, there's no hurry, it's not the first time. The good lady did not come down to our Mardi gras last winter.

DESPORTES: She felt a little out of sorts. Were there many balls?

WESENER: Oh, yes, there must have been some. As you know, I don't go to any, and my daughters to even fewer.

DESPORTES: But should it be allowed, Mr. Wesener, for you to deny your daughters all pleasures? How can they remain in good health?

WESENER: Oh, if they work, they'll stay healthy enough. My Marieel lacks for nothing, thank God, and she always has rosy cheeks.

MARIE: Yes, you can't change Papa's mind on this, even though I feel such a tightness in my heart now and then that I don't know if I can sit still for anguish.

DESPORTES: You see, if you allow Mademoiselle your daughter no pleasure, she will become melancholy.

WESENER: Eh, what? She has pleasures enough with her girlfriends. When they're all together, you can't hear yourself think.

DESPORTES: Permit me the honor of escorting Mademoiselle your daughter once to the theater. Tonight there's a brand new piece.

MARIE: Oh, Papa!

WESENER: No, no, absolutely not, sir! Please don't take this wrongly, but not one word more on the subject. My daughter is not used to going to theaters. It would just provide gossip for the neighbors. And with a soldier to boot!

DESPORTES: I am in civilian clothes. Who would know me?

WESENER: *Tant pis*![1] Once and for all, it's not proper for her to be seen anywhere with a man. She hasn't even made her First Communion yet. Should she be going to the theater and pretending to be a fine lady? In a nutshell, no! I shall not permit it, sir.

MARIE: But, Papa, if nobody knows the baron!

WESENER (*somewhat gently*): Will you be quiet? Nobody knows him. *Tant pis* if nobody knows him. You will *pardonner*, sir! I would be more than happy to serve you in any other capacity.

DESPORTES: Apropos, Mr. Wesener. Would you show me then some of your brooches?

WESENER: Immediately. (*Goes out*.)

---

[1]So much the worse!

61

DESPORTES: Listen, my angelic, my divine Marieel. We shall play a little prank on your father. There's nothing we can do today, but the day after tomorrow, they're doing an excellent show, *La chercheuse d'esprit*,[2] and the first *pièce* is *The Deserter*. You have a friend around here, don't you?

MARIE: Mrs. Weyher.

DESPORTES: Where does she live?

MARIE: Near here, at the corner by the fountain.

DESPORTES: I'll go there first, and then you'll go there, and then we'll go together to the theater.

(WESENER *returns with a large box of brooches.* MARIE, *smiling, gestures to* DESPORTES.)

WESENER: As you see, they're available at all prices. These go for one hundred talers, these for fifty, these for one hundred and fifty. Whatever you like.

DESPORTES (*examines each, and shows the box to* MARIE): Which would you advise me to get? (MARIE *smiles and, as soon as her father looks down to take one out, waves at* DESPORTES.)

WESENER: On my honor, this one is especially attractive.

DESPORTES: That is true. (*Holds it against* MARIE's *hair.*) Just see what a sparkle it has against such beautiful brown hair. Oh, Mr. Wesener, it looks so beautiful on your daughter. Would you do me the favor of letting her keep it?

WESENER (*smiling, takes it back from him*): I must ask you, sir—that won't do. My daughter has never in her life accepted a present from a young gentleman.

MARIE (*gaze fixed solidly on her work*): I wouldn't have been able to wear it anyway. It's too large for my hairstyle.

DESPORTES: So I'll send it to my mother. (*Wraps it up painstakingly.*)

WESENER (*putting the others away, growls somewhat secretly at* MARIE): Brooch indeed! You should never wear any such thing on your head. That's no sort of business for you. (*Silently, she continues working.*)

DESPORTES: So I'll take my leave of you, then, Mr. Wesener. But before I leave town, I'll settle the account.

WESENER: There's no hurry, sir, there's no hurry. I hope you will be so kind as to do us the honor again.

DESPORTES: With your permission. Adieu, Miss Marie. (*Leaves.*)

MARIE: Really, Papa, how could you!

WESENER: See here, I don't have to settle any account with you. What do you know of the world, my silly innocent thing?

MARIE: He certainly has a pleasant disposition, the baron does.

WESENER: Because he flatters you a bit and so on and so forth. One is the same as the next; you don't have to tell me how it is with soldiers. You'll find them in all the taverns and all the coffeehouses. They tell stories and before you know it, a poor girl is trash on everybody's lips: "Such and such a young lady is rather loose," and "I know about so and so," and "I'd like that one too."

MARIE: Papa! (*Begins to cry.*) You are always so crude!

WESENER (*pats her on the back*): You must not think so badly of me. You are my only joy, you little fool. That's why I worry so much about you.

---

[2]The Seeker of Spirit

MARIE: I wish you'd just let me worry about me. I'm not a little girl any more.

Scene Four

Armentières
The COLONEL, COUNT VON SPANNHEIM, *at a table with the chaplain,*
EISENHARDT. *A* YOUNG COUNT. *His* COUSIN. *The* COUSIN's TUTOR.
HAUDY. *A* CAPTAIN. MARY. OTHER OFFICERS.

YOUNG COUNT: Do you think we'll get such a good troupe here again soon?

HAUDY: It is to be hoped for, especially for our younger men. They say Godeau wanted to come.

TUTOR: In fact, it cannot be denied, that the theater is an almost indispensible thing for a garrison, *c'est à dire,*[3] a theater where taste prevails, as for example, with the French theater.

EISENHARDT: I don't quite see what the advantage is supposed to be.

COLONEL: You only say that, Pastor, because you've got those two white wattles under your chin. I know in your heart you think otherwise.

EISENHARDT: Pardon me, Colonel! I have never been a hypocrite, and even if that were a necessary vice in my profession, I think chaplains would still be an exception, because they have to deal with more sensible people. I love the theater myself, and very much like to go and see a good play. But all that notwithstanding, I don't think that it is such a wholesome institution for our officers.

HAUDY: For God's sake, Padre, or Pastor, or whatever you're called. Think of all the depravities that are prevented or restrained through the theater. Certainly officers have to have some diversion, don't they?

EISENHARDT: In moderation, Major! Better you should ask what sort of depravities are introduced to the officers by the theater.

HAUDY: We can settle this now. In a nutshell, sir (*Leans forward, both elbows on the table.*) I maintain before you here that a single play, even if it were the most dreadful farce, is ten times more useful—and not just for officers, but for the whole city—than all the sermons taken together, than anything that you and the likes of you have ever delivered or ever will.

COLONEL (*gestures at* HAUDY *indignantly*): Major!

EISENHARDT: If I were prejudiced in favor of my profession, I would be offended. But we shall put all that aside, because I consider neither you nor many of the men here qualified to pass judgment on the value of my profession to your lives. So let us keep to the subject of the theater and the astonishing benefits that it is supposed to have on officers. Just answer me one simple question: what do the men learn there?

MARY: Eh, do we always have to learn something? We amuse ourselves, isn't that enough?

---

[3]that is to say

EISENHARDT: Would God that you only amused yourselves, that you didn't learn anything! In fact, though, you imitate what you see before you and bring misfortune and damnation to whole families.

COLONEL: Pastor, your enthusiasm is laudable, but it does smack of the black cloth. Now, don't take this badly, but what family has been ruined by an officer? That now and then a girl has a child she shouldn't have had?

HAUDY: A whore will always be a whore, no matter whom she meets. If she doesn't become a soldier's whore, then she becomes a preacher's whore.

EISENHARDT: Major, it displeases me that you always drag the clerics along in your jokes, because you prevent me then from answering you candidly. You may think that there's personal bitterness in my words. But I swear to you, if I get excited, it is merely the subject of which we are speaking, and not your mockings and personal attacks on my profession. If we devote ourselves to wisecracks, we'll never get anywhere in the talk.

HAUDY: Oh talk, talk, prattle away. That's why we're here. Who's stopping you?

EISENHARDT: What you said was a thought worthy of a Nero or Oglei Oglu. And it may have caused horrors back then when it first appeared: "A whore will always be a whore." Do you know the other sex so well?

HAUDY: Sir, *you* will not teach me anything about them.

EISENHARDT: You know them, perhaps, from the masterpieces of your art, but permit me to say to you that a whore never becomes a whore unless she is driven to it. The desire is in all people, but every woman knows that her future happiness depends completely on it. Would a woman sacrifice her entire future if she were not forced to?

HAUDY: I wasn't referring to honorable girls.

EISENHARDT: Even honorable girls should be wary of the theater; that's where you learn the art of making them dishonorable.

MARY: What an evil mind you have!

HAUDY: The man also has a foul mouth about officers. Damn, if anybody else said this to me! Do you mean to say, sir, we stop being honorable men as soon as we enter the army?

EISENHARDT: I wish you much luck in your views. As long as I continue to see kept women and unfortunate burghers' daughters, however, I cannot retract my statements.

HAUDY: That deserves a rap on the knuckles.

EISENHARDT (*rising*): Sir, I carry a sword!

COLONEL: Major, I beg of you—Mr. Eisenhardt has done nothing wrong. What do you want from him? And the first man who comes too close to him—sit down, Pastor, he will give you satisfaction. (HAUDY *leaves.*) But you also went too far, Mr. Eisenhardt, for all that. There is no officer who doesn't know what honor demands of him.

EISENHARDT: If he has time enough to think about it. But what is before his eyes in the most recent plays? Aren't the most monstrous crimes against the most sacred rights of father and family painted in the most charming colors? Aren't the villains made to look as if they'd just fallen from heaven? Wouldn't that incite people, wouldn't that suffocate every bit of conscience left from their upbringing? How to betray a watchful father, or instruct an innocent girl in depravity—those are the sort of test questions they see answered there.

64

HAUDY (*in the entryway with the other* OFFICERS, *as the door swings open*): That damned blackfrock!

COLONEL: Let us go to the coffeehouse, Parson, you owe me a rematch in chess. Adjutant! Tell Major Haudy not to leave his quarters today. Tell him I'll return his sword myself tomorrow morning.

Scene Five

Lille

WESENER *sits, eating his evening meal with* MRS. WESENER *and* CHARLOTTE. MARIE *enters, very dressed up.*

MARIE (*throws her arms around* WESENER'*s neck*): Oh, Papa! Papa!

WESENER (*with his mouth full*): What is it? What's the matter with you?

MARIE: I can't keep it a secret from you. I went to the theater. What a marvelous thing it was.

(WESENER *shoves his chair away from the table and whirls around to face* MARIE.)

MARIE: If you had seen what I saw, you would not be angry, Papa. (*Sits in his lap.*) Dear Papa, what a marvelous thing it was. My head is still spinning. I won't be able to sleep a wink tonight from sheer excitement. The wonderful baron!

WESENER: What, the baron took you to the theater?

MARIE (*somewhat timidly*): Yes, Papa . . . dear Papa!

WESENER (*pushes her from his lap*): Away from me, you slut! Do you intend to be the baron's mistress?

MARIE (*face half turned away, almost crying*): I was at Mrs. Weyhern's . . . and we were standing at the door there . . . and he greeted us . . .

WESENER: Right, more lies. The hell with your lies. Get out of my sight, you godless soul.

CHARLOTTE: I could have predicted, Papa, that it would turn out like this. They have always had secret goings-on, she and the baron.

MARIE (*crying*): Just shut up, will you?

CHARLOTTE: Not on your say-so, I won't. Do you think you can give orders, after the way you've behaved?

MARIE: Just watch out yourself, you and your young gentleman, Mr. Heidevogel. If I behaved as shamelessly as you—

WESENER: Both of you shut up! (*To* MARIE.) Go to your room this instant. No dinner for you tonight—piece of trash! (MARIE *leaves.*) And you be quiet too. You're not simon-pure either. Do you think nobody knows why Mr. Heidevogel comes here so often?

CHARLOTTE: This is all Marie's fault. (*Cries.*) That godless little whore just wants to drag decent girls down with her.

WESENER (*thundering*): Shut up! Marie is getting far too haughty, to speak to you so, but you are jealous of your own sister. You're not as pretty as she; at least you should have behave better. Shame on you! (*To the* MAID) Clear the table, I don't want any more. (*Pushes away his plate and napkin, throws himself in his easy chair, and sits, lost in thought.*)

Scene Six
MARIE's *room*
MARIE *is sitting on her bed. She holds the brooch in her hand, toys with it, absorbed in reveries.* WESENER *enters. She starts up and tries to hide the brooch.*

MARIE: Oh, sweet Jesus—

WESENER: Now, now, don't act like a child. (*Paces back and forth a while, then sits down next to her.*) Now listen, Marieel! You know I'm kind to you. You just have to be honest with me, and you'll have nothing to be ashamed of. Tell me, has the baron said anything to you about love?

MARIE (*very secretively*): Papa! It's true, he is in love with me. You see, he even sent me this brooch.

WESENER: Thunder and lightning! Good God! My God! (*Takes the brooch from her.*) Didn't I forbid you to—

MARIE: But, Papa, I can't be so crude as to throw it back at him. I tell you, he would have gone raving mad if I hadn't taken it. (*Runs to her armoire.*) Here are even some verses that he wrote to me. (*Hands him a sheet of paper.*)

WESENER (*reads aloud*):
"You highest object of my purest drive,
I adore you, our love shall eternally survive.
Accept this assurance of my love so true,
You most beautiful light, every day again new."
You most beautiful light, ha, ha, ha.

MARIE: You wait, I'll show you something else. He also gave me a ring, a heart surrounded by little stones. (*Runs again to the armoire.* WESENER *looks at the ring indifferently.*)

WESENER (*reads aloud again*): "You highest object of my purest drive." (*Sticks the paper in his pocket.*) He has honorable intentions, I see. But listen, Marieel, to what I'm telling you. You must not accept any more presents from him. I don't like it, that he's giving you so many presents.

MARIE: It's just his kind heart, Papa.

WESENER: Give me the brooch. I want to give it back to him. Just let me do this, I know better what's right for you. I've lived longer in the world than you, my daughter. You can still go to the theater with him, but always take Madame Weyher along, and act as if I knew nothing about it. Just tell him that he should keep it all very secret, and that I would become very angry if I found out about it. But for God's sake no more presents from him, Miss!

MARIE: I know, Papa, that you would never advise me wrongly. (*Kisses his hand.*) You will see. I shall follow your advice in everything. And I shall tell you everything—of that you can be sure!

WESENER: So then, well and good. (*Kisses her.*) You may become a fine lady, foolish child. One never knows, how one might be elevated by a stroke of luck.

MARIE: But Papa! (*Somewhat softly.*) What will poor Stolzius say?

WESENER: You must not scare off Stolzius immediately. Listen—mm, I'll tell you later how to handle the letter to him. In the meantime, sleep well, little monkey.

MARIE (*kisses his hand*): Good night, Poppi! (*When he is gone, she heaves a great sigh, and stands by the window while she undresses.*) My heart is so heavy. I think there'll be lightning tonight . . . if it would only strike . . . (*Stares off into the distance, hands beating her bare chest.*) God! What wrong have I done? Stolzius! I still love you . . . but if I can improve my fortune . . . and if Papa tells me too . . . . (*Draws the curtain.*) If it strikes me, it strikes me. I would gladly die. (*Puts out the light.*)

Act Two
Scene One

Armentières
HAUDY *and* STOLZIUS, *strolling along the Lys.*

HAUDY: You must not let him bully you, good friend. I know Desportes. He's a
   rogue, who seeks nothing but his own amusement. He doesn't want to take
   your fiancée away from you.
STOLZIUS: But the gossip, Major! City and country alike are full of it. When I
   think of it, I could throw myself in the river.
HAUDY (*grasps* STOLZIUS *by the arm*): You must not lose heart, damn it!
   Everybody gets gossiped about. I am your best friend, rest assured of it, and I
   would certainly tell you if there were any danger. But it's nothing. You're
   just imagining it. See to it that the wedding will be this winter, while we're
   still here in the garrison. And if Desportes makes the slightest commotion, I
   promise you I'll be the man who'll spill his blood. Meanwhile, pay no
   attention to gossip. You know very well it's the most virtuous girls who get
   gossiped about the most. It's quite natural that the young fops try to get back
   at the girls they couldn't get anywhere with.

Scene Two

The coffeehouse
EISENHARDT *and* PIRZEL *in the foreground, on a sofa, drinking coffee.*
In the background, a group of OFFICERS, *talking and laughing.*

EISENHARDT (*to* PIRZEL): It's ludicrous, how they all swarm around poor
   Stolzius like flies around gingerbread. This one pulls him there, that one
   pushes him here, that one goes walking with him, this one takes him along in
   the cabriolet, that one plays billiards with him like a hunting dog who's caught
   the scent. And how obviously his drapery-shop prospered as soon as it was
   known that he was going to marry the pretty miss who recently came through
   here.
PIRZEL (*clasps* EISENHARDT's *hand with great energy*): Where does it come
   from, Reverend? Because people don't think. (*Stands in a very picturesque
   position, half-facing the* OFFICERS) A most perfect attitude. In this attitude I
   can either offend or not offend.
ONE OF THE OFFICERS (*turns around*): God, is he starting up again?
PIRZEL (*zealously*): If I can offend it (*Turns completely to face the group.*) it
   would stop being the most perfect.
ANOTHER OFFICER: Yeah, yeah, Pirzel, you're right, you're sure right.
PIRZEL (*turns back immediately to* EISENHARDT): If I cannot offend it— (*Grasps
   him by the hand and remains ramrod-stiff, in deep thought.*)

TWO OR THREE OFFICERS: Pirzel, what the hell? Are you talking to us?

PIRZEL (*turns and faces them, very seriously*): My dear companions, you are worthy creations of God; thus I cannot but respect you and honor you. I am also a creation of God; thus you must honor me as well.

AN OFFICER: We were about to tell you the same thing.

PIRZEL (*turns again to* EISENHARDT): Now—

EISENHARDT: Captain, I agree with you completely. But the question was, how can we get it into people's heads that they should leave poor Stolzius alone, and not place jealousy and mistrust in two hearts that perhaps could make each other happy for all eternity.

PIRZEL (*who had been sitting through this, stands again very hastily*): As I had the honor and the privilege of saying to you, Reverend! That happens because people don't think. Thinking, thinking makes the man. That is exactly my point. (*Grasps* EISENHARDT's *hand.*) Look, that is your hand, but what does that mean? Skin, bones, dust (*Feeling his pulse.*) There, there it's hiding. This is only the sheath; the sword is hiding inside—the blood, the blood! (*Sits down suddenly, because there is a great uproar.*)

HAUDY (*enters with a loud cry*): People, I have him now, the most pious son of God in the world. (*Bellows frighteningly.*) Madame Roux! Rinse out a few glasses and make us some good punch right away. He'll be here soon. I must ask you to please treat this fellow with every courtesy.

EISENHARDT (*bowing*): Who, Major, if I may be permitted to ask—

HAUDY (*without looking at him*): No one, a good friend of mine.

(*All the* OFFICERS *crowd around* HAUDY.)

AN OFFICER: Have you asked him if the wedding will be soon?

HAUDY: Fellows, you must let me handle things, or you'll spoil the whole business. He trusts me, I tell you, as if I were the prophet Daniel, and if one of you butts in, everything'll be shot to hell. He's jealous enough, poor soul, Desportes turns him into something absolutely inhuman, and it's only with the greatest difficulty that I've kept him from throwing himself in the river. My job is to rebuild his confidence in his girl. He has to know that she is not actually stormproof. Let this be a warning to you: do not spoil the fellow for me!

RAMMLER: How you do go on! I know him better than you. He doesn't miss much, believe me.

HAUDY: And you miss even less, I suppose?

RAMMLER: You think the way to ingratiate yourself with him is to tell him good things about his fiancée. You are wrong. I know him better; it's just the opposite. Oh, he'll pretend to believe you and take it all to heart. But if you make him suspicious of his woman, then he'll be sure that we're being quite straightforward with him.

HAUDY: What lofty politics, rednose! Do you want to drive the fellow mad? Do you think he doesn't have enough doubts nagging already? And if he lets them stay or hangs himself—it's all your doing. And the life of a man is certainly not a trivial matter. Right, Reverend?

EISENHARDT: Don't involve me in your war-council.

HAUDY: You must admit, however, that I'm right?

PIRZEL: My worthy brothers and comrades, do wrong to nobody. The life of a man is a blessing, that he has not given himself. Now, however, nobody has

69

a right to a blessing that was given him by another. Our life is such a blessing—

HAUDY (*grasps him by the hand*): Yes, Pirzel, you are the most honest man I know (*Sits between him and* EISENHARDT.) but for this Jesuit (*Embraces* EISENHARDT.) who would gladly be cock of the walk himself.

RAMMLER (*sits on* EISENHARDT'*s other side and whispers in his ear*): Chaplain, you should see what sort of joke I'm going to play on Haudy.

(STOLZIUS *enters.* HAUDY *leaps to his feet.*)

HAUDY: Ah, my good man! Come, I've ordered a good glass of punch for us. The wind here just cuts you to the bone. (*Leads him to a table.*)

STOLZIUS (*tipping his hat to the* OTHERS): Gentlemen, you will forgive my being so bold as to come to your coffeehouse. It is at the Major's request.

(ALL *tip their hats very courteously and bow.* RAMMLER *stands and draws closer.*)

RAMMLER: Oh, obedient servant, it is an especial honor for us.

STOLZIUS (*touches his hat again, somewhat coldly, and sits next to* HAUDY): There's such a sharp wind outside. I believe we're going to get snow.

HAUDY (*tamping his pipe*): I believe so too—you smoke, don't you, Mr. Stolzius?

STOLZIUS: A little.

RAMMLER: I don't know where our punch is, Haudy. (*Rises.*) What's taking that damn Roux so long?

HAUDY: You just tend to your own business. (*Thunders in a frightening voice.*) Madame Roux! A light here! And our punch, where is it?

STOLZIUS: Oh, Major, it would pain me deeply to cause you any inconvenience.

HAUDY: Not at all, not at all, good friend. (*Hands the pipe to him.*) Truly, the Lys air can be not at all conducive to good health.

RAMMLER (*sits with them at the table*): Have you heard anything from Lille? How's your little fiancée? (HAUDY *glares at him; he remains seated, smiling.*)

STOLZIUS (*ill-at-ease*): Your servant, sir. But I must beg most humbly your pardon. I don't know of any fiancée. I have none.

RAMMLER: Miss Wesener of Lille, isn't she your fiancée? Desportes wrote me that you two were engaged.

STOLZIUS: Mr. Desportes must know the situation better than I.

HAUDY (*smoking*): Rammler likes to shoot off his mouth, whether or not he knows what he's talking about.

ONE OF THE CROWD: I assure you, Mr. Stolzius, Desportes is an honorable man.

STOLZIUS: I never doubted it for a moment.

HAUDY: You people know a lot about Desportes. I take it as a good sign when a man is known to others. When he came to the regiment he was recommended to my care by his mother, and did nothing without asking my advice. But I assure you, Mr. Stolzius, that Desportes is a man of feeling and religion.

RAMMLER: We were schoolmates together. I have never in my life seen a man more bashful with women.

HAUDY: That is true; you're right there. As soon as a woman smiles at him, he's incapable of stammering out one coherent word.

RAMMLER (*with a pedantically clumsy pretense*): I believe, in fact . . . if I'm right . . . yes, he still corresponds with her. The day of his departure I read a letter that he wrote to a mademoiselle in Brussels, with whom he was—quite astonishingly—in love. He will marry her soon, I think.

ONE OF THE CROWD: But I can't understand what he's doing so long in Lille.

HAUDY: Damn it all, where the hell are our drinks? Madame Roux!

RAMMLER: In Lille? Oh, I can tell you that better than anybody. I know all his secrets. But it really shouldn't be discussed in public.

HAUDY (*annoyed*): Out with it already, idiot! Don't keep us in the dark.

RAMMLER (*smiling*): I can only tell you this much: he's waiting for someone he's going to ride off with secretly.

STOLZIUS (*stands, and lays the pipe down*): Gentlemen, I have the honor to take my leave of you.

HAUDY (*alarmed*): What? But where, good friend? In just a moment—

STOLZIUS: Please don't think ill of me. Something's just affected me this moment.

HAUDY: So what? The punch will do you good, I assure you.

STOLZIUS: I don't seem quite myself, Major. You will excuse me . . . pardon me . . . but I cannot stay here a moment longer or I'll faint—

HAUDY: That is the Lys air. Or was the tobacco too strong?

STOLZIUS: Good-bye. (*Leaves unsteadily.*)

HAUDY: Now you've done it! You damned ass-faces!

RAMMLER: Ha, ha, ha, ha! (*Ponders a while, pacing about.*) You stupid devils, don't you see that I took great pains to arrange all this? Reverend, didn't I tell you about this?

EISENHARDT: Leave me out of your game, please.

HAUDY (*to* RAMMLER): You are a politic goose. I'll wring your neck.

RAMMLER: And I'll break your arms and legs and throw them out the window. (*Paces about.*) You just don't know my strategem yet.

HAUDY: Yes, you're as full of tricks as an old fur is full of lice. You're a fellow worth spitting on, you and your machinations.

RAMMLER: And I'll wager, that once I get started, I'm going to get the better of you and all you people here with Stolzius.

HAUDY: Listen, Rammler! It's a shame that you're just a bit too intelligent, for it does you no good. You're like a too-full bottle that one upends but can't get anything out of, because one drop is always in the way of another. If I had a wife I'd let you sleep with her, if you could only persuade her to do it.

RAMMLER (*pacing very quickly to and fro*): You just wait and see what I'm going to do to Stolzius. (*Leaves.*)

HAUDY: The fool is so stupid, it's galling. He can't do anything but spoil other people's plans.

AN OFFICER: That's true; he mixes into everything.

MARY: His head is always full of schemes and intrigues, and he thinks everybody lives as sneakily as he does. Recently, when I was whispering to Reitz about whether he would lend me his spurs till the next day—well, if Rammler wasn't after me the whole day, asking me, for God's sake, to tell him what we were up to. I think there's a spoiled politician in him.

ANOTHER OFFICER: The other day I was standing behind a house, to read a letter in the shade. Rammler immediately concluded it was a love letter that somebody in the house had thrown down to me, and he spent the whole evening till midnight prowling about the place. I thought I would split my sides laughing. Nobody but a sixty-year-old Jew lives in the place, but Rammler placed sentries all over the street, who were supposed to lie in wait for me and give him a sign when I went in. I bought the whole story from one of the men for three livres. I thought I'd go mad laughing.

ALL: Ha, ha, ha, ha, and he thought there was a pretty girl in there.

MARY: Listen, you want to have a real laugh? Let's go tell the old Jew there's somebody out there who wants to steal his money.

HAUDY: Right, right, that he's in the direst peril. Let's go right over to him. Ha, this should be a comedy that the likes of you have never seen before. And you, Mary, keep putting into Rammler's head the idea that the most beautiful woman in all of Armentières lives there and that Gilbert has confided to you that he will go this very night to her.

Scene Three

Lille

MARIE, *on an easy chair, crying. A letter is in her hand.* DESPORTES *enters.*

DESPORTES: What's the matter, my golden Marieel? What's wrong with you?

MARIE (*about to hide the letter in her pocket*): Oh!

DESPORTES: For heaven's sake, what kind of letter can that be, to bring on tears like that?

MARIE (*somewhat more subdued*): Just see, what this fellow Stolzius wrote to me, as if he had a right to scold me. (*Begins crying again.*)

DESPORTES (*reads quietly*): He is an impertinent ass. Tell me, why do you keep up correspondence with such a beast?

MARIE (*dries her eyes*): I shall only tell you, sir, it is because he has asked for my hand, and I am as good as half-promised to him.

DESPORTES: He has asked for your hand? What could the ass have been thinking of? Wait, I shall answer the letter.

MARIE: Yes, dear sir! And you cannot believe what I've had to put up with from my father. He keeps drumming in my ear, I must not throw away my chances.

DESPORTES: Your chances! With such a lummox! What can you be thinking of, dearest Marieel, and what can your father be thinking of? I know the man's circumstances well. You were not meant to be a tradesman's wife.

MARIE: No, sir, nothing will come of this. You're trying to get around me with empty hopes. Your family will never permit it.

DESPORTES: That is my problem. If you have pen and ink, I shall answer the buffoon's letter. Just wait.

MARIE: No, I want to write him myself. (*Sits down at the table and gets out the writing materials.* DESPORTES *stands behind her shoulder.*)

DESPORTES: All right, I'll dictate to you.

MARIE: No, you won't do that either.

DESPORTES (*reading over her shoulder*): "Monsieur"—you should add "lout." (*Dips another quill and is about to add something.*)

MARIE (*covering the letter with both arms*): Sir— (*They begin to tease one another: as soon as she moves her arm, he makes a move to write. After much laughter, she takes the dripping quill and makes a big blot on his face. He runs to the mirror to wipe it off. She continues writing.*)

DESPORTES: I'll be lying in wait for you. (*He draws nearer. She threatens him with the pen. Finally she sticks the sheet in her pocket. He tries to stop her; they wrestle. She tickles him; he shrieks pitifully before he finally collapses, half-breathless, on the easychair.*)

WESENER (*enters*): Here, now, what's going on? We'll have people dashing in from the streets pretty soon.

MARIE (*recovers*): Papa, just see what kind of letter this clumsy boor Stolzius writes me! He calls me unfaithful! Think, as though I had tended pigs with him. I shall certainly answer him so that he shall not presume again, the insolent ass!

WESENER: Give me the letter—oh, there's Miss Zipfersaat. I'll read it down in the store. (*Exits.*)

(MISS ZIPFERSAAT *enters.*)

MARIE (*peevishly, curtsying here and there*): Miss Zipfersaat, I have here the honor to present to you a baron who is madly in love with you. Here, sir, is the young woman of whom we have spoken so much, and with whom you were so wildly infatuated with recently at the theater.

MISS ZIPFERSAAT (*embarrassed*): I don't know what you're going on about, Marieel.

MARIE (*with a deep curtsy*): Now you can make your declaration of love. (*Runs off to the next room, slamming the door behind her.* MISS ZIPFERSAAT, *quite embarrassed, goes over to the window.* DESPORTES *looks at her contemptuously, then watches for* MARIE, *who from time to time opens the door a crack. Finally she sticks her head out, disdainfully.*) Well, are you going to be finished soon? (DESPORTES *tries to squeeze himself between the door and the jamb.* MARIE *jabs him with a large pin; he screams and dashes off suddenly, in order to enter the room through another door.* MISS ZIPFERSAAT *paces, quite annoyed, while the shouts and exultations in the next room grow louder and louder.* WESENER's *old* MOTHER *creeps into the room with* MISS ZIPFERSAAT. WESENER's MOTHER, *glasses on her nose, sits in a corner by the window and knits and sings—or croaks, rather—in a rough, old voice.*)

MOTHER: A young girl is a die
    Thrown often on the table
    And the little rose from Hennegau
    Will soon attend God's table.

(*Works some stitches.*)

    The piper must be paid, my child,
    So smile while you can.
    And the little rose from Hennegau
    Is picked off by a man.

Oh, little child, it hurts me so.
You laugh and sing these weeks.
But soon a thousand little tears
Will wash your little cheeks.

(Meanwhile the tumult continues in the next room. The old MOTHER *goes in to quiet them.)*

Act Three
Scene One

Armentières
The JEW's *house*

RAMMLER (*accompanied by several people in disguises, whom he directs into position. To the last one*): When somebody goes in, cough. I'm going to hide myself under the stairs, so I can tail him. (*Crawls under the stairs.*)

AARON (*looking out the window*): Gad, vat incredible doings is outside my own house.

(MARY, *wrapped up in a coat, comes down the street, stands under the* JEW's *window, and whistles softly.*)

AARON (*softly*): Is it you, good sir? (MARY *winks.*) I'll open the door at once.

(MARY *goes up the stairs. Someone coughs softly.* RAMMLER *follows on* MARY's *heels, without being seen. The* JEW *opens the door;* MARY *enters.*) (*The scene changes to the inside of the house. The room is pitch-dark.* MARY *and* AARON *whisper to each other.* RAMMLER *slinks into the room closer and closer, but steps back instantly when one of them makes a sound.*)

MARY: He is here with us.

AARON: Oy veh!

MARY: Quiet, he won't do you any harm; just let him do whatever he wants with you. If he gags you, I'll be at your side in a minute with the sentries to see that he gets what he deserves. So go to bed.

AARON: But vat if he kills me, hah?

MARY: Don't worry, I'll be with you in a minute. He can't be convicted any other way. The sentries are ready here below; I'll just go call them in. Lie down. (MARY *leaves. The* JEW *lies down on the bed.* RAMMLER *creeps closer to him.*)

AARON (*teeth chattering*): Adonai, Adonai!

RAMMLER (*to himself*): I'm sure that is a Jewess. (*Aloud, as he tries to imitate* MARY's *voice.*) Ah, my little treasure, how cold it is outside.

AARON (*more and more softly*): Adonai, Adonai!

RAMMLER: You know me. I'm not your husband, I'm Mary. (*Takes off his coat and boots.*) I believe we're going to get snow, it's so cold.

(MARY *and a large crowd of* OFFICERS *with lanterns charge in, and burst into horrible laughter. The* JEW *sits up, terrified.*)

HAUDY: Have you gone mad, Rammler? Why are you trying to make out with that old Jew?

RAMMLER (*stands as if turned to stone. Finally draws his sword*): I will hack you into a thousand million pieces, every last one of you. (*Runs out in a fury. The* OTHERS *laugh all the more insanely.*)

AARON: Oy, Gad, I'm half dead. (*Rises. The* OTHERS *all run after* RAMMLER. *The* JEW *follows them.*)

75

Scene Two

STOLZIUS's dwelling
STOLZIUS sits, with bandaged head at a table, on which a lamp burns.
He holds a letter in his hand. His MOTHER *stands next to him.*

MOTHER (*suddenly losing her temper*): Can't you go to sleep then, you godless soul! Then talk, tell me what you want. The slut was never worthy of you anyway. What are you grieving about? Why whine about a little . . . army whore!

STOLZIUS (*with the most extreme indignation, rising*): Mother—

MOTHER: What else is she then, other—you! And you too, to get involved with such people.

STOLZIUS (*grasps both her hands*): Dear mother, don't curse her. She is innocent. The officer got her all muddled. Just see how she's written to me. It's enough to make me lose my mind. Such a good heart!

MOTHER (*stands and stamps her foot*): Such a slut! Off to bed, I order you! What's going to come of this? What's to become of you? I want to remind you, young man, that I am your mother.

STOLZIUS (*striking his breast*): Marieel! No, she is no more. She is not the same any more. (*Leaps up.*) Let me go!

MOTHER (*cries*): Where to, you godforsaken—

STOLZIUS: I want the devil who has misled her! (*Collapses on the chair, powerless, both hands in the air.*) You shall repay me! Oh, you shall repay me! (*Coldly.*) One day is like the other, what doesn't happen today will happen tomorrow, and all things come in due time. How does it go in the song, Mother, if a little bird carries away a grain of a mountain every year, eventually he'll carry away the whole thing.

MOTHER: You're raving. (*Takes his pulse.*) Just go to bed, Carl, I beg you, for God's sake. I'll cover you up warmly. Oh, God! What will come of this? Such a fiery fever—over such a little tramp!

STOLZIUS: Finally . . . finally . . . every day a grain of sand, a year has ten, twenty, thirty, a hundred . . . (*His* MOTHER *tries to lead him away.*) Leave me alone, Mother, I'm quite well.

MOTHER: Just come, please come. (*Drags him away with all her might.*) I won't let go, believe me.

Scene Three

Lille
MISS ZIPFERSAAT. *A* MAID *in* WESENER's *house.*

MISS ZIPFERSAAT: She is at home, but she's not seeing anyone? Tell me, when did she become so aristocratic?

MAID: She says she's busy. She's reading a book.

MISS ZIPFERSAAT: Just tell her I have something to say that is of great importance to her.

MARIE (*enters, a book in hand. In a careless tone*): Good morning, Miss Zipfersaat. Why don't you have a seat?

MISS ZIPFERSAAT: I only came to tell you that Baron Desportes left town this morning.

MARIE (*Quite beside herself*): What are you talking about?

MISS ZIPFERSAAT: You can believe it; he still owes my cousin seven hundred talers. When they went to his room, they found it cleared out. Just a scrap of paper on the table, where he told them they shouldn't make any effort to pursue him, that he had resigned his commission and was going to join the Austrian army.

MARIE (*runs about the room, sobbing. Cries out*): Papa! Papa!

WESENER (*offstage*): What is it?

MARIE: Come here right now, Papa!

MISS ZIPFERSAAT: Now you see what officers are. I should have warned you about them from the beginning.

WESENER: All right, what's so—your servant, Miss Zipfersaat.

MARIE: Papa, what are we going to do? Desportes is gone.

WESENER: Oh now, who's telling you such silly stories?

MARIE: He owed Miss Zipfersaat's cousin, the silk-dealer, seven hundred talers and left a note on the table that he's never in his life coming back to Flanders.

WESENER (*furiously*): What kind of godless, damned talk— (*Striking his breast.*) I'll make good the seven hundred talers. Understand, Miss Zipfersaat? And anything else that you wish. Our houses have dealt with each other for thirty years, but that that godforsaken dog in the manger—

MISS ZIPFERSAAT: It will make my cousin very happy, Mr. Wesener, if you take it upon yourself to preserve the good name of the baron.

WESENER: I'll go with you this minute. (*Looks for his hat.*) I'll shut the mouth of anybody who tries to drag the good name of my house in the mud. You can take my word for it!

MARIE: But Papa! (*Impatiently.*) Oh, I wish that I had never seen him. (WESENER *and* MISS ZIPFERSAAT *exit.* MARIE *throws herself in the easychair. After she has sat for some time in deep thought, she cries out anxiously.*) Lottie! Lottie!

CHARLOTTE (*enters*): So what do you want, that you're going on so?

MARIE (*rushes to meet her*): Lottie! My dear Lottie! (*Chucking her under the chin.*)

CHARLOTTE: God have mercy, now what's going on?

MARIE: You are my bestest little Lottiekins. Yes, you.

CHARLOTTE: You must want to borrow money again.

MARIE: I will do anything you ask.

CHARLOTTE: Oh, nonsense! I haven't time for this. (*Is about to leave.*)

MARIE (*stops her*): Just listen . . . only for a minute. Can't you just help me write a letter?

CHARLOTTE: I haven't time.

MARIE: Just a few lines . . . and I'll give you my pearls for just six livres.

CHARLOTTE: So who are we writing to?

MARIE (*embarrassed*): To Stolzius.

CHARLOTTE (*laughs*): Is your conscience bothering you?

MARIE (*half-crying*): Oh, stop!

CHARLOTTE (*sits at the table*): All right, then. What do you want to write to him? You know how much I hate to write.

MARIE: I have such a tremor in my hand—put that in on top or in a line somewhere. "My dearest friend—"

CHARLOTTE: My dearest friend.

MARIE: In your last letter to me you invited certain base remarks, as my honor was impugned.

CHARLOTTE: Impugned.

MARIE: Nonetheless, all expressions must not be weighed, but look instead at the heart—what should I say now?

CHARLOTTE: How would I know?

MARIE: Tell me, what's the right word?

CHARLOTTE: I won't know if I don't know what you want to tell him.

MARIE: That my heart and . . . (*Flings herself in the chair and begins to cry.* CHARLOTTE *looks at her and laughs.*)

CHARLOTTE: So what should I write to him then?

MARIE (*sobbing*): Write what you want.

CHARLOTTE (*writes and reads aloud*): "That my heart is not so inconstant as you have imagined"—is that all right?

MARIE (*leaps up and reads over her shoulder*): Yes, that's good, that's good. (*Embraces her.*) My old Lottiekins.

CHARLOTTE: Come on, let me write.

(MARIE *paces back and forth a few times, then suddenly dashes over to* CHARLOTTE, *rips the letter away from under her arm, and tears the paper into a thousand pieces.*)

CHARLOTTE (*infuriated*): Oh, now! You little tramp! After all I did—but that's the sort of *canaille*[4] you are.

MARIE: *Canaille vous même.*[5]

CHARLOTTE (*threatens her with the inkwell*): You—

MARIE: That's right, attack someone too miserable to defend herself.

CHARLOTTE: Slut! Why did you tear it up? And after I used my best handwriting!

MARIE (*furious*): Watch the insults!

CHARLOTTE (*also half-crying*): Why did you tear it up?

MARIE: Should I lie to him then? (*Begins to wail at the top of her lungs, and flings herself face down on a chair.*)

(WESENER *enters.* MARIE *stands, and flies to his side. She embraces him.*)

MARIE (*trembling*): Papa, dear Papa, what's going on? For God's sake, tell me.

WESENER: Don't be foolish. He can't have disappeared from the planet. This carrying-on of yours is in bad taste.

MARIE: But if he's gone—

---

[4]Scum!

[5]Scum yourself!

WESENER: If he's gone, he'll come back. I swear you've lost your mind and want to drive me crazy too. I've known his family longer than yesterday, and they won't let this business go on for very long. Go get our notary; I want to have him notarize this bill that I've signed, along with this copy of the *Promesse de Mariage,* and send everything to Desportes' parents.
MARIE: Oh, Papa, dear Papa! I shall run right down myself and fetch him. (*Dashes out head over heels.*)
WESENER: I swear, five minutes with that girl, God forgive me, and *Louis Quatorze*'s heart would be in his boots. But it's not going to go well for *Monsieur le Baron.* I'll stir things up at his father's, just you wait—where are you? (*Runs off after* MARIE.)

Scene Four

Armentières
A walkway on the now-abandoned town moat.
EISENHARDT *and* PIRZEL *are strolling.*

EISENHARDT: Mr. von Mary wants to spend the next six months in Lille. What could that mean? He doesn't have any relatives there, so far as I know.
PIRZEL: He is also not one of those who have the hang of things. Transitory, transitory. But the lieutenant colonel, now *there* is a man.
EISENHARDT (*aside*): Ah me, how can I bring this man out of his metaphysics? (*Aloud.*) In order to know man, one must in my opinion begin with women. (PIRZEL *shakes his head.*)
EISENHARDT (*aside*): Where the others have too much, he has too little. Oh soldiering, frightful infamy! What caricatures you make of men!
PIRZEL: You say, with women? That would be exactly as if one began with sheep. No, what man is— (*Rests his finger on his nose.*)
EISENHARDT (*aside*): He's going to philosophize me to death. (*Aloud.*) I have observed that you can't take a step outside your door this month without seeing a soldier caressing a girl.
PIRZEL: That is because people don't think.
EISENHARDT: But doesn't thinking sometimes hinder you in drilling?
PIRZEL: Not at all, not at all. That goes so mechanically. It's the others who don't have their wits about them; instead beautiful girls float before their eyes the whole time.
EISENHARDT: That must produce some strange battles. A whole regiment with its head in the clouds must do wondrous deeds.
PIRZEL: That all goes so mechanically.
EISENHARDT: Yes, but you also run mechanically. You must sometimes find the Prussian bullets a very rude awakening from your sweet dreams. (*They walk off.*)

Scene Five

Lille. MARY's dwelling.
MARY. STOLZIUS, *now a soldier.*

MARY (*drawing, looks up*): Who's there? (*Stares at him a long while, then rises.*) Stolzius?

STOLZIUS: Yes, sir.

MARY: What in hell are you doing here? And in that coat? (*Turns him around.*) How changed, how haggard, how pale. You could tell me a hundred times you were Stolzius and I wouldn't believe you.

STOLZIUS: It's the mustache, sir. I heard that you needed a servant, sir, and because the colonel trusts me, he has given me permission to come here, to help you enlist a few recruits if need be, and to serve you in any other way.

MARY: Bravo! You are a fine fellow! And it pleases me that you are in the service of the king. What can come of the Philistine life? And you have something to gain; you can live honorably and go far. I will look out for you, you can be sure of that. Come now, I want to get a room for you. You should spend this whole winter with me. I'll clear it with the colonel.

STOLZIUS: As long as I pay to have my sentry-duty done, nobody will have cause to fault me. (*They leave.*)

Scene Six

MRS. WESENER. MARIE. CHARLOTTE.

MRS. WESENER: It's a scandal, the way you're carrying on with him. I don't see any diffrence between the way Desportes treated you and the way you're treating him.

MARIE: What should I do, Mama? He's Desportes' best friend. He's the only one who can give us any news of him.

CHARLOTTE: If he didn't send you so many presents, you'd treat him quite differently.

MARIE: Should I throw the presents back in his face? I have to be civil to him; he's the only one who still corresponds with him. If I scare him off, fine things will happen. He'll intercept every letter that Papa writes to his father, just wait.

MRS. WESENER: No more talk. You shouldn't have anything to do with this one. I won't permit it.

MARIE: So come along, Mama! He's already ordered a horse and a cabriolet. Should he send them back?

MRS. WESENER: As far as I'm concerned.

MARIE: So you come along, Lottie. Oh, what do I do now? Mama, you don't know how much I endure for your sake.

CHARLOTTE: She's getting fresh again.

MARIE: You be quiet.

80

CHARLOTTE (*somewhat softly, to herself*): Army whore!

MARIE (*acts as if she didn't hear it. Continues to primp before the mirror*): If we offend Mary, we'll have only ourselves to blame.

CHARLOTTE (*loudly, as she quickly leaves the room*): Army whore!

MARIE (*whirls around*): Now you see, Mama! (*Wringing her hands.*)

MRS. WESENER: I can't help you. You brought it on yourself.

(MARY *enters.*)

MARIE (*quickly assumes a cheerful expression. Greets him with the greatest possible liveliness and cordiality*): Your servant, Mr. von Mary! Did you sleep well?

MARY: Incomparably, gracious Mademoiselle! I saw all of yesterday's fireworks again in my dream.

MARIE: They were certainly beautiful.

MARY: Indeed they must have been beautiful to win your approval.

MARIE: Oh, I am no connoisseuse of such things. I only repeat what I have heard from you. (*He kisses her hand. She makes a deep curtsy.*) You've caught us here in quite some turmoil. My mother will soon be ready.

MARY: Madame Wesener is coming with us, then?

MRS. WESENER (*drily*): Why not? Isn't there room for me?

MARY: Oh yes, I'll stand behind, and my Casper can go on ahead on foot.

MARIE: You know, Soldier, you're very much like a certain man I once knew. He also asked for my hand.

MARY: And you refused. Was Desportes responsible for that?

MARIE: He settled the score.

MARY: Shall we go? (*He offers his hand. She curtsies, and gestures toward her mother. He offers* MRS. WESENER *his hand.* MARIE *follows them out.*)

Scene Seven

Philippeville

DESPORTES (*alone, in a green room, stretched out writing a letter. A lamp is burning beside him. Mutters as he writes*): I'd better lay it on pretty thick or the letter-writing will never end, and my father's sure to intercept one. (*Reads his letter.*) "Your good father is angry at me, because I have let him wait so long for his money. I beg you, appease him until I find a suitable opportunity to reveal everything to my father, and to persuade him to consent to my possessing you, my beloved, eternally. I have the greatest fear that he has already intercepted one of your letters, for I see from your last one that you must have written many to me that I did not receive. That could ruin everything for us. May I ask that you not write any more to me until I have sent you a new address where I can safely receive your letters." (*Seals his letter.*) If I can get Mary really in love with her, then perhaps she'll forget about me. I'll write him not to leave my side, and that once I make my adorable Marie happy, he shall be her *cicisbeo*. Just wait. (*Paces up and*

81

down a few times, lost in thought, then leaves.)

Scene Eight

Lille. The residence of the COUNTESS DE LA ROCHE.
COUNTESS. *A* SERVANT.

COUNTESS (*glancing at her watch*): Hasn't the young man returned yet?
SERVANT: No, Your Grace.
COUNTESS: Give me the master key and go to bed. I'll see to the young man myself. What's Miss Cathy doing?
SERVANT: This evening she had a high fever.
COUNTESS: Go in then, and see if the mademoiselle is still awake. Tell her I'm not going to bed. I'll come at one to relieve her. (SERVANT *leaves.*)
COUNTESS (*alone*): Does a child have to drive its mother to the grave from pain? If you weren't my one and only, and I hadn't given you such a soft heart. (*A knock is heard. She goes out and returns with her* SON.)
YOUNG COUNT: But, Mother, where is the servant? Damned people! If it weren't so late, I'd go right to the watchman and break every bone in his body.
COUNTESS: Gently, gently, my son. How would you like it if I acted as rashly with you as you do with innocent people?
YOUNG COUNT: But this is not to be endured.
COUNTESS: I sent him to bed. Isn't it enough that the man has to tend to you all day long? Should he also give up a night's sleep for your sake? I believe you want me to look on the servants as beasts.
YOUNG COUNT (*kisses her hand*): Mother dearest!
COUNTESS: I must speak seriously with you, young man! You are beginning to darken my days. You know I have never restricted you. I have shared all your goings-on as a friend, never as your mother. Why have you started now to keep your affairs of the heart secret from me? You never kept any of your youthful follies secret from me before. And I, because I am myself a woman, was always able to give you the best advice. (*Regards him stiffly.*) You are beginning to become dissolute, my son.
YOUNG COUNT (*kissing her hand through tears*): Mother dear, I swear I have no secrets from you. You happened on me and Miss Wesener after supper, and you jumped to conclusions because of the time and the way we were talking. She's a nice girl, and that is all.
COUNTESS: I don't want to know any more. As long as you believe that you have cause to keep something from me—but remember that from now on you will have only yourself to blame for the consequences of your actions. Miss Anklam has relatives here. I know that Miss Wesener does not have the highest reputation, not through her own fault, I believe, the poor child is said to have been deceived—
YOUNG COUNT (*kneeling*): Just that, Mother dearest! Even her misfortune, if you knew the circumstances—yes, I must tell you everything. I feel that I

82

have a share in the girl's fate . . . and yet . . . how easily she was deceived! Such a light, open, trusting heart. It tortures me, Mama, that she did not fall into better hands.

COUNTESS: Son, leave the sympathizing to me. Believe me (*Embraces him.*) I have no harder a heart than you. But sympathizing won't be so dangerous for me. Hear my advice and follow it. For the sake of your peace of mind, don't see her any more. Leave the city, go visit Miss Anklam, and rest assured that no harm will come to Miss Wesener here. You have left her in the care of her tenderest friend—me. Do you promise me this?

YOUNG COUNT (*regards her a long time, tenderly*): Good, Mama. I promise you everything. Only one word, before I go. She is an unfortunate girl; that is certain.

COUNTESS: Calm yourself. (*Clapping him on the back.*) I believe it more than you can say.

YOUNG COUNT (*rises and kisses her hand*): I know. (*Both exit.*)

Scene Nine

MRS. WESENER. MARIE

MARIE: Let it be, Mama! I want to torment him good.

MRS. WESENER: Now what? He has forgotten you. He hasn't been here in three days, and everybody says he's in love with little Madame Duval, on Brüssler Street.

MARIE: You cannot believe how kind the count has been to me.

MRS. WESENER: Oh, fine, he's also supposed to be engaged.

MARIE: So I'll torment Mary with it. He's coming this evening after supper again. If only he wanted us to meet his Madame Duval!
(*A* SERVANT *enters.*)

SERVANT: The Countess de la Roche wishes to know if you are receiving guests.

MARIE (*in the most extreme consternation*): Oh, heavens, the count's mother! Tell her—Mama, tell me, what should he say?
(MRS. WESENER *is about to leave.*)

MARIE: Tell her, please, it will be a great honor—Mama! Mama! Say something!

MRS. WESENER: Cat got your tongue at last? Tell her it would be a great honor for us. We are, to be sure, in the greatest disorder here—

MARIE: No, no, wait! I'll go to the carriage myself. (*Goes off with the* SERVANT. MRS. WESENER *exits.*)

83

Scene Ten

The COUNTESS *and* MARIE *re-enter.*

MARIE: You will forgive us, Your Grace. Everything is in such a state here.

COUNTESS: My dear child, you don't need to go to any fuss for me. (*Takes her by the hand and sits down with her on the sofa.*) Look upon me as your best friend. (*Kisses her.*) I assure you that I take the most righteous interest in everything that happens to befall you.

MARIE (*wiping her eyes*): I don't know how I have deserved this special favor that you bestow upon me.

COUNTESS: No favor, I assure you. I am glad that we are alone. I have much, much to tell you that is in my heart, and also much to ask you. (MARIE, *very attentive, joy in her face.*) I love you, my angel! I cannot restrain myself from letting you see it. (MARIE *kisses her hand fervently.*) Your whole demeanor is so open, so charming, that your misfortunes become doubly painful to me. Do you know, my new dear friend, that there's much, much talk about you in the town?

MARIE: I certainly know that there are evil tongues everywhere.

COUNTESS: Not only evil. Some also speak well of you. You are unfortunate, but you can take comfort in the fact that you were not brought to your ill-fortune through any fault of your own. Your only mistake was that you did not understand the way of the world, that you didn't understand the divisions that lie between the different social classes, and that you've read *Pamela,* the most dangerous book that a person of your class can read.

MARIE: I don't know the book at all.

COUNTESS: Then you've trusted the talk of young people too much.

MARIE: I have trusted only one too much, and it is still not certain that he will be untrue to me.

COUNTESS: Good, dear friend! But tell me, how did you come to pursue a man above your class? You thought your figure could carry you further than your playmates. Ah, dear friend, that should have made you even more cautious. Beauty is never a means on which to base a good marriage, and no one has more cause to tremble than a pretty face. A thousand dangers strewn with flowers, a thousand admirers and not one friend, a thousand merciless traitors.

MARIE: Oh, gracious lady, I know that I am hideous.

COUNTESS: No false modesty. You are beautiful and heaven has punished you for it. There were people above your class who made promises to you. You saw no difficulty at all in climbing a rung higher; you scorned your companions, you believed it unnecessary to acquire other endearing qualities; you shrank from work; you were disdainful of men of your own class; you became hated. Poor child! How happy you could have made some fine upstanding burgher, if you had ensouled these marvelous features, this captivating, bewitching being, with a humble humanitarian spirit. How you would have been worshipped by all of your class, imitated and admired by all people of quality. But you wanted to be envied by your peers. Poor child, what were you thinking of? For what miserable fortune did you want to trade all these advantages? To be the wife of a man who would be hated and scorned by his whole family because of you? And for the sake of this most dangerous game of chance, you risked your fortune, your honor, your life itself. What were you thinking of? What were your parents thinking of? Poor betrayed child, abused through vanity! (*Presses her to her bosom.*) I would give my blood for this not to have happened.

MARIE (*crying on the* COUNTESS's *hand*): But he loved me.

COUNTESS: The love of an officer, Marie. Of a man used to every type of depravity and inconstancy, who stops being an honest soldier as soon as he becomes a faithful lover, who swore to the king to be only a soldier, and who collects a salary from him for exactly that. And you believed that you would be the only person in the world he would be true to, despite his parents' wrath, despite his family's pride, despite his vow, despite his character, despite everything? That means you wanted to turn the world upside down. And now that you see that it has come to nothing with this one, you think you can carry out your plan with somebody else. You don't see that what you consider to be love from these people is nothing more than sympathy for your plight—or something far worse. (MARIE *falls to her knees before her, buries her face in the* COUNTESS's *lap, and sobs.*) Make up your mind, child! Unfortunate child, there is still time. The abyss can still be avoided. May I die if I can't pull you back! Give up all attempts to gain my son. He is promised; Miss Anklam has his hand and his heart. But come into my household. Your honor has been greatly impugned; this is the only way to reestablish it. Become my companion, and resolve not to see any man for a year. You shall help me raise my daughter. Come, we shall go to your mother right away and ask her permission.

MARIE (*raising her head heartrendingly from the* COUNTESS's *bosom*): Dear lady! It is too late.

COUNTESS (*excitedly*): It is never too late to become sensible. I'll settle a thousand talers on you as a dowry. I know that your parents have debts.

MARIE (*still on her knees, falls halfway backwards, with clasped hands*): Ah, Your Grace, permit me to think about all this . . . that I may explain all this to my mother.

COUNTESS: Good, child, do your best. You should have enough diversions with me. I'll have you instructed in drawing, dancing, and singing.

MARIE (*collapses, face down*): Oh too, too magnanimous lady!

COUNTESS: I must leave. Your mother would find me in a most peculiar state. (*Quickly exits, then stops outside and peeks through the door at* MARIE, *who still lies as if in prayer.*) Adieu, child!

Act Four
Scene One

MARY. STOLZIUS.

MARY: I should tell you frankly, Stolzius, if Desportes doesn't marry the girl, then I will. I'm absolutely mad about her. I have already tried to dispel the idea, well, you know, with the Duval woman. And I don't like those goings-on with the count at all, or that the countess has taken her into her house. But none of that means anything. I can't get this foolishness out of my heart.

STOLZIUS: Doesn't Desportes write to her any more?

MARY: Oh sure, he writes. His father tried recently to force him to marry somebody else, and even had him jailed for fourteen days on bread and water. (*Striking his head.*) And now that I think of how recently she went walking with me in the moonlight and bewailed her fate, how she sometimes would leap up in the middle of the night, when melancholy thoughts pushed themselves forward, and go off in search of a knife.

(STOLZIUS *trembles.*)

MARY: I asked her if she loved me. She said she loved me more tenderly than all her friends and relatives, and pressed my hand against her breast.

(STOLZIUS *turns his face to the wall.*)

MARY: And when I asked her for a little kiss, she said if it were in her power to make me happy she would certainly do so. However, I would first have to get permission from Desportes. (*Suddenly seizes* STOLZIUS.) Devil take me, if I wouldn't marry her if Desportes would let her go.

STOLZIUS (*very coldly*): She is supposed to be on very good terms with the countess.

MARY: If I only knew how I could manage to speak to her. Make inquiries about it.

Scene Two

Armentières
DESPORTES, *in prison.* HAUDY *with him.*

DESPORTES: I really don't mind being in prison, as long as nobody finds out that I am here.

HAUDY: I shall forbid all our men to speak of it.

DESPORTES: Above all, don't let Mary find out.

HAUDY: Or Rammler. Who claims to be such a great friend of yours, and says he deliberately joined the regiment a few weeks later to give you seniority.

DESPORTES: The fool!

HAUDY: Oh, listen, the other day there was another high old time with him, which

86

was just delicious. You know Gilbert is lodging with an old, bent, cross-eyed widow, merely because of her beautiful cousin. Now every week to please her, he gives a concert in the house. Well, Rammler got drunk at one and, because he thought the cousin slept there, he followed his usual tricky style, and sneaked off after supper to the widow's bedroom, undressed, and lay down on the bed. The widow, who was also somewhat tipsy, first lighted the way home for her cousin, who lives in the neighborhood—and we all thought Rammler had gone home—then the widow went up to her room, and was about to lie down on the bed when she finds my Monsieur there, in the most extreme consternation. He excused himself by saying he hadn't understood the layout of the house. She transported him downstairs without further ado, and we all laughed ourselves sick. He asked her and us for God's sake not to tell anybody anything about what happened. But you know how Gilbert is. He told everything to the cousin, and she put it firmly into the old widow's head that Rammler was in love with her. In fact, he's even rented a room in her house, probably in order to persuade her not to press any charges. Now you should see him and the old crone in society together. She simpers and flirts and twists up her wrinkled old shrivelled face at him, till you could die. And he with his red aquiline nose and the fixed frightened eyes—you can't think about it without bursting out laughing.

DESPORTES: When I am free again, my first steps will be to Gilbert. My mother will write to the colonel at once that the regiment should make good my debts.

Scene Three

Lille
A little garden at the COUNTESS's *residence*

COUNTESS (*on a pathway*): What is the girl up to, going out so late in the garden? I'm afraid, I'm afraid it is something prearranged. She draws distractedly, she plays the harp distractedly, she's always daydreaming when her language tutor says something to her—ssh, do I hear someone? Yes, she is over in the gazebo, and someone is talking to her from the street. (*Puts her ear against the green wall of the garden. Offstage.*)

MARY'S VOICE: Can it be allowed, that you forget all your friends and everyone who was ever dear to you?

MARIE'S VOICE: Ah, dear Mr. Mary, I am so very sorry, but it has to be so. I assure you, the countess is the most charming woman on God's earth.

MARY: But it's as if you're in a convent there. Don't you ever wish to rejoin the world? Do you know that Desportes has written? He is inconsolable, he wants to know where you are and why you don't answer him.

MARIE: Oh? Ah, I must forget him. Tell him that he should also forget me.

MARY: But why? Cruel Mademoiselle! Is it permissible to treat friends so?

MARIE: It can't be any other way. God, I hear somebody down in the garden below. Adieu, adieu. Just don't flatter yourself— (*Descends.*)

COUNTESS: So, Marie! You're having a rendezvous?

MARIE (*extremely agitated*): Oh, Your Grace! It was a relative of mine . . . my cousin, and he had only just found out where I was.

COUNTESS (*very serious*): I heard everything.

MARIE (*almost on her knees*): Oh God! Please forgive me just this once!

COUNTESS: Girl, you are like a sapling in the evening air; every breeze bends you. What can you be thinking of, that you here, right under my nose, try to spin your web again for Desportes? That you have a rendezvous with his very good friend? If I had known this, I wouldn't have taken you in.

MARIE: Forgive me just this once!

COUNTESS: I shall never forgive you when you act against your own best interests. Go. (MARIE *leaves, despairingly.*)

COUNTESS (*alone*): I don't know if I can, in good conscience, take away all the girl's romantic little dreams. What charm does life have left if our imagination doesn't enter in? Eating, drinking, pursuits without prospects—without self-created pleasure they are only a slow death. She senses that too, and only imagines herself happy. If I could find out some way to unite her fantasy with my cleverness, to force her heart, not her head, to obey me.

Scene Four

Armentières

DESPORTES (*in prison, hurriedly pacing up and down, a letter in his hand*): If she comes to me here, all my prospects are ruined. Ashamed, the sport of all my comrades. (*Sits and writes.*) My father must not see her!

Scene Five

Lille. WESENER'*s house.*
WESENER. A SERVANT *of the* COUNTESS.

WESENER: Marie run away! I am dead! (*Dashes out. The* SERVANT *follows.*)

Scene Six

MARY'*s quarters.*
MARY. STOLZIUS, *standing, quite distraught.*

88

MARY: So let's set after her, damn it. I am to blame for everything. Straight off and get some horses here.

STOLZIUS: If we only knew where—

MARY: To Armentières. Where else could she be? (*Both leave.*)

Scene Seven

WESENER's *house*
MRS. WESENER *and* CHARLOTTE, *in bonnets.* WESENER *returns.*

WESENER: It's no good. She's nowhere to be found. (*Smacks his hands together.*) God! Who knows where she drowned herself!

CHARLOTTE: But still, who knows, Papa—

WESENER: No. The countess's messengers have returned, and it's still not half an hour that they noticed she was missing. They rode off in all directions. She couldn't have disappeared off the face of the earth in so short a time.

Scene Eight

Philippeville

DESPORTES' RIFLEMAN (*holding a letter from his master in his hand*): Oh! There comes a pretty piece of game right into the trap. She wrote to my master she was coming to him in Philippeville (*Reads in the letter.*) on foot. Ah, the poor child! I shall refresh you.

Scene Nine

Armentières
A concert in the house of MRS. BISCHOF. *Various* LADIES, *including*
MRS. BISCHOF *and her* COUSIN, *in a circle around the orchestra.*
Various OFFICERS, *including* HAUDY, RAMMLER, MARY, DESPORTES,
GILBERT. *The* OFFICERS *and* LADIES *converse.*

MADEMOISELLE BISCHOF (*to* RAMMLER): So you also reside here, sir? (RAMMLER *bows silently, blushing redder and redder.*)

HAUDY: He's taken a room on the second floor, exactly opposite your cousin's bedroom.

89

MADEMOISELLE BISCHOF: So I've heard. I wish my cousin all the best.

MADAME BISCHOF (*squints and smiles coquettishly*): Hee, hee, hee! The baron wouldn't have come to reside here, if Mr. von Gilbert hadn't recommended my house so. Of course I treat all my gentlemen in such a way that they have nothing to complain about.

MADEMOISELLE BISCHOF: I believe you must get on well with each other.

GILBERT: Nonetheless, there was a slight to-do between them, otherwise Rammler wouldn't be staying here.

MADAME BISCHOF: Oh? (*Holds her fan before her face.*) Hee, hee, hee, since when, Mr. Gilbert, since when?

HAUDY: Since the last concert, as you well know, Madame.

RAMMLER (*pulls at him*): Haudy!

MADAME BISCHOF (*strikes* HAUDY *with her fan*): Naughty Major! Must you babble about everything?

RAMMLER: Madame! I don't know at all, how we are supposed to have become so familiar with each other. I deny—

MADAME BISCHOF (*very angry*): So, sir? So now you want to be uppish? You should consider it a great honor if a woman of my age and character is familiar with you, and not put on airs.

OFFICERS: Ah, Rammler! Shame, Rammler! You shouldn't treat Madame like that.

RAMMLER: Madame, keep still, or I'll break your arms and legs and throw you out the window.

MADAME BISCHOF (*rises, enraged*): Sir, come here! (*Grabs him by the arm.*) Come here this instant! Try, just try, to do me an injury!

ALL: Into the bedroom, Rammler, she's challenging you!

MADAME BISCHOF: If you carry on any longer, I'll throw you out of the house. And the way to your commandant is not far. (*Begins to cry.*) Think of it, to be so impertinent in my own house! The impertinent boor!

MADEMOISELLE BISCHOF: Now calm down, Cousin. The baron didn't mean anything by it. He's just joking, so calm down.

GILBERT: Rammler, be reasonable, I beg of you. What sort of man are you, to insult an old woman?

RAMMLER: You can all— (*Runs out.*)

MARY: Wasn't that fun, Desportes? What's the matter with you? You're not laughing.

DESPORTES: I have an astonishingly bad shooting pain in my chest. This cold of mine is going to kill me.

MARY: Isn't that just a sympathetic reaction? Did you see how he went all black and blue around the nose from anger? Anybody else would have just had fun with the old slut.

(STOLZIUS *enters and tugs at* MARY's *sleeve.*)

MARY: What is it?

STOLZIUS: Please don't be offended, Lieutenant! Would you come for a moment into the next room?

MARY: What's going on? Have you discovered something?

(STOLZIUS *shakes his head.*)

MARY: So then. (*Takes a few steps forward.*) So tell me here.

STOLZIUS: Last night the rats ate your best undershirt. As I opened the linen-cupboard, two, three leaped out at me.

MARY: So? What do I care? Set some poison out.

STOLZIUS: But I must have a requisition with your seal on it.

MARY (*annoyed*): Why are you telling me about this now?

STOLZIUS: I won't have time later, Lieutenant. I have to handle the delivery of the uniforms.

MARY: Here's my watch; you can use the seal on that. (STOLZIUS *leaves.* MARY *rejoins the company.*)

(*The* ORCHESTRA *strikes up a symphony.*)

DESPORTES (*seated in a corner, off by himself*): Your image is incessantly before me. Damn it all! Away with these thoughts! Can I help it, if she becomes one of those? She couldn't have hoped for anything better. (*Rejoins the company, coughing miserably.* MARY *rams a stick of licorice in* DESPORTES' *mouth.* DESPORTES *jumps.* MARY *laughs.*)

Scene Ten

Lille. WESENER'*s house.*
MRS. WESENER. *A* SERVANT *of the* COUNTESS.

MRS. WESENER: What? The countess has taken to her bed from overexcitement? Please convey our humble respects to the countess and her daughter. My husband has traveled to Armentières, because the people wanted to seal up everything in the house because of the guarantee, and he heard that Baron von Desportes was supposed to be there with the regiment. And we are truly sorry that the countess is taking our misfortune so to heart.

Scene Eleven

Armentières

STOLZIUS (*pacing in front of an apothecary, It is raining*): Why do you tremble? My tongue is so weak that I fear I won't be able to get a word out. He will see it in me. Then must they who suffer injustice tremble, and only they who do injustice be happy? Who knows against what fencepost she's starving right now? Go in, Stolzius! If it's not for him, it's for you. That's all that you wanted. (*Goes in.*)

91

Act Five
Scene One

On the way to Armentières

WESENER (*resting*): No, I won't take any mail-wagon. I'll just lie here forever. My poor child has cost me enough. Even before she went to the countess's, she had to be the grand lady, and brother and sister were not to reproach her for it. My business has lain idle for two years. Who knows what Desportes is doing with her? What he has done with us all! Without a doubt, she is with him. One must trust in God. (*Remains lost in thought.*)

Scene Two

MARIE (*on another road to Armentières, resting under a tree. Pulls a piece of dry bread from her pocket*): I have always believed that one could live on nothing but bread and water. (*Gnaws at the bread.*) Oh, if I only had a drop of the wine that I so often threw out the window . . . that I used to wash my hands in when I was giddy. (*Suffers spasms.*) Oh, the torment . . . a beggar, now. (*Looks at the piece of bread.*) I can't eat it, God knows. Better to starve to death. (*Throws the bread away and struggles to her feet.*) I shall crawl as far as I can, and if I collapse, so much the better.

Scene Three

Armentières. MARY'*s quarters.*
MARY *and* DESPORTES *sit, undressed, at a small, set table.*
STOLZIUS *removes the napkins.*

DESPORTES: As I was telling you, she was a whore from the very beginning. She was only good to me because I gave her presents. I got so much in debt because of her, it's astonishing. She would have taken everything I own if I had let the game go on any longer. Anyway, before I expected it, I got a letter from her. She was coming to see me in Philippeville. Now imagine the spectacle that would have taken place if my father had managed to see her. (STOLZIUS *changes the napkins again, in order to have a reason to remain in the room.*) So I wrote my rifleman and told him he should meet her and confine her to my quarters, until I returned to Philippeville and fetch her away secretly. For if my father ever saw her, she'd be as good as dead. *But* my rifleman is a strong, robust fellow, and the time will certainly grow heavy on their hands, all alone in the room. What he is doing to her now, I'll wait to hear. (*Laughs derisively.*) I let him know privately that it certainly wouldn't

92

bother me.

MARY: Desportes, that is indecent.

DESPORTES: Eh, indecent—call it what you want. Isn't she going to be well enough provided for, if my rifleman marries her? For such a little—

MARY: The countess thought very highly of her. And damn me, Brother, I'd have married her if the young count hadn't gotten in my way. She also liked him a lot.

DESPORTES: Then you'd have had a pretty yoke around your neck. (STOLZIUS *exits.*)

MARY (*calling him back*): See to it that the gentleman gets his wine soup soon. I don't know how it happened that she came to know the man. I think, in fact, she wanted to make me jealous because I'd been sulking for a few days. None of this would have mattered, but one time I came—it was on the hottest of the dog days, and she was wearing, because of the heat, only a sheer, sheer, little dress of muslin, through which her beautiful legs could be seen. Every time she went through the room, the little dress fluttered so about her—listen, I would have sacrificed heaven to sleep one night with her. Now imagine, of all the ill-luck, the count arrived that very day and, well, you know the girl's vanity. She acted absolutely insane. I don't know whether it was to embarrass me or because such girls don't know where they are when a gentleman of high position condescends to smile at them. (STOLZIUS *enters, serves* DESPORTES, *and, deathly white, places himself behind* DESPORTES' *chair.*) I was like glowing iron that all of a sudden goes cold as ice. (DESPORTES *devours the soup greedily.*) All appetite for her left me. From that time on, I've never been on good terms with her. In fact, I hear she's run away from the countess's.

DESPORTES (*still eating*): Why do we keep talking about the little bag of bones? I tell you, Brother, you'd make me very happy if you didn't mention her any more to me. Such *ennui,* to hear of her.

STOLZIUS (*behind the chair, his face twisted*): Really?

(BOTH *look at him, astonished.*)

DESPORTES (*holds his chest*): I'm getting pains . . . Ayee!

(MARY *stares fixedly at* STOLZIUS, *without saying a word.*)

DESPORTES (*throws himself in an armchair*): Ayee! (*Suffers spasms.*) Mary!

STOLZIUS (*springs to him, grabs him by the ears, and whirls his face around, pressing it close to his own. With an awful shriek*): Marie! Marie! Marie!

(MARY *draws his sword and is about to run* STOLZIUS *through.*)

STOLZIUS (*turns coldbloodedly and grasps* MARY's *sword*): Don't trouble yourself; he's already dead. I'll die happy, since I can take him with me.

MARY (*leaves the sword with him, and dashes out*): Help! Help!

DESPORTES: I'm poisoned.

STOLZIUS: Yes, betrayer, you are. I am Stolzius, whose fiancée you turned into a whore. She was my fiancée. If you can't live without ruining girls, why did you turn to those who can't resist, who believe every word you say. You are avenged, my Marie! God cannot condemn me. (*Sinks to the floor.*)

DESPORTES: Help! (*After a few spasms, he also dies.*)

Scene Four

WESENER *walks along the Lys, lost in thought. It is dawn.*
A veiled WOMAN *plucks at his sleeve.*

WESENER: Leave me alone. I don't go in for such things.

WOMAN (*almost inaudibly*): For God's sake, alms, sir!

WESENER: To the workhouse with you! There's a horde of slovenly urchins. If I were to give you all alms, I'd never be through.

WOMAN: Good sir, I've gone three days without a crust of bread to stick in my mouth. Have the grace to lead me to a workhouse where I can get one swallow of wine.

WESENER: You miserable trash! Aren't you ashamed to ask that of a respectable man? Go, go, chase after your soldiers.

(*The* WOMAN *goes off without answering.*)

WESENER: To hear her sigh so deeply . . . my heart has become so hard. (*Pulls out his purse.*) Who knows where my daughter is begging alms right now? (*Runs after the* WOMAN *and hands her, trembling, a coin.*) There's a guilder for you—but do yourself some good with it.

WOMAN (*begins to cry*): Oh, God! (*Takes the coin and collapses to the ground, almost fainting.*) How can that help me?

WESENER (*turns away and wipes his own eyes. Finally, quite beside himself*): Where do you come from?

WOMAN: That I may not say. But I was a respectable man's daughter.

WESENER: Was your father a jeweler?

(*The* WOMAN *is silent.*)

WESENER: Your father was a respectable man? Stand up, I shall take you to my house. (*Tries to help her to her feet.*) Didn't your father live somewhere in Lille? (*At the last word, she embraces him.*) Oh, my daughter!

MARIE: My father! (BOTH, *still embracing, collapse, half-dead, on the ground. A crowd of people gather around them and carry them away.*)

Scene Five

The COLONEL'*s residence*
The COLONEL, COUNT VON SPANNHEIM. *The* COUNTESS DE LA ROCHE.

COUNTESS: Have you seen those two unfortunates? I haven't had the heart. One look would kill me.

COLONEL: It has aged me ten years. That in my corps—! I shall make good all the man's debts and pay an additional thousand talers as his indemnification. Subsequently I shall see what I can get out of the villain's father for the family his son destroyed.

COUNTESS: Worthy man! Accept my warmest thanks in these tears. You are the

94

kindest, most gracious being! What hopes I had already begun to have for her!

COLONEL: These tears do you honor. They soften even me. And why shouldn't I cry? I who would fight and die for the fatherland. To see a burgher of the same fatherland and his whole family brought to the most irredeemable destruction through one of my men!

COUNTESS: Those are the consequences of having unmarried soldiers.

COLONEL (*shrugs his shoulders*): How can it be helped? Even Homer, I think, said a good husband would be a bad soldier. And experience bears him out. I always have a thought of my own, every time I read the story of Andromeda. I see the soldiers as the monster, to whom from time to time an unfortunate girl must willingly be sacrificed, so that the remaining wives and daughters remain unharmed.

COUNTESS: What are you talking about?

COLONEL: If the king would establish a hothouse of army-girls—of course they would all have to renounce voluntarily the elevated ideas that women form about eternal ties.

COUNTESS: I doubt that a woman of honor could persuade herself to do so.

COLONEL: They must be Amazons. One honorable instinct, it seems to me, would counterbalance the other. The delicacy of womanly honor, against the idea of being a martyr to the state.

COUNTESS: How little you men know the heart and dreams of a woman.

COLONEL: Of course the king must do his best to make this position both glorious and laudable. He must allot them good salaries, and the children would belong to him. Oh, how I wish that just one man could be found to present this idea to the court. I would provide him with all the information he needs. The defender of the state would thereafter also be its salvation. Maintaining its external security would no longer compromise its internal safety. And in the society that we have up to now despoiled, peace and well-being and joy would prevail.

THE CHILDMURDERESS

BY

HEINRICH LEOPOLD WAGNER

1777

DRAMATIS PERSONAE

MARTIN HUMBRECHT, *a butcher*
MRS. HUMBRECHT
EVCHEN HUMBRECHT, *their daughter*
LISBET, *their maid*
MASTER HUMBRECHT
MAJOR LINDSTHAL
LIEUTENANT VON GRÖNINGSECK
LIEUTENANT VON HASENPOTH
LANDLADY *of "The Yellow Cross"*
MARIANEL, *a maid at "The Yellow Cross"*
MRS. MARTHAN, *a washerwoman*
PUBLIC PROSECUTOR
TWO JAILERS
CLERK, *nonspeaking role*
MAGISTRATES, *nonspeaking roles*

The action takes place in Strassburg, over a period of nine months.

Act One

A seedy room in "The Yellow Cross," an inn.

(*How this room is furnished is to be gathered from the dialogue itself. Off to the side is a door, which leads to another room.*)

(LIEUTENANT VON GRÖNINGSECK *leads* MRS. HUMBRECHT *by the hand into the room.* EVCHEN, MRS. HUMBRECHT's *daughter, follows. The women are wearing dominoes; he, a fur mantle. All are in masks.*)

MARIANEL (*sets a lamp on the table. As she leaves*): Have you ordered already? (LIEUTENANT *signals yes.* MARIANEL *leaves.*)

MRS. HUMBRECHT (*removing her mask*): Captain! Can you assure me . . .

VON GRÖNINGSECK (*tosses off his mantle, mask and hat*): Of everything, my dear Mrs. Humbrecht! Of everything! A kiss, my little one, that is my right after a ball. (*Pulls* EVCHEN's *mask off as well.*) Don't be so bourgeois! A kiss, I say! (*Kisses her. To* MRS. HUMBRECHT.) Now, now, I am not yet a captain, and I don't want to pretend to be what I'm not.

MRS. HUMBRECHT (*curtsies*): As you wish, Major! Serve me!

VON GRÖNINGSECK: Bravo! Bravo! Much better! Ha, ha, ha!

EVCHEN: Oh, Mother, don't try to play the grand lady. Major is higher than captain; you really don't know anything. The lieutenant has already been boarding with us a whole month—

VON GRÖNINGSECK: A month and three days, my child! I have counted every minute.

EVCHEN: Imagine! Does time hang so heavily on your hands then?

VON GRÖNINGSECK: Not yet! But it might very well soon, Evchen, if you don't—

EVCHEN: Evchen! Since when did you become so familiar?

VON GRÖNINGSECK: Don't quarrel, Evchen! Don't quarrel! You mustn't take anything I say tonight the wrong way. I have had a bit too much to drink.

MRS. HUMBRECHT: What I wanted to ask, Lieutenant, is can you assure me that this is a respectable establishment?

VON GRÖNINGSECK: May the devil tear me alive, Mrs. Humbrecht, if everybody of the *beau monde* doesn't come here daily. Just look around, see how shabbily the room is furnished?

MRS. HUMBRECHT: Exactly!

VON GRÖNINGSECK: Exactly, of course, exactly! That implies that all the good rooms are already taken. Do you believe then—*pardieu!*[1]—that Lieutenant von Gröningseck would normally enter such a pigsty? Three chairs and a table that you wouldn't dare touch! (*Lurches forward, knocking the lamp and the table over. The lamp goes out.*)

MRS. HUMBRECHT: My God, the lamp! Lieutenant, the lamp!

VON GRÖNINGSECK (*mimicking her*): The lamp! The lamp! Don't sweat it, this isn't the only damn lamp! Where's the candlestick? (*Searches.*)

EVCHEN: Here, I have it.

---

[1] By God!

VON GRÖNINGSECK: Where? Where?

EVCHEN: Here, for heaven's sake! You're reaching right past it. Honestly!

MRS. HUMBRECHT: What is it? What's the matter?

VON GRÖNINGSECK: Oh, nothing, nothing. (*Takes the candlestick and goes to the door.*) *Holà, des flambeaux!*[2] (*An old* WOMAN *holds a lighted candle out to him, without really letting herself be seen. He lights his own by it.*)

EVCHEN (*wiping her hands on her handkerchief*): Lord, now my hands are all covered with tallow. (*Secretly throws a threatening look at* VON GRÖNINGSECK; *he smiles.*)

MRS. HUMBRECHT: If there's nothing else—

VON GRÖNINGSECK (*rights the table, places the lamp on it*): That was, *ma foi,*[3] a capital joke! Even as I was talking about the crippled dog, the blackguard fell to the floor. We would have missed the best part. *Le diable m'emporte, c'est charmante, c'est divin!*[4] Just look at the frame there: half-bed, half-sofa. I do believe it's some army cot they stole from an old-folks' home. Ha, ha, ha! I bet you didn't have a bridal bed as pretty as this, Mrs. Humbrecht! To be sure, there's only a straw sack (*Tests it with his hand.*), but well-stuffed—resilient!

MRS. HUMBRECHT (*somewhat angry*): See here, Lieutenant! In front of my daughter—

VON GRÖNINGSECK: I must kiss you. Are you looking askance, Evchen? Once more, back to the fun with Evchen! So! All good things come in threes. (*Lets go of* EVCHEN; *offers her his hand; looks fixedly into her eyes; says to her.*) That was punishment for your tactless "Honestly!" (EVCHEN *laughs, shakes hands.*)

MRS. HUMBRECHT (*during this pantomime*): I could just eat you up, the little fool. You have to be good to him whether you want to or not. He's like quicksilver: first here, then there.

MARIANEL (*enters*): Do you wish to be served now?

VON GRÖNINGSECK: But of course, *pardieu!* The sooner the better, and the more the better.

MRS. HUMBRECHT: Come, Eve! I must slip my domino off a bit; I'm getting so warm in the chest.

EVCHEN: Me too, Mother. (*Takes the lamp from the* MAID *and goes with her* MOTHER *to the adjoining room.*)

VON GRÖNINGSECK: So much the better (*Softly.*) for me! (*Calls after them.*) Should I act as chambermaid? I certainly know how to deal with this.

MRS. HUMBRECHT: Oh, yes! That would be lovely. No, a personal chambermaid would be much too aristocratic for us.

EVCHEN: We can manage without you, Mr. Bluecoat! (*Pushes him away from behind her* MOTHER, *and shuts the door.*)

VON GRÖNINGSECK: So how the hell did you wind up here, Marianel? Aren't you working at the coffeehouse on the corner any more? That little room there was very cozy.

---

[2]Hey, a light!

[3]By my faith

[4]Devil take me, it's charming, it's divine!

MARIANEL: I'm glad you brought that up, devil-child! Really glad. You still owe me a Christmas present. Pay up now or I'll tell them all about you.

VON GRÖNINGSECK: I? Owe you? Didn't I always give you your little taler when—

MARIANEL: Yeah, sure, you paid every time! But how often did I have to cover up for you? Right? Don't you remember, you boozer, Sunday before Christmas, how you were making such a racket at midnight? Like you wanted to storm the house? How I secretly let you in at the back door, and how I made you tea, and how you spat on me over and over and—

VON GRÖNINGSECK: And . . . and . . . shut the hell up. Here are six livres, you carrion. But now you have to do one favor.

MARIANEL: Anything, anything, my precious! Tell me! Tell me! (*Tries to cuddle him.*)

VON GRÖNINGSECK (*pushes her from him*): That's not necessary now. When a soldier has a croissant to eat, he doesn't need army bread.

MARIANEL: Think about it, my precious. You're in rotten shape now, but you can be happy and back to your old self again.

VON GRÖNINGSECK: Yes, I think so too, my stupid. I didn't mean to sound so rude. Now, here is a little packet. Take it, and when I call for punch, put the little powder inside in the first glass you set on the table.

MARIANEL: Go to the frigging devil, and take your goddamn powder with you! You want *me* to poison the people for you? You think I have no conscience, you hellhound?

VON GRÖNINGSECK: Now just listen to me, Marianella! Damn it, listen to me or—it's not a poison. It's a little sleeping-powder, if you want to know. And here's a large taler.

MARIANEL: Oh, well, that's something else. Give it here. (*She grabs at the money; he sticks it back into his pocket.*)

VON GRÖNINGSECK: Here is the powder. Now, don't screw things up. When I leave, you'll get the taler.

MARIANEL: Why not now?

VON GRÖNINGSECK: A whore is never to be trusted.

MARIANEL (*as she leaves*): Nor a whore's trick. If there weren't any of your sort around, all maidens would be quite virtuous. You're a fine one to insult! First you carve yourself a God, then you crucify Him.

VON GRÖNINGSECK: Shut up and do what I tell you!

MARIANEL: It won't do you a hell of a lot of good. (*Leaves.*)

VON GRÖNINGSECK: That's my problem! Things might get out of hand, if I can't get rid of the old bat. (*To* EVCHEN, *who has returned, followed by her* MOTHER.) Yes, *ma chère*, that's right. That's lovely, lovely! *Le diable m'emporte,* you do look appetizing! Such sheer, light clothing! On my honor, you have grown into a beauty. So thin, everything standing out so much.

MRS. HUMBRECHT: Now, Lieutenant, how do *I* look? All right for the show?

VON GRÖNINGSECK (*without looking at her*): Superb! Superb! The gown flatters you.

MRS. HUMBRECHT: Yes, that's what you say. Thoughts are free is what you think. If only there were a mirror here!

VON GRÖNINGSECK: How divinely beautiful in disarray your hair is, my darling! I can't gaze upon you enough. Ah, the floating tresses! (*Kisses her and leads her, his arm around her waist, to the table. Sits next to her.*)

MRS. HUMBRECHT (*observing herself during this*): You're almost right, Eve, I should have put my domino back on. Now I see; before, I couldn't. I couldn't tell by the lamp, but my collar is too dirty.

EVCHEN: I tried to tell you, but you wouldn't listen.

VON GRÖNINGSECK: You look fine, both of you. You look fine, Mrs. Humbrecht, you look fine. You look fine.

MRS. HUMBRECHT: Oh well, then. As long as it's good enough for you. (*Goes over to him and toys with his epaulettes.*) I figured, under the mask, nobody can tell if my collar is dirty or not, and if I put on a fresh one, sure as anything it'd get crumpled.

VON GRÖNINGSECK: An exemplary housekeeper, by my faith! (*Lets go of EVCHEN's hand, seizes MRS. HUMBRECHT and sets her between his legs.*) *Très bonne ménagère!*[5] Aren't you tired then, after the ball, little woman?

MRS. HUMBRECHT: Oh, who could be tired, there's always something to see! Always something new! I think I would have been able just to sit in one spot the whole night and the whole day through, not eating or drinking.

EVCHEN: Not I! I don't find any fun in just watching.

VON GRÖNINGSECK: You'd rather get in on the fun, is that it?

EVCHEN (*innocently*): Yes!

MRS. HUMBRECHT (*laughs so hard she leans forward onto the* LIEUTENANT's *chest; her face is turned away from* EVCHEN. *He plays with* MRS. HUMBRECHT's *necklace; she presses his hand and kisses it.*): She didn't understand you. You mustn't misinterpret her naivety. (*Straightens herself.*) You really are too wicked. If you only knew!

(MARIANEL *brings in food, wine, and glasses. Sets them down. Leaves.*)

VON GRÖNINGSECK: *Allons,*[6] let's eat! Take your places, my dears. Breakfast is served. Dig in! (MRS. HUMBRECHT *sits down. He serves her.*) Here, Madame—

MRS. HUMBRECHT: Oh, bosh! I've told you before, I'm not Madame, I'm just plain old Missus. Go ahead, serve yourself.

EVCHEN: What can you be thinking of? How could I possibly eat all of this? (*About to return her portion to the serving dish.*)

MRS. HUMBRECHT: Now stop that! Behave! What you can't eat, you can stick in your pockets. Right, Lieutenant? I mean, it's already paid for.

VON GRÖNINGSECK: Right, little woman! (*Pinches her cheek and leers at* EVCHEN.) *Ma foi,* you have the mind of an angel. Surely you know how to help yourself. *Pardieu!* The muscatel is magnificent! (*Lurches.*) To our health! To your future husband, Evchen!

MRS. HUMBRECHT: Oh, she's still got plenty of time. She's only eighteen years old.

VON GRÖNINGSECK: Already three years lost!

MRS. HUMBRECHT: Now really! I was nearly twenty-four when I married Mr.

---

[5]A very good housekeeper!
[6]Come on

Humbrecht, and all my girlfriends laughed at me for marrying so young.

VON GRÖNINGSECK: Gothic times! Gothic customs! (*Lurches.*) Now to the wedding night, Mrs. Humbrecht!

MRS. HUMBRECHT: Hee, hee, hee! You are trying to get me tipsy. No, no, it won't do you any good. Well then, to the honor of my dear husband; I give myself the honor— (*About to rise.*)

VON GRÖNINGSECK (*restrains her*): No ceremony! We have to finish the bottle. Then we can have a nice little glass of punch on top.

MRS. HUMBRECHT: Take care and watch out! That could be a pretty mess. No, no, if you don't mind, we really should be leaving.

VON GRÖNINGSECK: Leaving? Already? Are you out of your mind, little lady? (*Flings his arm around her neck.*) Truly then we *would* be making a public display of ourselves. (*Looks at his watch.*) Only half past two! The whole neighborhood would laugh at us if we came home from a ball at only half past two. Stop imagining trouble, Mrs. Humbrecht. I won't let you budge from here for another hour. Then we'll go right back to the ball. I still have the ticket-stubs.

EVCHEN: Oh yes, Mother! Back to the ball!

MRS. HUMBRECHT: Oh well, then. I'll permit it only because I want to let you have a good time, and because the lieutenant is doing us such a great honor. Your fool of a father never lets you out of the house like this.

VON GRÖNINGSECK: Now you're talking sense. When one partakes of pleasure only rarely, he should make the most of it. Besides, tonight is the last ball of the year. Come on, Evchen! Don't sip it like that. The glass must be drained. (EVCHEN *finishes her glass.*) Well done! For that you get a kiss. (*Kisses her.*) Holà! la maison![7] (MARIANEL *opens the door.*) Punch! (MARIANEL *leaves.*)

EVCHEN: What kind of drink exactly is punch, Mother?

MRS. HUMBRECHT: Oh . . . yes, well . . . there's some . . .

VON GRÖNINGSECK: What, Evchen? You don't know what punch is? You've never tasted it? You people live like the mendicant monks. Eighteen years old, and this is your first ball, and you don't know what punch is? Ah, nectar! A drink fit for the gods! *Le diable m'emporte s'il n'est pas vrai*![8] If I were the king of France I could not conceive of a more delicious hooch than punch. It is and will always be my favorite drink, so help me God. *Ah, le voilà*! (MARIANEL *brings three bar-glasses on a salver. He takes them from her one at a time. With the first that she gives him, he asks.*) Is everything there?

MARIANEL (*With a deep curtsy*): Exactly as you ordered it, sir. (*Pinches him, unseen by the others, on the arm. He looks at her haughtily and gestures that she should leave. She curtsies again and leaves, biting her lips to keep from laughing.*)

MRS. HUMBRECHT (*holds the glass to her nose*): Oh yes, that would finish me, by God! I'd better not have a drop of that. It smells so strong, God forgive me, I could get sloshed on the smell alone.

VON GRÖNINGSECK: Just the opposite, little woman, just the opposite! I give you

---

[7]Hey! Service!

[8]Devil take me if it's not true.

my *parole d'officier*,[9] or my *parole de maçon*,[10] whichever you want, that I have been drunk two or three times in an afternoon, and each time it was punch that restored me.

EVCHEN: Yes, your stomach is used to such things, but I've never drunk anything strong.

VON GRÖNINGSECK: Good! So I'll capitulate: Evchen drinks as much or as little as she wants, and I'll finish what she doesn't take as well as my own. Mama, however, must empty her own glass. That way everything's in proportion. *Allegro!* To arms! (*He hands each her glass, then takes his own. He raises his glass; they drink.*)

EVCHEN (*spits the drink back out*): Pfooey! Wow, does that burn!

MRS. HUMBRECHT: You rude—! Is that how one treats a gift from the gods? (*Takes a larger gulp herself.*) This is delicious. Almost like Rossoli.

VON GRÖNINGSECK: More or less, to be sure! I'm glad you like it, dear lady. But one thing, Evchen, you must promise me. When we go back to the ball, you must dance no allemand with anyone else but me, however many quadrilles you want.

MRS. HUMBRECHT: Is that so? She can't do that. She's forgotten all that.

VON GRÖNINGSECK: Not at all! She dances only too well, makes her figures, turns and steps with too much *grâce*, too charming, too captivating. I cannot see you with anyone else without secretly becoming very jealous.

MRS. HUMBRECHT: Ooh, you do love to tease. Though she *did* take lessons for three years with Sauveur.

VON GRÖNINGSECK: With Sauveur! *Pardieu!* Now I am not at all surprised. I have also been a student of his. *C'est un excellent maître pour former une jeune personne!*[11] To his health! (MRS. HUMBRECHT *and he drink.*) But *comment diable*[12] did you wind up with Sauveur? He's always busy with counts and barons.

EVCHEN: There were three barons and a wealthy Swiss who boarded next to us at Mrs. Schaffner's. They needed female partners, so they invited me along.

VON GRÖNINGSECK: Damn me, the fellows didn't have bad taste. How long ago was that?

MRS. HUMBRECHT (*yawning*): Oh, it must have been five years or so, I think.

EVCHEN: Yes, at least that many. Maybe even six.

VON GRÖNINGSECK: That's close enough. So you were then only twelve years old, and you'd already caught the eyes of barons.

EVCHEN: Oh, Mother! I hope you're not about to go to sleep?

VON GRÖNINGSECK (*supports her with one arm around her neck; with the other hand he brings her glass to her lips*): The rest, just a bit more, Mrs. Humbrecht.

MRS. HUMBRECHT (*pushes the glass away*): Not another drop! (*He sets it aside.*) I can't keep my eyes . . . open . . . any . . . long . . . (*Falls asleep against the* LIEUTENANT'*s chest.*)

---

[9] word as an officer
[10] word as a Mason
[11] He's an excellent master for shaping a young person.
[12] how the devil

EVCHEN: Good God! What's wrong! (*Leaps up, frightened, and tries to rouse her* MOTHER.) Mother! What's the matter with you? Can you hear me? Can you hear me? God in heaven! I hope she's not ill!

VON GRÖNINGSECK: Calm down, Evchen. It doesn't mean anything. In a quarter-hour, she'll be as awake as ever. The punch did it. She's not used to it.

EVCHEN (*shakes her again*): Mother! Mother! I think she must have fainted, or else she's dead.

VON GRÖNINGSECK: Fainted! Dead! Balderdash! Feel her pulse. She just drank a little too quickly, that's all. Come on, Evchen, help me get her on to the bed. She's really too heavy for me. (EVCHEN *and he carry her to the bed and lay her across it.*) *Pardieu*! We made fun of this bedframe before, but now we're glad we've got it.

EVCHEN (*quite disturbed*): I still don't know what's going on! If only I could get her home!

VON GRÖNINGSECK (*sits down next to* MRS. HUMBRECHT, *draws* EVCHEN *to him*): Don't be a child, *ma chère*! Nothing else is going to happen. We still have time to get back to the ball. (*Gazes at her fixedly.*) Do you still like me, Evchen?

EVCHEN: For heaven's sake, don't look at me like that. I can't stand it.

VON GRÖNINGSECK: Why can't you, my little fool? (*Kisses her hand passionately, looking deeper and deeper into her eyes with each kiss.*)

EVCHEN: That's why! I won't! (*He is about to embrace her and kiss her. She struggles, breaks free, and runs into the next room.*) Mother! Mother! I am lost!

VON GRÖNINGSECK (*hurrying after her*): You shouldn't run away from me! (*Slams the door shut behind him. Offstage pandemonium. The old* LANDLADY *and* MARIANEL *enter; they behave as if they hear nothing. By and by it grows quiet.*)

LANDLADY: Clear away fast. Look at how the old marmot there is sleeping.

MARIANEL: If you had only let me have my way, I know who'd be sleeping there now. *Then* we would have been able to nab something!

LANDLADY: Yeah, nab! You and the devil go nab! Officers are the right ones for you. A year ago one from the *Corps royal* lost a trifling little ring. The bastard wanted to fleece me! He'd have had me turn the house upside down if Christine hadn't found it again in the mattress. You and your officers can go to hell! But I'm not coming along—what are you sticking in the mattress? Huh? Back to your dust mop! What are you sticking there? Can't you tell me?

MARIANEL: Shh! Shh! A snuffbox. We'll share it. It belongs to the old marmot there.

LANDLADY: Really? It's not the lieutenant's?

MARIANEL: No, really, I'm sure.

LANDLADY: So go on and get out—march! The bottles can stay there. If he asks for the bill, tell him one and a half louis d'ors. (*Leaves.*)

MARIANEL: Fine! And a half for me makes two. (*Clears everything away and tiptoes out.*)

EVCHEN (*bursts in from the adjoining room and flings herself on her* MOTHER):

Mother! Cruel mother! Sleep, sleep forever. Your daughter is a whore! (*Falls sobbing onto her* MOTHER's *bosom. The* LIEUTENANT *paces a few times up and down the room. Finally he stands next to her.*)

VON GRÖNINGSECK: Have you taken leave of your senses, Mademoiselle? Do you want to be a prostitute? To let the whole world know what's happened between us?

EVCHEN (*straightens herself. Her face is hidden, however, in her handkerchief*): Go! Go, tormentor! Devil in angel's clothing!

VON GRÖNINGSECK: You've been reading novels, right? It would be an eternal shame if you weren't a heroine yourself.

EVCHEN: Joke away, thief of my honor, joke away! Yes, I've read novels. I read them in order to learn about you monsters, to be able to protect myself from your wiles—and now look! God! God! Your sleep is not natural, Mother. Now I understand.

VON GRÖNINGSECK: For heaven's sake, pull yourself together! You certainly aren't the first.

EVCHEN: That you've ruined? I'm not . . . not the first? Oh, say that just once more . . .

VON GRÖNINGSECK: Not the first, I say, who gave in before she was married. From this moment on, you are mine. I swore so already in the bedchamber, and repeat it again here by all that is holy. On my knees, I repeat it. In five months I shall be of age. I shall lead you to the altar then, and proclaim you publicly to be mine.

EVCHEN: How can I trust you after what's happened? But of course I must. I'm as despicable as you, more, more! I can't become any worse, can't sink any lower. (*Wiping away her tears.*) Good, Lieutenant, I shall believe you. (*Stands.*) Get up and hear my conditions! Five months, you said! Good! That's how long I'll choke back every emotion. No one will learn of my disgrace from my face. But!—are you really and truly in earnest, what you've sworn to? Well, have you been struck dumb? Yes or no?

VON GRÖNINGSECK: Yes, yes, Evchen! As true as I'm standing here!

EVCHEN (*kisses him, but tears away as soon as he kisses her*): Listen! May these kisses be the rings that we exchange in promise of our marriage. But from now on, until the minister says "Amen," from now on—listen to what I am saying—do not be so bold as to even kiss my finger. Else I shall hold you to be a perjurer, who sees me as a fallen woman, to whom he owes no respect, whom he can play with as he wants. As soon as I sense this, I shall reveal the whole story to Father or Mother. It doesn't matter which one, right? To whomever, I'll tell everything that happened, even if they should trample me to dust! Do you understand? Why so silent, sir? Are you surprised at what I said? Now go call the coachman!

VON GRÖNINGSECK: You astonish me, Evchen! This tone!

EVCHEN: Offended virtue speaks. It must speak so. Now everything depends on you to prove that you have spoken truly.

VON GRÖNINGSECK (*about to embrace her*): Angel child!

EVCHEN (*draws back*): Are you insulting me, betrayer? Can you say angel without thinking of the fallen ones? Brought down by you!

(LIEUTENANT VON GRÖNINGSECK *leaves*.)

(*The curtain falls.*)

Act Two

(*Living room in the* HUMBRECHTS' *house. Plain middle-class furnishings. A piano is off to the side.*)

(MARTIN HUMBRECHT *sits, quite grumpily, in a corner, his head propped up by his hand.* MRS. HUMBRECHT *is working.*)

MRS. HUMBRECHT: I really don't know who you think you are, Husband! You, you grudge your daughter a little sunshine, much less any other pleasure.

HUMBRECHT: You're right, dear. You're always right.

MRS. HUMBRECHT: It's true, isn't it? Look at him sitting there, with a face like a garden spider. If we dare once every six months to sample some pleasure outside this house, right away you fly off the handle.

HUMBRECHT: You're right, dear, you're always right. I advise you, however, with the best of intentions—to shut up. I swear, I shall never again leave this house, even if everything here goes to blazes!

MRS. HUMBRECHT: Now what are you going on about? You haven't any cause to complain about me. I don't debase you, I don't waste your money, I never get out of the house—

HUMBRECHT (*laughs in her face*): Oh, you're the model of the ideal wife; everybody in town knows it. Eternal shame that you're not Catholic. Why, eventually you could be canonized! Saint Mrs. Humbrecht, pray for us! Ha, ha, ha!

MRS. HUMBRECHT: Joke all you want. I am, and always will be, what I am.

HUMBRECHT: Who could deny it? You are, and through all eternity will be, a—

MRS. HUMBRECHT: A what? Come on, if you know anything to say, out with it! Can you show me where I have neglected you in the slightest? Aren't my eyes always everywhere, always checking?

HUMBRECHT: Oh yes, checking everything except the one thing they should be checking. You give your daughter too much freedom, no matter how many times I warn you.

MRS. HUMBRECHT: And you don't give her enough. It's a big deal if she goes *once* to a ball. Now really, where's the harm, eh? Aren't there a great many virtuous people at balls?

HUMBRECHT: It's not right for middle-class people. I've lived fifty decent years, I've never been at a ball, and I'm still alive. (MASTER HUMBRECHT *enters.*)

MRS. HUMBRECHT: You're right on time, Cousin. My little girl won't have her piano lesson today, so you can help me bring my husband to his senses.

MASTER: I'm sure, Cousin, you're quite capable of doing that without my help. However (*Seeing the white collar lying off to the side.*) may I ask if your daughter is ill?

HUMBRECHT: Not at all, Cousin! Not at all! She's just beginning to follow the latest fashion, make day out of night, and turn everything upside-down.

MASTER: That would mean, then, she's still asleeep?

MRS. HUMBRECHT: It's nothing to worry about, Cousin. Last night we were at the ball, Eve and I, the lieutenant from upstairs just wouldn't leave us in peace. Every Sunday during Carnival season he had begged us very insistently to do him the honor. Yesterday he came again and invited us, and since it was the last ball, as he said, which decent people could attend—since on *mardi gras*, only wigmakers go, as he said—he wanted to be absolutely sure not to be refused—

HUMBRECHT: And because I had just gone off on some business, they grabbed their chance and were off shaking their tails at the ball.

MRS. HUMBRECHT: Now, is there anything wrong with that, Cousin?

HUMBRECHT: There you're asking the right man! What would a cleric know of balls? He knows as much about them as about bulls. And I'll be hanged if he knows the difference between a bull and an ox!

MRS. HUMBRECHT: Don't be ridiculous. The men have been around, they hear tell of what *mores* are. Tell him frankly, Cousin, is there anything so sinful about going to balls?

MASTER: To answer your question, I must distinguish, my esteemed Cousin, first the going to balls itself, and second, the various other conditions that go along with it or could go along with it. Considering the first point, I see nothing sinful in going to balls in itself; it's a delight and, according to the new theology, which however is at bottom also the oldest and most natural, delight is also a form of divine service—

HUMBRECHT: Cousin! Cousin! Take care that all you blackfrocks aren't thrown to the devil, once this new divine service is introduced!

MASTER: I'm only saying, delight is a type of divine service. It doesn't exclude all the other types, however, and consequently we teachers are not yet superfluous. Nonetheless, putting aside this argument, which I could better explain to you at another opportunity, that is, in clearer exegesis, I wish—with your permission, Cousin—to use the Socratic method, and thus I pose two questions to you. First, do you believe then that so many thoroughly righteous mothers, upstanding women, even women of the aristocracy, themselves would go to balls *and* take their daughters there, if their consciences bothered them about it?

MRS. HUMBRECHT: Right, Cousin! Exactly!

HUMBRECHT: As far as I'm concerned, they may have a conscience as broad as the town square! But what does the aristocracy have to do with me? I have a position of my own, and everyone should stick to his own! And I never said that going to balls is fit for nobody. *My* family shouldn't be going to such things, is what I say. Let those who belong at such doings dance about. Who's to say no? For the aristocratic ladies and gentlemen, landowners and their ladies, who because of their great position don't know what to do with the time that God gave them, such doings may be very pleasant ways to kill the hours. Who would stop them? But tradesmen's wives and decent middle-class daughters should keep away from all that. They can go to weddings and guild banquets and that sort of thing if they're so eager to wear their shoes out dancing. They don't have to seek out places to put their honor and good name in jeopardy. When, however, a sugar-sweet fellow in a uniform, or a little baron—God have mercy on him—takes a middle-class girl to such places, it's ten to one that he will not bring her back home in the same condition she was when she left.

MRS. HUMBRECHT: Oh, Husband! Are you crazy! You really don't believe that our daughter—

HUMBRECHT (*mimicking her*): You really don't believe—that that little brat! I only believe what I know. But if I *did* believe such a thing. (*Makes two fists.*) God in heaven! How I would thrash you!

MASTER: No, Cousin! Not that! You will not, I hope, fly into a rage over a matter that is so insignificant, one that remains completely within the class of those that the most stringent casuist must consider neither good nor bad.

HUMBRECHT: Are there many such "matters" in your catechism?

MASTER: Several! And I am so convinced that going to balls should be reckoned as one of them that I will tell you—just between us—I was there myself.

HUMBRECHT (*leaping up angrily*): So that's what your church school comes collecting at our church doors twice a year for! (*As he leaves.*) Adieu, Cousin! And I'll be damned before I throw another *sols* in your bowl. *Adieu!* (*Leaves.*)

MRS. HUMBRECHT: You did not handle that very well, Cousin! I'm afraid you've ruined things for a long time with my husband.

MASTER: Is he really in earnest?

MRS. HUMBRECHT: Oh, absolutely. He is totally of the old world. You just can't imagine what a cross he is for me to bear! Two years ago, at the beginning of winter, we just missed separating by a hair—God forgive me!—because I wanted to exchange my fur collar that he had inherited from his grandmother for a more stylish one. And only eight days earlier, when Evchen was supposed to attend a christening, he insisted with all his might and main, that she had to wear the golden bonnet. But nobody wears them any more except at best a gardener's or a linen-weaver's daughter! No, you might have confessed, Cousin, but you shouldn't have announced it.

MASTER: As long as I need not reproach myself for having done something, I can speak of it. Of course, there are some distinctions. My superiors, for example, in order to prevent wrongdoing, must totally forbid some things, which they wouldn't if there were no danger at all. It wouldn't be wise to draw their attention to these activities. But otherwise I make little secret of the fact that I consider it rather my duty to see everything and test everything before passing judgment on it.

(LIEUTENANT VON GRÖNINGSECK *enters hastily and dashes up to* MRS. HUMBRECHT. MASTER HUMBRECHT *rises.*)

VON GRÖNINGSECK: Quite a *tête-à-tête*! Lovely! I'll tell your husband, Landlady, if you don't find a way to stop me!

MRS. HUMBRECHT: Hee, hee, hee, hee, hee! Go ahead, my husband knows all about it. He's already left.

VON GRÖNINGSECK: So! (*Sings.*) "The good man, the decent fellow"—do you know the song? No? I must teach it to you. I'm sure I've seen this gentleman before.

MRS. HUMBRECHT: This is my cousin. He gives my Evchen piano lessons.

VON GRÖNINGSECK (*carelessly takes a pinch of snuff*): Yes, yes. Mr. Pianoteacher, yes.

MASTER: Your servant, sir! (*The* LIEUTENANT *takes* MASTER HUMBRECHT's *chair and sits close by* MRS. HUMBRECHT. MASTER HUMBRECHT *gets another chair and sits on her other side.*) With your permission, Cousin.

VON GRÖNINGSECK: No ceremony! *Pardieu!* I do believe this was *your* chair. Oh, I *do* beg your pardon, Mr. . . . . Pianoteacher.

MASTER: I am only a piano teacher to my friends, to whom I am more than happy to extend the favor. I do not have to stand for—

VON GRÖNINGSECK: As you wish, as you wish. It wasn't intentional, Abbé!

MRS. HUMBRECHT: If you only knew, Lieutenant, what sort of row I've been having with my husband over the ball. Oh, you just can't imagine!

VON GRÖNINGSECK: *Comment*?[13] Because of the ball? *C'est drôle!*[14] On my honor, that's insane.

MRS. HUMBRECHT: And think of it: here's my cousin, who I thought would help me bring my husband to his senses, and instead drives him even crazier!

VON GRÖNINGSECK: I'm so sorry for you! However, Mr. Blackfrock must be used to that sort of thing.

MRS. HUMBRECHT: Everything would have been fine, you see, he had told him the truth quite skillfully. But then in the passion of the moment he let it slip that he had been at the ball himself, and then of course my husband didn't want to hear any more. That's what did it. That alone!

VON GRÖNINGSECK: Ho, ho! The abbé himself at the ball. I really wouldn't have believed it of you. No, sir!

MASTER: And why not, sir?

VON GRÖNINGSECK: Hm! Because of the coat.

MASTER: Really! Since you like to give yourself such airs, you should know that this prejudice shows you off rather badly. If you had been closer to the hub of France, or even at the intellectual courts of Germany, you would know that prelates of the first rank in no way consider themselves obligated to renounce their right to the pleasures permitted to man. If our church would only begin to think so sensibly and behave so sensibly, there would be fewer religious fanatics and consequently fewer mockers of religion!

MRS. HUMBRECHT: Oh, Cousin!

VON GRÖNINGSECK: Damn, what a sermon! *Ma foi*, you're going to get the first position of tutor that's mine to give.

MASTER: I doubt it. The father who is willing to entrust his son to me—after talking to me for fifteen minutes—is yet to be born.

VON GRÖNINGSECK: Why? Now you're making me curious.

MASTER: You're making a joke, sir.

VON GRÖNINGSECK: *Parole d'honneur!*[15] No! I repeat, you're making me very curious about your reasons.

MASTER: To explain it all at once is impossible. In general, I can say that nowadays my educational axioms would hardly win approval.

MRS. HUMBRECHT: Oh, Cousin! You don't think as old-fashionedly as my husband.

MASTER: Quite the contrary! My thoughts are far too modern to escape prosecution.

VON GRÖNINGSECK: A little test, Master. Just one example. I like to hear things like this. I think they are called "paradoxes," right?

MASTER: I would, for example, at the critical moment in which a boy becomes a young man, begins to be aware of his own feelings and to sense the physical reasons for his existence—a moment that is a critical stumbling-block for the virtue of almost all young people, a dangerous rock—

---

[13]What?

[14]How amusing!

[15]Word of honor!

MRS. HUMBRECHT (*rising*): This is all over my head, gentlemen. I'm going to find my daughter. (*Leaves.*)

MASTER : I would, I was about to say, treat my student in these years in a manner that was exactly the opposite of what is customary. Instead of leaving him in his ignorance to some mere chance that certainly leads astray nineteen out of twenty, I would be careful to make him aware of the greatness, the nobility of his destiny.

VON GRÖNINGSECK: Certainly others have suggested that.

MASTER: But more! To instill in him forever a dreadful repugnance for all crimes of this type, I would imitate the Spartans, who in order to warn their youth of the perils of drunkenness showed them a few drunken slaves to laugh at. I myself would accompany my student to licentious and degenerate places. The insolent, self-seeking, vile behavior of the venal prostitutes would certainly make an imperishable mark on his tender, still uncorrupted heart, a mark that no temptation could ever erase.

VON GRÖNINGSECK: You may be right. For all that, though, the treatment seems damned drastic to me.

MASTER: To be sure, it is. But all other preventive measures can be overthrown by a glass of wine, a dissolute friend, an unfortunate moment. To be even surer, I have another prescription up my sleeve.

VON GRÖNINGSECK: Namely?

MASTER: The nearest military hospital or sanatorium for the incurably ill. The young man, when he has suitably absorbed the prior scenes and reflected on them, and is then led to this living hell, and sees before his very eyes the pitiful, horrible consequences of a single misstep, a single intemperance of this type—if he's not restrained forever, he has neither head nor heart.

VON GRÖNINGSECK: You're getting excited, Master. I like that. I hate everything about the phlegmatic temperament. Pardon me, if my first impression of you was not a true measure of your merit. We must talk further. Give me your hand on it!

(MASTER HUMBRECHT *gives him his hand trustingly, as* MRS. HUMBRECHT *and* EVCHEN *enter.*)

MRS. HUMBRECHT: Eh, look at that! How nice! Already such good friends?

VON GRÖNINGSECK: Now I know your cousin. Before, the clothing fooled me. Good morning, Mademoiselle Evchen.

MASTER: Are you all slept out, little cousin? (EVCHEN *lowers her eyes, blushes, curtsys, and sits down to work.*) Such red eyes! Were you crying?

MRS. HUMBRECHT: Not at all. You know, Cousin, he who seldom rides—she's not used to staying up late, that's all.

VON GRÖNINGSECK: I am so terribly sorry if I . . . or the ball . . .

EVCHEN (*interrupting*): You are very kind, Lieutenant.

MRS. HUMBRECHT: So don't be so surly! I don't know what's with her today. If I hadn't been with her every minute, if I didn't know that she had enjoyed everything fine and good, I'd wonder if some misfortune had befallen her.

VON GRÖNINGSECK: If I could only offer something for your reassurance . . . amusement, I mean . . . Mademoiselle . . . it would be my pleasure . . .

EVCHEN (*with a forced smile*): I'll look forward to that, Lieutenant. I hope you keep your word.

111

VON GRÖNINGSECK: Absolutely! (*Looks at his watch.*) *Pardieu*! I've scarcely enough time to make the parade.

MASTER: I'll go with you. It seems that today my little cousin has no head for music.

EVCHEN: No! Today, no. I have a headache.

(*The* LIEUTENANT *and* MASTER HUMBRECHT *leave.*)

MRS. HUMBRECHT: Oh, child, child! I beg you, for God's sake, not to mope around so. If your father comes back—you know how he is—and sees you so depressed, he'll start in all over again about the ball.

EVCHEN: You're right, Mother. (*With a deep sigh.*) If only you hadn't fallen asleep! Then—

MRS. HUMBRECHT: Go on! Then *what*?

EVCHEN: Then you wouldn't be any more awake than I, or at least I'd seem as awake as you.

MRS. HUMBRECHT: Infant! A little sleep would do you good! Didn't you say yourself I didn't sleep long?

EVCHEN: No, not long, but longer than—

MRS. HUMBRECHT: I'm going to lose my temper! Do I have to throttle each word from your throat one at a time? (*Mocking her.*) "No, not long, but longer than—" Than *what*?

EVCHEN: Oh, well, than me! Isn't that right?

MRS. HUMBRECHT: Oh, what's the use? Look, Evchen, do your mother a favor and wipe that gloomy expression off your face. Your father already thinks that we went to the ball more for my sake than for yours. If he sees you so thoroughly miserable, I'll be the one he yells at again, for sure. Now, Evchen, won't you be a dear for me? There isn't anything else wrong, is there?

EVCHEN: I'll do what I can.

MRS. HUMBRECHT: Good God, something else! Do you know where my snuffbox is?

EVCHEN: No. You mean the silver one with gold trim?

MRS. HUMBRECHT: That's it. The one your father gave me for an engagement gift. I can't figure out what I—

EVCHEN: You had it in your hand yesterday morning. I saw it.

MRS. HUMBRECHT: Oh, God! If I've lost it! I'll go this instant and search through everything again. If I don't find it, I'll have it advertised after dinner. (*Leaves.*)

EVCHEN: Poor Mother! All that fuss over a box! If only that were the biggest loss! Fatal moment! Unhappy ball! How low I have fallen! My burden alone! I wanted to pull my braids out by the roots, but I was ashamed to in front of the maid doing my hair. May nobody see me, no man look me in the eye! If the hope weren't there . . . my only hope . . . he swore it to me, twice, three times! Be still, my heart! (*Frightened.*) My God, I hear my father! Every word from him will be a dagger in my heart. How he thunders! By Heaven! Could he have already learned of my downfall? (*Turns from the door in anguish and covers her face with her hands.*)

HUMBRECHT (*to his* WIFE, *who has entered with him*): That piece of trash! That goddamned, pigheaded—! I want her out of this house this instant! Did you hear me? I said this instant! I won't eat a bit in peace as long as the little tramp is under my roof! So are you going to tell her or not? If I have to do it, I can't be sure I won't throw her down the stairs headfirst!

EVCHEN: My god! That means me!

MRS. HUMBRECHT: At least tell me why! I have to be able to give her a reason. Up to now you've never had any cause to complain about her.

HUMBRECHT: Reason! *I'm* supposed to give *you* a reason? You should be ashamed of yourself for being such a poor landlady and not keeping order in your own house. Because she's a slut! A whore! *That's* the reason!

EVCHEN (*leaping up*): I can't bear it any longer! (*Falls suddenly at her* FATHER*'s feet.* HUMBRECHT, *who hadn't seen her, jumps, startled.*) Father! Dearest father! Forgive me! (*Wordlessly, she lets her head sink to the ground.*)

MRS. HUMBRECHT (*Grabbing her by the arm*): Eh, girl! What's the matter with you? Are you dreaming? Get up. I swear, she must have thought you were talking about *her.*

HUMBRECHT: The fool! What a fright she gave me! Falling before me like a sack of potatoes! Get up! Get up! (*Helps her to her feet.*) I can't stand grimaces, you know that. I had made up my mind to scold you thoroughly, but now it's just as if I hadn't a dram more bad temper in me. I believe the fright has wiped out everything. Well? Aren't you going to thank me for my leniency? This time you escaped. But if it ever happens again—thunder and lightning! Just once more and I'll break every bone in your body, so you won't get much pleasure a third time.

EVCHEN: I swear to you, Father! If I had it to do over, I wouldn't.

HUMBRECHT: Really? You wouldn't? Now that's my good girl, Evchen! That's wonderful. So you're sorry, eh? Come here and let me kiss you! What? You blush when you kiss your father? Why should you be so upset? But I forget that the mamsell was at the ball. In the future you'll stay at home. The balls will go on very nicely without you.

EVCHEN: Mamsell!

MRS. HUMBRECHT: Don't be so hard on her! Look how she's shaking!

HUMBRECHT (*taking her hand*): Does the word bother you, Daughter? I'm glad! One must never want to be more than one is! And now, Wife! We almost didn't get to the most important thing—even if you do only know it because I have to tell you. The pretty young girl in back let a sergeant take her measurements. Her mother knows about it and lets them do as they please. The whole neighborhood is worked up over it. Now—march! Terminate her lodging. Now you understand why, right? Better the whole rear section stay empty our whole life long, abandoned to mice, rats, and owls, than harbor any more such riffraff. I wouldn't let my own daughter stay in the house one more hour if she went so far astray. (MRS. HUMBRECHT *leaves; he calls after her.*) I want her packed up by sunset or I'll fling everything out the window and the both of them, mother and daughter, right after them! (*Turns to* EVCHEN.) You, go set the table. (*Leaves.*)

EVCHEN: His own daughter! Those few words are my sentence of condemnation! What a treasure a clear conscience is! (*Beating her breast as she leaves.*) But that's gone! Everything's gone! (*Leaves.*)

113

Act Three

(LIEUTENANT VON GRÖNINGSECK's *room in the* HUMBRECHTS' *house. A bathroom off to the side.*)

(LIEUTENANT VON HASENPOTH *stands before the mirror, whistling.* VON GRÖNINGSECK *sits, lost in thought, in an easychair.*)

VON HASENPOTH (*turning away from the mirror*): To hell with all those melancholy thoughts, Gröningseck! Come, the weather's beautiful. Have a cabriolet brought. Let's take a boat ride.

VON GRÖNINGSECK: Go by yourself. I'd rather stay at home.

VON HASENPOTH: Always and ever at home. How can you stand it? This whole summer you didn't go anywhere unless you had to with the company. I'd like to live that way too. Like a Carthusian! Really! Ten times better a bullet in the brain!

VON GRÖNINGSECK: To each his own.

VON HASENPOTH: Fine! But this moping around isn't your normal style. Only for the last four or five months . . . since the last carnival. That's it! I remember, *that's* when you began this Capuchin life. Why? Just why, that's all I want to know. Just give me a reason! Are you in love? Are you homesick?

VON GRÖNINGSECK: Homesick? Are you crazy?

VON HASENPOTH: Has to be one of them. If it's not homesickness, it must be love. And . . . when I see you in the light . . . no, it's not possible! I mean, what I don't know is *who?* In this whole, dear, long time I don't believe you've spoken to three women. Once every four weeks, for appearance's sake, you pay your respects to the marshall. And as soon as you make your obeisance you stand way off from everyone, like Nicodemus. Elsewhere you're never seen with anyone. If I didn't know for sure that you'd had the little Humbrecht wench, I'd think—

VON GRÖNINGSECK: Had? I? Who said that?

VON HASENPOTH: Take it easy, Gröningseck, take it easy! We're speaking as friends, just between us. You don't think I'm some kind of child who can be persuaded that red is green?

VON GRÖNINGSECK: Haven't I already sworn to you several times exactly the opposite?

VON HASENPOTH (*laughs*): An excellent proof! You're crazy enough in love not to confess your conquest to me. When I could have directed the whole siege from my room!

VON GRÖNINGSECK: I have nothing to confess!

VON HASENPOTH: Your ardor indicates the opposite and besides—to put it bluntly—how can you expect me to think she's a vestal virgin? You both sneaked away from the ball at two, and it wasn't till five that I heard the carriage pull up.

VON GRÖNINGSECK (*very serious*): Talk about something else, please!

VON HASENPOTH: And the sleeping powder that I delivered to you. If you didn't use it, why haven't I gotten it back?

VON GRÖNINGSECK: Because . . . because I . . . misplaced . . . lost . . . oh, I threw it to hell. Now stop it, Hasenpoth, not one word more if we're to remain friends!

VON HASENPOTH: I believe you would be able to break a lance for her. To play Don Quixote for her.

VON GRÖNINGSECK: Possibly.

VON HASENPOTH: But not with me? Your countryman? Your *compagnon de débauche*?[16] Hear me, Brother! I certainly hope that you have not pushed foolishness to its limits and really fallen in love with the girl. May the devil tear me apart, that would be against all *esprit de corps*. I wonder if that's why you're spending so much time with the blackfrock, the cousin from the house. Well? Good! So you don't lack the means to have your fill of her soon. You live under the same roof—or if that's not convenient, should I find you two a time and a place? I am ingenious.

VON GRÖNINGSECK: Like Satan! I know!

VON HASENPOTH: At least you've put it to the test. You would never in your life have thought of the sleeping powder.

VON GRÖNINGSECK: Powder! Powder! That damned powder! I wish I'd never seen it, or you, or this house, or anything! I wish it had turned to poison in my pocket and that I'd died from it as soon as I touched it!

VON HASENPOTH: What the hell kind of talk is that? Are you sorry you did it? It's because of it you were able to—

VON GRÖNINGSECK: Yes! Yes! Devil take you! I followed your accursed teachings to the letter! I have—if you want to know—desecrated an angel and become a monster.

VON HASENPOTH: A prank! A prank! Little brother! A childish prank! Priest's prattle! You did what you set out to do. Well and good! You ought to be pleased with yourself.

VON GRÖNINGSECK: If she'd been one of the run-of-the-mill lot, who wouldn't be good for anything if we didn't need them for our games—yes! Then I'd be happy. But she's not like that. You should have seen her, should have heard her, at the instant, the critical instant that follows the pleasure, when the greatest beauty disgusts us. You should have seen her. How mighty in her weakness! How great her virtue, even after I had taught her what depravity was! And I, how small! How—oh, I can't bear to think of it!

VON HASENPOTH: Can grimaces make you so tenderhearted? You poor simpleton!

VON GRÖNINGSECK: Grimaces! You're saying I can't tell grimaces from true expressions? The distempered gravediggers, the embellished, varnished dolls, that you see stinking everywhere around here—*there* one finds grimaces! But not in a simple nature!

VON HASENPOTH: Simple or not simple! I say a woman's a woman, and in this matter, even the inexperienced ones give us food for thought. I've met few women who didn't passionately want to be taken by storm, and not a one that didn't cry a few crocodile tears after the overthrow! It's born into them!

VON GRÖNINGSECK (*with smoldering rage*): Ultimate libertine! You can thank my guilty conscience that I listen to you so indulgently. I'm a coward, a

---

[16]companion in debauchery

115

poltroon . . . but I still can't guarantee I'll listen to much more of your talk! I may no longer be enough at peace to be deliberately valiant, but rage may make me foolhardy. Do you understand?

VON HASENPOTH: Better than you understand *me*. I assure you, I was speaking of course only of the women whom I—

VON GRÖNINGSECK: Ha! Of the frivolous ones, fifty of which on the subtlest scales of conscience wouldn't weigh an ounce. But I beg to remind you, Lieutenant, . . .

VON HASENPOTH: If we're speaking seriously, you don't need to be so formal! It sounds so strange to me—

VON GRÖNINGSECK: Let it be! But mark this, Hasenpoth! We shall never be at ease with one another again if you fail to do what I expect. To a sensible woman, of course, it matters very little what you and the likes of you or others think of her. Your praise is a stigma. In your disapproval lies inner greatness. But it matters to *me*, what you say of the girl whose name you earlier let fall from your unwashed lips. Not a word! Just listen to me. So you no longer fail to recognize that—

VON HASENPOTH: Someone's coming.

VON GRÖNINGSECK (*looking around*): The master! I met him out walking. Don't you breathe a word of this! He doesn't know anything about it. (MASTER HUMBRECHT *enters*.) Bravo! Master Humbrecht, how wonderful! You don't forget me when you visit your relatives.

MASTER: Certainly not, you know that. When I haven't seen you in a few days, I feel a real lack.

VON GRÖNINGSECK (*shaking his hand*): I'm glad for that. How are things with the family?

MASTER: You live here in the house and ask me that?

VON HASENPOTH: Good point! To inquire of an outsider about the people in your own house may be all right in Paris or London, but here? If the lieutenant weren't such a night owl, out trying all manner of things, he'd go look for himself and—

VON GRÖNINGSECK: And! Perhaps I have my reasons? Yes, Master Humbrecht! I ask you because as their cousin you already have their trust and access. As good as my landlord may be at heart, he and I are not good for each other. He has his own whims, as well you know . . . and I can be rather hot-tempered. In the long run it wouldn't be good.

MASTER: So you should wait till he's not home. My cousin and her daughter—

VON GRÖNINGSECK: —have my best wishes, Master, Evchen especially, and that's exactly why I don't want to get them in trouble. Since the carnival I have been with them some four or five times, and unfortunately once or twice he wasn't there, and—ugh! Was there ever a row!

MASTER (*laughs*): He just can't forgive your escorting his women to the ball. As he said to me—

VON GRÖNINGSECK: Have you seen your little cousin?

MASTER: Not for two whole weeks, I think. She sits in her room constantly. Melancholy eats at her. I can't make head nor tail of it. Asking, praying—everything's in vain! It makes her father even more intolerant.

VON GRÖNINGSECK: Merciful God! I! I!

MASTER: Sympathize with her? Oh, you do have a kind heart.

116

VON GRÖNINGSECK: That's it, Master Humbrecht! Yes! You took the words right out of my mouth. Kind! Yes, that's my heart, all right. So full of—

VON HASENPOTH (*who, during this, has been whistling. To* VON GRÖNINGSECK): Don't let the cat out of the bag! (*To* MASTER HUMBRECHT.) Has she been like this for long?

MASTER: Well, I can't fix the time exactly. It came in stages. Unfortunately, it gets worse every day. Her favorite book is Young's *Night Thoughts*, in the French translation.

VON HASENPOTH: May God have mercy on her! If I had to read a single page of that, I'd be as melancholy as the Englishman and hang myself by my garter.

VON GRÖNINGSECK (*scornfully*): You! But my dear Master! As much beauty as Young may have for a cheerful, tranquil soul, at peace with herself and the world around her—you would know this better than I—this reading is hardly appropriate for a discontented, world-weary, lifeless heart, without which melancholy could not occur. Shouldn't you as a friend—

MASTER: Take it away? I tried that already, because I happen to think exactly as you do on the matter. But she wailed so long, that she was going to die from grief and oppression—in short, I was happy to give it back.

VON GRÖNINGSECK: God! God! Is there no solution! I'm sorry for her from the bottom of my soul, the dear child! What if—ah, what good will it do? Most things are a matter of time . . . still . . . it might be tried! At least here's a civility that can't offend her even if it can't help her. As soon as you see her *alone* again, Master, would you tell her for me that I am very concerned for her well-being and have often asked about it. Asked *you* about it, and that I hope she will again be cheerful and lively, and the sooner the better. She can absolutely— (*Stuck.*) —oh, well, it sounds like an empty compliment, but it comes truly from the heart. She can depend on me absolutely to be always at her service, now or in the future. Tell her that, would you, Master? Word for word! And better a little more than a little less!

MASTER: Gladly, Lieutenant! I thank you for your interest, but before long you will—

VON HASENPOTH: Put crazy ideas in your head? Not at all, Master! You judge him wrongly: his heart is colder than ice. But nonetheless he is so soft that if he sees somebody suffering or only hears about it—well, I still don't know how he could let himself become a soldier. All the gossip is about a woman—

VON GRÖNINGSECK: Good God! You pompous ass, will you never shut up! Don't forget, Master. Tell her as a courtesy, if for no other reason.

MAJOR LINDSTHAL (*enters*): Furlough! Furlough! Von Gröningseck! Your furlough papers have arrived. I've got them here.

VON HASENPOTH: Furlough! You asked for a furlough?

MASTER: You're going to leave us?

VON GRÖNINGSECK: Oh, Major, you are doubly welcome! (*To* MASTER HUMBRECHT.) I'm only going home for a short time.

VON HASENPOTH: When did you ask for that? Damn! A furlough! And I didn't know a thing about it.

VON GRÖNINGSECK: A great crime, truly! I asked the inspector himself for it at the general review.

MAJOR: And I also wrote to the secretary and can say, without flattering myself too much, that I have the *congé*,[17] properly signed, in my pocket. *Preuve de cela!*[18] Here it is! (*Hands the papers to* VON GRÖNINGSECK.)

VON GRÖNINGSECK: Thank you for your act of friendship.

MAJOR: If it's an act of friendship, as I hope, and as I hope you take it, then no thanks is necessary. Thanks are for alms.

VON GRÖNINGSECK: Your double graciousness puts me to shame.

MAJOR: Paperla, paperla, pap! Another stupid word that I've never been able to tolerate: shame! A lowdown cad, when you tell him to his face he is a cad, *he* is put to shame, but never an honorable man.

MASTER (*aside, to* VON HASENPOTH): A singular man! His mood pleases me.

VON HASENPOTH: The best or the craziest man in the whole regiment, as you wish.

MAJOR: Rid yourselves of such tasteless words, gentlemen! It will trouble you little now, but once a bad habit's established, it's damnably hard to break. Apropos! Today I saw a capital joke! In the *auberge*[19] where I eat, and devil take me, I wouldn't take a thousand gold pieces not to have seen it. Perhaps you already know the story, gentlemen? (VON GRÖNINGSECK *and* VON HASENPOTH *look at one another and shake their heads.*) No? That surprises me. It's spreading like wildfire from mouth to mouth. So much the better! Now you'll hear the plain unvarnished truth, for I saw the whole thing myself, and may the devil tear me apart alive if I change a word of it! Yesterday afternoon, while I was drinking my glass of liqueur—to aid digestion—at the "Mirror," I saw two officers through the window that faces the courtyard. One was from Lyon, and the other from Anhalt, playing a game of piquet. It was razor-sharp, I can assure you, at stake were three pounds and all honor cards were paid for. As it's my favorite game, I went out and watched things for a while. I sat behind the officer from Anhalt who was already losing terribly. In my whole life I've never seen such poor luck. Every moment he went down pique and repique, and God knows, his little talers were running away. Damn it, it was a pleasure to see. Meanwhile Lieutenant Wallroth from Salis stood behind the other one, facing me. He watched three or four plays, going first red, then white in the face. I thought he was *moitié*[20] with my man, and the loss bothered him. All of a sudden—God only knows how he caught on so fast!—he leaped on the pile of money that lay between them and pushed everything, big and small, to the officer from Anhalt, saying: "Sir, this money is yours! It's not right; you've been the dupe in this game. Three times this man has kept the ace up his sleeve. I've seen him do it myself." Well, before he'd even finished talking, just listen, just listen! The officer from Lyon gave him such a smack in the face that the whole room rocked. They grabbed for their swords, but they were stopped by Osterreid and his waiters. We all just stood there, thunderstruck. The *chevalier de fortune* finally slunk off, without our being aware of it, and a bit later the honest Swiss did too. "Fortunate *retour*!"[21] I

---

[17]furlough

[18]Here's the proof of it!

[19]tavern

[20]halves, gone halves with

[21]reverse

thought to myself, for certainly somebody would have been set on his ass. But *pardieu,* no! Wallroth went to the commandant, reported the whole thing, and the crooked officer is stuck in *pontcouvert.*[22] Dismissed and kicked out of his regiment in shame and degradation—it's the least that'll happen to him.

VON GRÖNINGSECK: The blackguard deserved it, too! And Wallroth?

MAJOR: He will *bon gré, mal gré* [23] have to quit too.

MASTER: But why, Major? Didn't he behave as any decent man would?

MAJOR: Decent and not decent! *You* don't understand. A man of honor wouldn't have run to the commandant, but would have just quietly asked to meet his man somewhere alone. Now I'm just reporting what happened. Today at noon Wallroth arrived at the *auberge* for lunch. As usual thirteen or fourteen of us were already there. As Wallroth entered the room, his neighbor turned his—Wallroth's—plate over. Wallroth sat down, as if he didn't understand, and turned it right side up. Then one after another stood, just as if a signal had been given, and left for sanctuary. Finally I also left. You should have seen the face he made. I'd like to have a picture of it. Then you could see, how stupid one looks when one is truly ashamed.

VON GRÖNINGSECK: I feel sorry for the poor devil.

MAJOR: Me too. However! You do understand, sir, why he has to quit? Before, he'd have only had to tangle with one man. Now he has fourteen against him. If he wanted to stay, he'd have to duel with them all.

VON HASENPOTH: Naturally! They had all insulted him.

MASTER: But . . . dueling is forbidden.

MAJOR: Forbidden! Pah! The ban doesn't matter to us! Or to any soldier!

MASTER: You'll permit me, Major! Are you not also a citizen of the state, a subject of the king, as much as any other? And didn't you swear to our king, at his coronation, to give no quarter to any dueller, without exception?

MAJOR: That may well be true, Master. I have faith in every honest officer that he will not intentionally offend the king or go against his command. But do we want then to let every Bohunk ride roughshod over us? We cannot endure these daily insults silently, even at meals, as you see with Wallroth—

MASTER: Must you break the law?

VON GRÖNINGSECK: There's no other way, my dear Master! Does that surprise you? At one time I would have agreed with you. We other *epaulettes* have only two paths once we are insulted, with or without cause—we risk our lives or our honor!

MASTER: That is a contradiction. In order not to be considered dishonorable, a law-abiding man must break the law, and place his head on the executioner's scaffold. Unbelievable!

MAJOR: Not unbelievable at all! Not at all! Better to lose one's life than one's honor. The scaffold does not dishonor a man. Only crime can do that, and a crime that one is forced to commit is not a crime. If I'd been in Wallroth's place, I'd have dueled before I let that insult go by. Better to fight with the whole garrison—one after another, of course. If he still demands satisfaction from me, he'd have it today, even if a thousand scaffolds or a thousand

---

[22]confinement

[23]whether he wants to or not

gallows stood nearby. If you want to eliminate all contradictions, Master, or make all the crooked straight, go ahead! You have my blessing. *A l'honneur,* gentlemen! Before you go, Gröningseck, I shall see you again?

VON GRÖNINGSECK: Of course.

MAJOR (*as he leaves*): Without saying farewell then— (VON GRÖNINGSECK *accompanies him to the door.*)

MASTER: The major speaks—

VON HASENPOTH: As becomes a soldier, and you, as becomes a man of your profession. Each in his own way may be right.

VON GRÖNINGSECK (*returns*): Yes, Master, quite so! You don't know what a trial it is for us to remain honorable, how carefully, how circumspectly we must measure every step. But (*In flattering tones.*) the learned argument has not caused you to forget my instructions?

MASTER: Certainly not! To remove any doubt, I'll leave now and find an immediate opportunity to speak to my little cousin.

VON GRÖNINGSECK: Do that and I'll be forever in your debt. I only believe I have the right to ask this kindness of you because I know that I would do the same for you. (*Grips the* MASTER'*s hand. The* MASTER *leaves.*)

VON HASENPOTH: Hellfire and damnation! Gröningseck! You've never conducted yourself so stupidly. Anyone could read the whole secret in your eyes. If the master were to the slightest degree a mistrustful—

VON GRÖNINGSECK: Oh no, he's far too goodhearted.

VON HASENPOTH: And the instructions you gave him!

VON GRÖNINGSECK: I made them very ambiguous. With great pains, I assure you. But if he repeats them exactly as I gave them to him, it will have a good effect. Evchen will understand every word, and perhaps she will be comforted. For I don't know any sure way to send her a letter.

VON HASENPOTH: You mean you've never written to her?

VON GRÖNINGSECK: No. Since I've been in the house, I haven't spoken to her for a moment without witnesses. So I have to seize any opportunity I can.

VON HASENPOTH: So tell me, what really went on between you two? As far as I can see, her melancholy has some physical cause.

VON GRÖNINGSECK: Oh, that it has, to be sure! She's pregnant. I've been around too much to be able to deny it. But half a *confidence* is good for nothing. She's pregnant by me. Do you know what that means? By *me* she's pregnant, so you can—I should hope—figure out what I had to do with her, and what I will do, what I must do. I shall marry her.

VON HASENPOTH: You?

VON GRÖNINGSECK: I! That's the least I can do for her.

VON HASENPOTH: Lieutenant von Gröningseck and the Humbrecht girl! Impossible!

VON GRÖNINGSECK: Why, if I may ask? Why? Why impossible?

VON HASENPOTH: To begin with, as a lieutenant—

VON GRÖNINGSECK: I can resign, so where's the impossibility? It will not be difficult to have her as my wife. I've squandered a lot, but I've also saved some. I'm going to take control of the rest of my possessions; that's why I'm taking the furlough. I'm now of age and can take control at any time. As soon as this is in order, I'll come back and ask for my Evchen. When I take off the blue coat for good, she'll be mine. I know it.

VON HASENPOTH: You want to give up everything then?

VON GRÖNINGSECK: Everything! Everything! Rather than drag the pains of hell along with me! But one more thing! Mark this, Lieutenant, mark this. (*Takes him by the hand.*) You are the only one to whom I have opened my heart. Not a word of this has crossed my lips before. Your plans pushed me into this abyss. I don't reproach you. You misjudged the angel. I too! And I should have known her better. I alone! Not you! Now you must also help me wriggle out of this again. I don't believe I am trusting too much to your virtue. *But* if I am deceiving myself, and even a suspicion of what I have told you comes to light before the proper time—then, Hasenpoth (*Lets go of his hand and recoils.*) you or I will go to the devil in revenge! Now let me go! I must catch my breath and make preparations for the trip. We'll talk later. (*Goes off into the bath.*)

VON HASENPOTH: If you, with all your inflated ideas of virtue, take her as your wife—then let Satan make me run the gauntlet of his whole army of devils, back and forth, twenty-four times. No, Mr. von Gröningseck! I must first sift things out. (*As he leaves.*) I'll shuffle these cards myself. Better than that dummy at the "Mirror." Just wait. (*Leaves.*)

Act Four

(EVCHEN's *bedroom. At the right is a door. Opposite the door are windows, which face the street.*)

(*As the curtain rises,* MRS. HUMBRECHT *is closing the windows.* EVCHEN *is reading.*)

MRS. HUMBRECHT: Still I see and hear nothing of him.

EVCHEN: He's hardly likely to come this late, Mother! Go to bed! The gates have already been shut a long time.

MRS. HUMBRECHT: Who knows? Couldn't he get in through the servants' passage? It hasn't yet struck eleven.

EVCHEN (*sighing*): I hadn't thought of that.

MRS. HUMBRECHT: Again a sigh! Didn't you promise me to stop all this eternal moaning and groaning? Be a man of your word!

EVCHEN: Oh, if only I *were* a man!

MRS. HUMBRECHT: Why?

EVCHEN: I'd set off straightaway for America and join their fight for freedom.

MRS. HUMBRECHT: And leave your father and mother back here alone? Pfui, Evchen! I know why you're talking this way. You don't love us any more.

EVCHEN: How can you think that, Mother!

MRS. HUMBRECHT: How? Because you no longer trust your parents. Where there is no trust, there can be no love.

EVCHEN (*agitated*): Mother!

MRS. HUMBRECHT: Nothing else. I'm sorry I have to tell you this. Before, if you hurt your little finger, you'd come running to me to complain about it. Now—may God forgive you!—you get gooseflesh if you just catch sight of one of us.

EVCHEN: It's not true! You do me the greatest injustice in the world, Mother, when you say that! I love you just as much as ever . . . but . . .

MRS. HUMBRECHT: Well?

EVCHEN (*timidly*): But . . . there are things that one cannot reveal to anyone.

MRS. HUMBRECHT: Why not?

EVCHEN: Because they aren't yet ready. Because one can't admit them even to himself.

MRS. HUMBRECHT: Nothing but mystery! If your father heard an answer like that he'd be furious. You know he can't stand keeping things secret. Well, neither can I. Yesterday, before he rode off, I thought he was going to go raving-mad. When he'd set you so sweetly on his lap, talked to you so sweetly, pressed you to his heart, and squeezed you.

EVCHEN: And pushed me off again, so that I staggered off to bed.

MRS. HUMBRECHT: That was your own stubborn fault. It hurt him; I could see it in his eyes. But on the stairs he swore that if you were still hanging your head so low and wouldn't tell him why, then he would no longer recognize you as his child. He said: "I will not let myself be dragged about any more by her whims like a calf on a rope."

EVCHEN: As true as God lives! Mother, it's no whim! Would that it were! I

122

cannot admit to myself the source of my sorrow. But to tell the truth, Mother, the vehemence with which you've tried to discover it, by reading it in my eyes or by pressing it out of me with threats or caresses, has contributed greatly to my melancholy, or head-hanging, as you call it. You mean well, I know you do. I can tell, and suffer doubly because of it. I can give you at present no thanks for your tenderness. Just try this, Mother! Let me linger a while in my dreaming. Act as if you didn't notice anything at all. Leave me to myself, and tell Father to do the same. Only for a little while! Perhaps everything will clear up. It *must* clear up, and then I shall be your daughter again, or—

MRS. HUMBRECHT: Or?

EVCHEN: A child of death.

MRS. HUMBRECHT: Another thrust to the heart! Oh, Evchen! Evchen! You're going to send me to an early grave!

EVCHEN: No, Mother! No! Not you! More likely me, if you don't give me any peace. Just try what I ask, I beg you. Everything will turn out all right. (*Flings her arms around her* MOTHER's *neck*.) Here, hanging around your neck, I implore you—don't block your daughter from the one path that can save her!

MRS. HUMBRECHT (*extricates herself*): Your father! I hear him.

EVCHEN: Promise me!

MRS. HUMBRECHT (*taking a lamp from the table, turns toward her husband*): What else can I do? I have no choice.

HUMBRECHT (*enters, wearing boots and spurs*): What the hell are you sitting up here for, woman! Letting the house below go unattended!

MRS. HUMBRECHT: I only came up this minute to see how she was doing.

HUMBRECHT: Delightful! Now the mother has to go to the daughter! Couldn't she just as easily have come to you? And she's standing there as if she'd lost the grace of God! Can't even say "Good evening" to her father!

EVCHEN (*timidly*): Good evening, Father.

HUMBRECHT (*scornfully, mimics her*): Good evening, my dearest daughter!

MRS. HUMBRECHT: You're always snapping at her. No wonder she's afraid of you.

HUMBRECHT: Afraid? Of me? Balderdash! Aren't I her father? Well, Evchen, aren't I? Do I have to weigh each word before I say it when I'm talking to my own child? I'll be damned before I do anything like that!

MRS. HUMBRECHT: Idiot! Who said anything like that? Only your tone—

HUMBRECHT: My tone! My tone! I admit it's not one of the sugar-sweet, butter-smeared types that our silver-tongued gentlemen use to squawk their compliments! But I assume my daughter after seventeen or eighteen years would have gotten used to it! By all that's holy, I am hardly a man-eater! Come here, Evchen, come! Have you been a good girl? Have you confessed to your mother? That's it! You have!

EVCHEN (*agitated*): Dearest father!

MRS. HUMBRECHT: Yes, yes, she has! Now leave her in peace. You'll hear all about it later.

HUMBRECHT: That's wonderful! That's right! (*Kisses her.*) Now you are doubly dear to me. Was it worth all the trouble, though? All the moping about?

MRS. HUMBRECHT: You'll hear all about it later, I said.

HUMBRECHT: I should be very angry that you didn't do me the courtesy. Only yesterday I thought I'd have to use sorcery to get it out. Then, no doubt, my tone was to blame. Will you be my pretty and lively Evchen again?

EVCHEN: As much as I can.

HUMBRECHT: Back into society, going to church? Not always sitting in your stall?

MRS. HUMBRECHT: Pooh! What questions! Things will work out: one after another. It's time now to go to bed. It's already struck twelve. Come on, husband! (*Pulls on his sleeve.*) Good night, Evchen.

HUMBRECHT: *Busoir, busoir!* Tonight I'm going to saw wood, wife! (*Breaks free, turns, and takes* EVCHEN's *hand.*) May God forgive you all the sleepless nights that you have given us for some time! I know He has counted all my sighs and all your mother's tears. May He not count them against you, my child. None! Otherwise they'd start all over again. (EVCHEN *embraces him, crying. She kisses him.*) Now, sleep well! (*Both* PARENTS *leave.*)

EVCHEN (*looking after him*): Poor man! Good, unfortunate father! (*Sighs deeply.*) I fear, I fear, you still have sleepless nights ahead! Your wrath terrifies me, but—God knows!—not so much as your love! (*Sits down and reads for a while.*) No use! It's no use. I read and read, but when I close the book (*Slams it shut.*) I can't remember a word of what I read. (*Lays the book aside. Paces excitedly a few times back and forth.*) Gröningseck! Gröningseck! What you have to answer for!

VON GRÖNINGSECK (*who meanwhile has slunk in. He is fully dressed, but without hat or sword. He places his lantern on the table and throws himself at her feet*): I know it, my dearest, my most precious! I want to answer for everything, to make everything good.

EVCHEN (*shrinks back*): How? You dare . . . at midnight? What do you want? What are your intentions?

VON GRÖNINGSECK: The purest, the most virtuous that ever a man had. To give you back your peace of mind.

EVCHEN: Can you? Can you make things that happened unhappen? Or do you intend to swear falsely before God and deceive me again?

VON GRÖNINGSECK: No, Evchen! Truly, no! The latter I would not, the former I cannot. And nonetheless I wish I could. With my blood I would buy back the unfortunate moment when I madly—

EVCHEN: It's burned deep enough in my soul. You don't need to remind me of it. Or are you so satanic as to be both seducer and accuser?

VON GRÖNINGSECK (*leaps up*): For the love of heaven, what a horrible monster you take me for! I came here—

EVCHEN: At a time, at an hour, at which you would not have come if you had the slightest respect for me.

VON GRÖNINGSECK: Forgive me! Evchen! I swear to you, just the opposite! I know and respect your delicacy, and I hesitated long before I decided on this untimely visit. I had to take the risk! I owed it to you and me to speak to you alone, once more, before I leave here.

EVCHEN: You're leaving?

VON GRÖNINGSECK: As soon as possible, in order to return in good time and ask you properly for your hand.

EVCHEN: Are you serious, Gröningseck? Is this your heart speaking? I seem to recall, you swore this to me before.

VON GRÖNINGSECK: And repeat it here with all solemnity! As soon as I realized that you were not the type I had mistaken you for in my recklessness, my first instinct was to make all the amends in my power to your offended virtue! And it shall remain, when all other instincts cease with my last breath. May you find some comfort in this promise. I shall not go back on my word. But you, Evchen! You have not kept your word to me.

EVCHEN: What do you mean?

VON GRÖNINGSECK: Didn't you promise me to control your features? That nobody would notice anything?

EVCHEN: It's true, I promised to try very hard. I did too, and—

VON GRÖNINGSECK: And so I never came into the room when you didn't blush all over! Was it anger, contempt, or loathing?

EVCHEN: None of them, Gröningseck! I loved you from the moment I met you. Now I can say it to you. Otherwise you would not have found me to be so weak. You cannot hate me for having the hope of becoming yours. But I have not yet learned to stifle the little voice of conscience that nagged me. If I could, I would blush doubly for myself.

VON GRÖNINGSECK: Divine child! (*Grasps her hand and presses it to his lips.*)

EVCHEN (*pulls it quickly back*): I thought you had only one word. Is it oblivion?

VON GRÖNINGSECK: Oblivion! Outpouring of the soul! Call it what you will! I must seal my oath of eternal fidelity with a kiss on your hand. (*Is about to kiss her hand with force; she pushes him away.*)

EVCHEN: No, Lieutenant! That's just affectation. A kiss on the hand is nothing, I know, and yet it can lead to anything. If you can't keep your word in trivialities, how can I trust you in more serious concerns? At least I shall spare you one perjury. Those who have been burned learn to be careful with fire . When do you plan to return here?

VON GRÖNINGSECK: Two months will more than do.

EVCHEN: Two months! My heart will not always be quiet in that time. But there's no other way. I must put up with it. I shall not order you to hurry; if your heart does not command you to, I shall be lost anyway.

VON GRÖNINGSECK: I shall certainly make haste.

EVCHEN: Gröningseck! Yes, I believe you. I trust your integrity. But who can guarantee me the future? No one! Not even you! None of us has read his fate in the Book of Providence. An inner voice, which I try in vain to still, tells me that mine is written in blood!

VON GRÖNINGSECK: Evchen! How can that come to pass?

EVCHEN: How? In the easiest, simplest way possible. If you don't keep your word.

VON GRÖNINGSECK: That is impossible.

EVCHEN: Time will tell. Meanwhile I'll suppose—hear me out—that you don't keep your word, that you abandon me to my fate, to the whole burden of scandal that lies in wait, the wrath of my family, the fury of my father. Do you believe that I shall wait for all this? No! I would seek out the most horrible wilderness, far away from everyone who has a human appearance. I would hide myself in the thickest shrubs, and only drink the rain of heaven, in order never to see my face in the brook, the reflection of an immoral being. If heaven should work a miracle and preserve me and the wretched creature—an orphan even before it has a father—I would, as soon as it began to stammer, instead of repeating "Father" or "Mother" in its ear, say the dreadful words "whore" and "perjurer," until it repeated them clearly. Then in a fit of rage at this insult, I would be driven to put an end to my misery and its. Wouldn't that be bloody, Gröningseck?

VON GRÖNINGSECK: Only too much. My hair stands on end. I am a soldier. I was in the field very young. I have witnessed many frightening scenes. But never such a—

EVCHEN: You have only to order and I shall carry it out!

VON GRÖNINGSECK: May God protect you! I shudder at the very thought! For God's sake, Evchen! Give up all this melancholy preoccupation! Put it out of your mind! Trust yourself to me, to my word of honor, to what remains of my feeling and virtue. If there's even a spark left, you will blow it into a flame.

EVCHEN: Good, Gröningseck! So be it! I promise you.

VON GRÖNINGSECK: Do you also promise me to maintain your composure during this time?

EVCHEN (*meditatively*): I wouldn't like to promise more than I can do.

VON GRÖNINGSECK: You can do it, darling! As soon as you believe in me, that I can be an honorable man.

EVCHEN: If I don't want to betray myself, and make my parents suspicious, I shall have to do so. You can't believe how close they are to guessing, how much they have plagued me! More than once the fatal secret has trembled on my lips. Only fear—

VON GRÖNINGSECK: Maintain your silence. I implore you, I tremble when I think of your father. Use every power, summon up every bit of cheerfulness, so as not to arouse suspicions. No one has an idea—

EVCHEN: I trust the master least of all. His eagle eyes have rattled me more than once. The message you gave him yesterday haunted his mind. I saw it, so pretended as if I weren't the least bit concerned.

VON GRÖNINGSECK: Could he be base enough to harm you?

EVCHEN: Oh, no! He never intends me any harm. Perhaps only too much good. As far as I can tell, he has secret designs on me. My mother may encourage him. Clerics are accustomed to choosing their wives while they're still probationers. When in ten or fifteen years they get a village parsonage, they don't want to take long looking for a wife.

VON GRÖNINGSECK: By that time perhaps we could offer him our daughter.

EVCHEN: Take care that she is not ashamed of her mother. Now go! The neighbors aren't used to seeing my light on for so long.

VON GRÖNINGSECK: Is Evchen also concerned?

EVCHEN: When it's not right here (*Pointing to her heart.*) when it rebukes us, then one can be afraid of his own shadow. Now go, I say! Tomorrow you can see me again with my mother. You will say a proper farewell to her.

VON GRÖNINGSECK: See you! But not speak!

EVCHEN: I will understand every look. (*She goes to the door.*) Two months, you said?

126

VON GRÖNINGSECK: Two months at most! I swear to you again by the moon and all the stars that shine in the heavens. My last look, when I board the carriage tomorrow, will swear it to you again. Only trust me, my darling! (*Presses* EVCHEN's *hand and leaves*.)

EVCHEN (*opens the door halfway, sticks her head out, and calls out in a muffled voice*): Gröningseck! One more thing! (*He returns. She kisses him*.) I won't be able to do that tomorrow. (*He leaves. She locks the door tightly after him*.)

(The curtain falls.)

Act Five

(*The room of Act Two. Daybreak.*)

(EVCHEN *stands before the mirror and puts on a cap.* LISSEL, *her maid, enters.*)

LISSEL: Hey! Heavens! Where are you going so early, Miss Evchen? The fog stinks of brimstone.

EVCHEN: That doesn't matter. It couldn't be anything else around Michaelmas. I just want to slip out somewhere quick. Lissel! Run and get me your cotton cloak. Hurry! Run!

LISSEL: What are you going to do with it?

EVCHEN: What do you think? Put it on! You'll get it back again. In the meantime you have my taffeta one. Go ahead, wear it until I come back. So go! I must leave now before people are up.

LISSEL: Why? Do you have an appointment?

EVCHEN: Yeah, sure. Don't keep me waiting any more! Go! (LISSEL *leaves.*) Where shall I go? I don't know myself. As far as my feet shall carry me. Gröningseck, Gröningseck! It should be hard for you to kick against the pricks! The letter you wrote me! Do I still have it with me? (*Searches in her pocket and pulls it out.*) Yes! (*Reads it through once.*) To send Hasenpoth with such a letter, portraying me as an out-and-out whore! I don't understand the mocking of the place where we got closer acquainted. I don't want to understand! (*Puts the letter away again.*) All things considered—oh, I must fly! (*Catches sight of the portrait of her parents.*) Ha! You dears, are you there too? Here on my knees I thank you for all the love and kindness you have shown me. (*Crying.*) I repay you badly. Don't curse me! Just don't curse me!

LISSEL (*returns.* EVCHEN *leaps up*): I hear your father already up and about in their room.

EVCHEN: Haste, then! For God's sake, hurry! Throw it over me, so I'm not recognized so easily. Now the cape over that. (*As she leaves, she turns around once more.*) The cloak, Lissel! Keep it until I come back. Do you hear? (*From the other side of the door.*) Don't give it up till I come back! (*Leaves.*)

LISSEL (*straightening up the room*): Till! Till! God only knows what's going on with her. Something's got to be wrong. I've never seen her act so crazily. What if something terrible's happened to her? Such a good, decent girl! It would break my heart. (*About to leave with* EVCHEN's *cloak.* MASTER HUMBRECHT *bursts in hastily.*)

MASTER: Has Mr. Humbrecht already left, miss?

LISSEL: Gone! Hardly. He's only just got up.

MASTER: So much the better. I didn't miss him. Tell him I have something urgent to discuss with him and that he should come here immediately.

LISSEL: Right away, Master Humbrecht. (*Leaves.*)

MASTER: I would give something to be outside this house again. I'm risking a lot. Nonetheless, if it's to prevent a great misfortune . . . if it *is,* as I am entitled to guess, then it's better that I break the news to my cousin gradually, rather than that he hears it from strangers, or finds out for himself. He wouldn't know how to contain his wrath.

HUMBRECHT (*in nightshirt, nightcap, and worn-out shoes*): Good morning, Cousin! Where the hell have you come from?

MASTER: Straight from home. I left especially early in order not to miss you.

HUMBRECHT: It must be a matter of great importance.

MASTER: I wish it were not so. You are a man—?

HUMBRECHT: At least I've proved it to my wife.

MASTER: No jokes, if you please. You are a man of reason?

HUMBRECHT: I have as much common sense as it takes to run my house.

MASTER: Good! Pull yourself together, Cousin, and listen to what I have to tell you! I am personally concerned . . . perhaps I am mistaken . . . but it is nonetheless my duty—

HUMBRECHT: Not so much preamble, Master! Get to it!

MASTER: First you must give me your word as an honorable man, that you will hear me out quite patiently, and not move from the spot before I am finished.

HUMBRECHT: What the hell kind of sermon is this going to be? As far as I'm concerned, you have my word. Here's my hand on it.

MASTER: Now to the point! Were you at St. Clausen's church yesterday, Cousin?

HUMBRECHT: No, I wasn't. But my family was: I wouldn't tolerate anything else.

MASTER: It was a catechism sermon.

HUMBRECHT: That could be.

MASTER: The text was the Ten Commandments.

HUMBRECHT: So, what else? I still don't see any rhyme or reason to this.

MASTER: Have patience! The minister lingered especially on the seventh commandment.

HUMBRECHT: The seventh? Wait a minute, which one is that? Thou shalt . . . thou shalt . . . thou shalt not commit adultery. Right?

MASTER: Exactly. And in addition, as you know, four times a year, the minister reads from the pulpit the decrees of our king against duelling, burglary, and infanticide.

HUMBRECHT: I knew that before I was old enough to button my clothes. What's your point?

MASTER: Now you shall hear it. In addition, you know—

HUMBRECHT: I know! I know! That I'm about to go crazy and leave you standing here if you don't get on with it.

MASTER: You promised me earlier not to go off half-cocked. You must keep your word. I was about to say, you know that the women's pews are exactly across from the organ, at least in part—

HUMBRECHT: Yes! And that you young men almost go blind during the divine service from gawking at the young girls! I know that too! Many a time I've worried about it. I'd like to be a preacher just once, for twenty-four hours. I'd have the sexton drive you and your spy-glasses out of the temple!

MASTER: If you don't choose to listen, Cousin—

HUMBRECHT: Yes, yes, I'm listening.

MASTER: I was standing by the organ, and could thus look my little cousin directly in the face.

HUMBRECHT: My Evchen?

MASTER: Yes. By chance, I was looking at her rather steadily during the sermon, exactly at the part that I have already mentioned. She blushed fire-red, then instantly went deathly pale, like a linen-cloth. Then she cast her eyes downward, and sat through the rest of the sermon absolutely rigidly. Finally, when the ordinance against infanticide was read, she fainted dead away.

HUMBRECHT: So? Then she was carried out of the church into the fresh air, and then she came to, and now she's as good as new.

MASTER: It is however—I'm sorry I have to say this—a matter for concern.

HUMBRECHT: Concern! I see nothing to be concerned about. When a young innocent thing has her ears filled with such trash as adultery, whoring, and fornication, and when a few tasteless louts are staring her straight in the eye as she listens—I see no cause for concern if she becomes dizzy, and red and white from annoyance.

MASTER: But the fainting! Right at that point!

HUMBRECHT (*removes his nightcap deferentially*): Don't take this the wrong way, Cousin. One can see that you've been a student. You learned men always want to see more than other people. But you do it like all bleary-eyeds: when you face the sun you see everything double and nothing clearly. Devil take it! Can people order up faints and tell them when to come?

MRS. HUMBRECHT (*comes running in*): You're shouting so loud, Husband, that people are gathering outside the door.

HUMBRECHT: I've got reason to be boiling over. This liberal arts fellow comes to me first thing in the morning and growls an earful about some blushing and fainting by our Evchen yesterday, and I think he's trying to make something of it.

MRS. HUMBRECHT (*turns up her nose and shrugs her shoulders*): What's to make of it? She didn't feel well. I don't know what else you can make of it.

MASTER: Actually, I came here to speak with your husband alone—however, as long as you're here! I know you are aware of my interest in your daughter. You have even encouraged me . . . (*Stammering.*) but . . . as your husband doesn't want to trust my skill in observation . . . I want . . . I must . . . (*Opens his purse, and looks for something.*)

MRS. HUMBRECHT: My God! What kind of observation? Martin!

HUMBRECHT: How would I know? If I read him right, he thinks we're calves' heads, with no eyes, and our Evchen—at least a whore.

MASTER (*dismayed*): Cousin!

MRS. HUMBRECHT: What! My Evchen? Master! Do you know what you are saying? Eh! Just what I expected! I'd pledge on my own life that my daughter is honorable. No decent man shall deny it, not even you, Master! But I shall no longer call you cousin. (*Places her hands on her hips.*) Is this the thanks for all the love and care that we—that my husband has shown you? After he paid for your music lessons, and made you so comfortable when you entered the seminary? The little piano you taught Evchen—is that your whole thanks for that master's ring on your finger? If we hadn't been there, you certainly wouldn't have been able to graduate. Not on your stipendium alone. How long have you been so greedy, eh?

HUMBRECHT (*grabbing her*): Woman! Woman! You're making six times more

130

noise than I did.

MRS. HUMBRECHT (*breaking free*): Haven't I the right? Anyone who casts slurs on Evchen's honor stabs me to the quick.

MASTER: Cousin, for God's sake! I'll say goodbye. (*About to leave.*)

HUMBRECHT: Was that all that you wanted to tell me?

MASTER: No! But (*Indicating* MRS. HUMBRECHT.) as long as she's here, I'll stay silent.

HUMBRECHT: Dearest! Leave us alone for a bit. Come! (*Takes her by the arm.*) Just a little while!

MRS. HUMBRECHT: Ten horses wouldn't drag me away from here! I'm not moving! I want to hear everything he has to say about my Evchen.

MASTER: I don't want to say anything against her, Cousin, I swear to you. You know that I am interested in her. It is precisely because of that I believed myself obligated to report to you one thing and another that you don't yet know . . . perhaps couldn't know. Now I don't believe it myself. I do, however, owe you a great deal for all the kindnesses you just this moment threw in my face so bitterly. I am thus obligated to tell you, and it is your duty to verify it. This note was sent to me last night. Read it yourself. I wouldn't have taken any notice of it, if it weren't for what happened in church. (*Gives the* HUMBRECHTS *the note, keeps the envelope, stuffing it finally in his purse.*)

HUMBRECHT: Maybe the devil can read this scrawl, but to me it looks like hen's scratchings. (*Hands it back.*)

MASTER: Give it here. I'll read it aloud, word for word. Just see, however, that you don't blame me again for it.

MRS. HUMBRECHT (*stamping her foot*): Well, read it, read it!

MASTER (*reads, pointing to the words with his finger.* HUMBRECHT *to one side, his wife on the other*):
"Dear Sir:
You are a Humbrecht and may have more sense than all the others in your family who bear that name. So ask Evchen Humbrecht, your little cousin, if she is really stupid enough to believe that I would really marry her. If she thinks back and remembers the place where we made our acquaintanceship, she will certainly not be able to demand anything of me. If her father doesn't fork over one hundred talers to place her child in a foundling-home, then if need be, I'll find a way. It concerns you as well.
Von Gröningseck
P. S. This letter requires no answer. None would reach me."
(MASTER HUMBRECHT *glances sideways at the others, holding the paper in his hand.*)

HUMBRECHT: Gröningseck! That was that Bavarian officer who lodged with us.

MASTER: The very one! Who took Evchen to the ball—

MRS. HUMBRECHT (*rips the letter out of his hand*): Yes, that's the one! But whoever wrote this infamous forgery here, *him* I don't know. (*As she speaks, she tears the letter into a thousand pieces and stamps on it.*) If I knew, I'd scratch his eyes out.

HUMBRECHT: Woman! What do you know of this? Call the girl down here. Now I'm angry we can't give her the letter to read herself. (*About to gather up the pieces.*) You are damned quick, woman!

MRS. HUMBRECHT: Read! What for? So it can kill her, or God knows what else? Isn't it a scandal and a mockery, that such an old ass like you can go on so about this childish prattle? All right, if I hadn't been constantly with her—but I was!

HUMBRECHT (*imperiously*): Get her! Or I will! (MRS. HUMBRECHT *makes a face like an ass's at* MASTER HUMBRECHT *and leaves.*) Cousin! (*Clapping him on the shoulder.*) Just between us! I didn't want to say so in front of my wife, but . . . if it's true, what you've read to me, if that creature doesn't clear out of this house, I'll break every bone in her body and her bastard's too.

MASTER (*gravely*): Cousin! If you have only a glimmer of religion in you, get a hold of yourself! I didn't come here to be eyewitness to a crime. Besides, it's not yet over. If Gröningseck was my friend, as he often maintained, the tone of this letter is a mystery to me. Taking into consideration the other circumstances, however, the matter deserves further investigation. Though, as I said, so that you don't make a mistake . . . perhaps it is also—

JAILER (*enters*): Be you Mester Humbresh, the butcher?

HUMBRECHT: I am.

JAILER: Mester Proshecuter sent me wid da box here. You should look at it to see if you recognize it.

HUMBRECHT: I recognize you at least. Aren't you Hans Adam, the beadle from Goat Alley?

JAILER: Yeah, right! But we's called jailers, not beadles.

HUMBRECHT: To hell with the title! I ask you, are you the same one who thrashed a poor child of five to death last spring in front of Baker Michael's door? Claiming privilege of profession?

JAILER: Hey! What's to cry about? It's more, I think, a blow went the wrong way.

HUMBRECHT: Wait, you scoundrel! I've plenty more to charge you with. If you're a beast, go off in the forest with the other wild animals! (*Picks up a Bengal cane, and thrashes him soundly.*) Now go, blackguard! I've carried this grudge against you a long time. I'm glad you've returned right at this time for your thrashing!

JAILER (*who, during the thrashing, drops the box*): Okay, okay! Ya won't ged off free for the thrashin'! (*Rubs his back.*)

HUMBRECHT: Get off free? Didn't you kill the child and get off free? Nobody made a peep, you tyrant! Hang on, I'll rub your back even better if you haven't had enough yet—

JAILER (*running out*): Okay, okay! I got yer point! (*Leaves.*)

HUMBRECHT (*throws the cane into a corner*): He sure came at the right time! Damn it all! To thrash a child of five so long in his rage till it died. And why? Because it begged a crust of bread, so it wouldn't have to steal one. Thunder and lightning! I should have thrashed the dog even harder.

MASTER: But consider, Cousin, the matter might have been badly explained to you.

HUMBRECHT: No! Let it cost me a few hundred guilders. I'll pay it gladly! I vented all my anger on that scoundrel!

MASTER: And insulted his authority.

HUMBRECHT: Authority! Authority! I have the greatest possible respect for my authority. But the beast doesn't have so much for his. Didn't he and his partner attack in the most vicious manner possible a poor journeyman in the same straits? Kicking him in the privates till he died three hours later? And that's supposed to be order, eh?

MASTER: They will soon be avenged! Cousin, Cousin! Be careful!

HUMBRECHT: Why? I tell the truth and shame the devil!

MRS. HUMBRECHT (*dashes in, tearing her hair*): Martin! Martin! Oh, my God! Evchen is nowhere to be found.

HUMBRECHT: What? Not to be found? Oh, now I believe it all! Did you really look for her? In her room? In the kitchen?

MRS. HUMBRECHT: Everywhere! Everywhere! I was even down in the slaughterhouse. I haven't a breath more. Merciful God, what could it mean?

MASTER: Has nobody seen her then? Yesterday she was—

MRS. HUMBRECHT: Ah! I was up with her very late.

MASTER: And this morning?

MRS. HUMBRECHT: I thought she was still asleep, like before. But according to her maid, she left the house quite excitedly first thing this morning. I hope she hasn't thrown herself in the river! These past few weeks she's been so melancholy—

HUMBRECHT: The devil take the melancholy! I feel like I've been kicked in the head by an ox. Check with all her friends this instant. See whether or not she's there. I'll want to dash over to your sister's myself. (*She is about to go; he runs past her, calling*): Just a minute, I want to talk to the maid myself. I'll be back in a moment, Cousin! (*Leaves.*)

MRS. HUMBRECHT (*on her way back, trips over the box. Gawks at it and picks it up*) My God! My snuffbox, that I advertised for? How did it get here?

MASTER: A jailer brought it, from the police. Your husband, who said he'd harbored a long animosity toward the man, thrashed him. He dropped the box from fright and ran off.

MRS. HUMBRECHT: Everything's coming at once! (*Pockets the snuffbox.*) Who would have thought it, Cousin! (MASTER HUMBRECHT *shrugs.*) But still I cannot believe, cannot believe it. She was always so gentle and pious, like a lamb! You know yourself how many hundreds of times I've said she must be a minister's wife. I never let her out of my sight. She never spoke to that goddamned lieutenant—God be gracious to me—without my being there.

MASTER: In his letter though he mentions a rendezvous—

MRS. HUMBRECHT: Well, he didn't have one with her, and couldn't have had one, any more than with me.

HUMBRECHT (*returns*): It's all over! She's not there either.

MRS. HUMBRECHT: Merciful God! I'm a dead woman!

HUMBRECHT: Now we can only fall at our cousin's feet and beg him to forgive our insults.

MASTER: I understood. I let it go in one ear and out the other. (*Glances at his watch.*) Now I must go; as soon as my duties permit, I'll be back. Now no excesses! Everything may still turn out all right. Goodbye. (*Leaves.*)

HUMBRECHT (*throws himself on a chair*): This has been quite a morning! (*His wife wrings her hands and cries.*) This could stop one's heart! Thank God, I have nothing to reproach myself for. I've preached to you often enough of virtue and order! I've read you sermons often enough, woman, when you gave her too much freedom! Well, now you have it!

MRS. HUMBRECHT (*imploringly*): For the love of heaven, Martin! Dear Martin, no reproaches! Not now when I'm ready to die this instant! I did my duty as much as you!

HUMBRECHT: Well, bully for you! That may be a great comfort, but not for a father's heart! (*Smites his forehead. The door opens. The* PUBLIC PROSECUTOR *enters, accompanied by two jailers.* HUMBRECHT *jumps at the sound.*)

HUMBRECHT: Who are you, sirs? What do you want here? Whom are you looking for?

PROSECUTOR: Take it easy, my friend! You're not going to thrash me as you did that honorable fellow there.

HUMBRECHT: *Him,* an honorable fellow? He may be a blackguard, a tyrant, but not a—

MRS. HUMBRECHT: Be quiet, Martin! The Public Prosecutor!

JAILER: There, you heard it yourself, Mester Proshecuter! There, you heard it, and there's his cane.

PROSECUTOR: Be quiet! You'll get your compensation.

HUMBRECHT: You then are the Public Prosecutor?

PROSECUTOR: I am he. I sent earlier—

HUMBRECHT: Oh, Mr. Prosecutor! Forgive me. You cannot think badly of an honest townsman if he has the honor not to know you. I would think it's always a good sign if one doesn't have much to do with our highly commendable police force.

PROSECUTOR: No ceremony, my friend. It doesn't suit you.

HUMBRECHT: I am Martin Humbrecht, butcher and decent townsman through and through, and for the money that I have to pay over to the city, even the mayor addresses me as "Sir."

PROSECUTOR: I understand, Mr. Humbrecht. We shan't argue over protocol. I sent a man to you earlier. He is in the service of the police, if you don't already know, and anyone who attacks him attacks the entire profession—but that will come to a hearing at some other time. Now I only stopped by to learn if you acknowledged as yours a certain box that the gentleman showed you?

HUMBRECHT: I don't know anything about any box. Did he show me a box? I must have been blind.

JAILER: Yeah! From anger! My back can tell ya.

MRS. HUMBRECHT: Yes, Martin, this is it. It was lying there on the floor. (*About to hand it to him.*)

HUMBRECHT: That? But that's yours. How did our most esteemed police come by it?

MRS. HUMBRECHT: I lost it.

PROSECUTOR: At least that's what you claimed when you reported it missing.

MRS. HUMBRECHT: And your man there presumably found it? Here's the tip I promised. (*Searches in her pocket.*)

PROSECUTOR: No, not he, Mrs. Humbrecht. I did, and you can put away the tip. I am, of course, not obligated to say how I brought the matter to light. But that you don't take me for some kind of sorcerer, I shall confess how it all happened. My position carries with it the responsibility of having my eyes and ears everywhere. I heard about this very box's being reported, and I noted down the description as I generally do. Then some days ago we recovered the box—among other things—from a low-class woman who was trying to cross the Rhine. So I sent for the crier and took his statement as to whom it belonged, *ad protocollum.* Still, it was necessary that you verify it. That has now been done, and now I must ask for it back again.

MRS. HUMBRECHT: Why? It's mine, isn't it?

PROSECUTOR: Of course it was! Now, however, it belongs to the *corpus delecti* and must remain in the hands of justice as evidence until the verdict. If you then want to pay the expenses *pro rata,* you can get it back again. (MRS. HUMBRECHT *gives him back the box.*) Meanwhile I can tell you—just between us—you didn't lose the box, it was stolen. The woman admitted everything.

HUMBRECHT: Stolen! Where? By whom?

PROSECUTOR: In a certain house where your respectable wife probably would rather not have been.

HUMBRECHT: Every minute something new! Woman, you want to tell me about this? Come on! Where did you and your snuffbox part company?

MRS. HUMBRECHT: No matter what you do to me, I can't say anything except I must have lost it at the ball.

PROSECUTOR: You would do better to speak out, Mrs. Humbrecht, your dearest will find out soon enough. In the "Yellow Cross"—remember now?

HUMBRECHT: In that whorehouse? Why?

PROSECUTOR: Bah! You can assume she didn't go there for breakfast.

MRS. HUMBRECHT (*dismayed*): Breakfast! Yes, we did have breakfast. Where, I don't know . . . but the lieutenant assured me we were in an honest house.

PROSECUTOR: And gave you, in all *honnêteté,*[24] a sleeping powder.

HUMBRECHT (*gnashing his teeth*): By Beelzebub and his living grandmother! You beast! I could wring your neck! (*Lunges at her; the* PROSECUTOR *steps between.*) Now at last my eyes are wide open. This was all dreamed up by the devil! That damned ball! Beast! Damned, accursed beast! You made your daughter a whore!

MRS. HUMBRECHT (*choking*): I! Almighty God knows that I am as innocent as the child in the womb—

LISSEL (*bursts into the room*): I can't find her anywhere. (*She catches sight of the* PROSECUTOR, *becomes confused, and is about to run away. Suddenly she runs up to* HUMBRECHT *and falls to her knees before him, sobbing.*) Ah, my esteemed, beloved master! I beg you for God's sake . . . I will confess everything gladly, tell everything. Only don't send me to the workhouse.

HUMBRECHT (*takes a step toward her*): To the gallows with you!

LISSEL: Ah, dear heaven above! Consider, sir, how very young I am.

HUMBRECHT: What's wrong with you? Did *your* mother ever take you to a whorehouse?

LISSEL: Oh, never! She's not so ungodly.

HUMBRECHT: Listen to her, Mrs. Humbrecht, listen to her! A lovely, little song!

---

[24]respectability, propriety

I'll sing it to you often.

(MRS. HUMBRECHT *clasps her hands to her head. Is about to speak, cannot, and leaves.*)

PROSECUTOR (*who up to now has been speaking privately with the* JAILERS, *to* LISSEL): Admit everything now that you know about the case or my men here will take you to a place where we will find ways to make you talk.

LISSEL: Ah, my most gracious, most respected Mr. Prosecutor, I don't know anything at all, except that she pinned up her braids first thing in the morning, put on a cap and left. She gave me her cloak, her taffeta one, and said I should keep it myself until she came back. She told me that three times in exactly those words, and that I had to give her my cotton one, then she was about to leave, and then she turned around at the door again and said: "Lissel! Until I return." May I be struck dead if I'm not telling the truth! Now have mercy on me, most gracious Mr. Prosecutor! I don't know anything else, except that I have the cloak in my trunk, as she told me to. As God is my witness, I didn't steal it. If you torture me, I won't know any other words to say.

PROSECUTOR: Who is this "she" then?

LISSEL: Who? Why, our young Miss! Miss Evchen!

HUMBRECHT: Your Miss and the devil's! The whore, Mr. Prosecutor, smelled trouble and left this morning. (*Agitated.*) If only the devil doesn't press her so hard that she—that would be a fine trip to Heaven!

PROSECUTOR: We must prevent that! Men, you know your duty! (JAILERS *are about to leave.*) Halt! Something else! What does your cotton cloak look like?

LISSEL: Brown, with red and green stripes, and yellow flowers.

PROSECUTOR: Got it.

JAILER (*to the other*): Praise God, now we can pick up a few groschen!

SECOND JAILER: So give me the marks that we're looking for again, Mr. Smarts.

JAILER: Go to hell! You think I don't know! A cap, a brown coat, and . . . and . . . oh, shoot, I know it all. I can see her already.

(*The* JAILERS *leave.*)

PROSECUTOR: (*meanwhile, to* HUMBRECHT): Mr. Humbrecht! You are a hotheaded, wild man! Control yourself and forget about breaking any necks. Take this as a warning! (*As he leaves.*) You, young girl, I advise to stay honest. This house has corrupted you. (*Leaves,* LISSEL *with him.* HUMBRECHT *falls, as if struck, onto a chair, his hands on the table, his head on them.*)

(*The curtain falls.*)

Act Six

(MRS. MARTHAN's *room. In the background, a pitiful bed, no curtains.*)
(MRS. MARTHAN *is ironing. She lays each piece, as she finishes it, in a basket.* EVCHEN *is sitting on the bed, holding her* CHILD, *who is crying.*)

EVCHEN: Poor, poor baby! No, I can't bear it any longer. (*Places it on the bed.*) Oh, dear Mrs. Marthan! I beg you, for God's sake, just one solitary half-slice of bread. Just a quarter. Please give it to me and a few spoons of milk, so I can make a bit of mush.

MRS. MARTHAN: Get it from where and not steal it? If you stand me on my head, not a penny will fall out of my pockets. You know yourself that I scraped together my last few pennies today to buy the little baby some army bread.

EVCHEN: Saviour of the world! He's going to starve to death!

MRS. MARTHAN: Give him something to drink.

EVCHEN: If only I could! But it's all dried up. Not a drop more to be pressed out. My anguish has absorbed it all. (*Goes away from the bed.*) I can't face my misery. If I do, I'll go crazy.

MRS. MARTHAN: Take care and beware! You'll wind up in an asylum. You know something, Miss?

EVCHEN: Are you speaking to me, Mrs. Marthan?

MRS. MARTHAN: Who else? Shouldn't I call you Miss? Curious! So many highborn and lowborn women go about in the city, with already three, four, or so little dollbabies boarded out, but they'll scratch somebody's eyes out, or hang a slander suit around his neck if he didn't call them Miss! I believe though, God forgive me, that you are not like other people. What's happened has happened. Weeping and wailing won't change anything, and a child, I think, is always better than a calf. If you can't get a job right away as a housemaid, I'll recommend you as a wet-nurse.

EVCHEN: If I only had milk for the wretch!

MRS. MARTHAN: How is it possible? Where could it come from? For the five weeks that you've been with me, God forgive me, you've cried a gallon of tears. And you still don't eat or drink anything. I don't want to think that it's not good enough for you. Who won't take the least, doesn't deserve the best, right? That bowl of meat soup I left evening before yesterday because I had to go do some washing for my wages. Why didn't you heat it up and eat it? God knows, I deprived my own mouth of it for you! Such a good, strong soup! Fit for a prince! A whole pound of the best beef, and two calves' feet! But no, you let it spoil there. Now I'll have to feed it to the cat. Isn't that sinful? Doesn't it look like you're trying to kill yourself? Can you take the responsibility for that? (*Goes out to get a hot iron.*)

EVCHEN: Ha! To take responsibility, that is the question! Were it not for that, for fear of eternally, eternally . . . my mortal frame would have been long gone. (MRS. MARTHAN *returns.*) You are absolutely right, Mrs. Marthan! Absolutely right! But think of my position. Think of the poor little wretch here, abandoned by God and the world—

MRS. MARTHAN: Don't say that! Ever, ever! You're sinning again. God has never abandoned anybody, and He's not going to begin with you and your child. I'll gladly do anything I can. Like I said, as soon as the councillor's wife's time comes, I'll bring you to her as the wet-nurse. I have some influence with her, that I'm sure of.

(*The* CHILD *cries again.*)

EVCHEN (*runs to the bed*): Merciful God! It's going to cry itself to death from hunger. (*Takes the* CHILD *in her arms and rocks it.*)

MRS. MARTHAN: There! That's right! Try to quiet it a bit. As soon as I'm finished with the wash, I'll return it, and maybe I'll pick up a few groschen. But stop moping around so. You might be a plaything for the wicked one, from whom God preserve us. Take a prayerbook and read it well—say yes, you can. In the little cupboard there's "The Way to Heaven and the Way to Hell." It's really beautiful, I tell you, my sainted husband during his last sickness learned it almost by heart. Where did you last work before trouble befell you? I always say, it's not right for an employer to throw a poor servant in unfortunate circumstances out of the house. We are all sinners. A bigger misfortune's likely to happen and then the master or mistress also has that on his conscience. So where'd you work last?

EVCHEN: Where? (*Agitated.*) At . . . at . . . you wouldn't know them.

MRS. MARTHAN: Who knows? So tell me! I won't tell anyone.

EVCHEN: At . . . at Butcher Humbrecht's.

MRS. MARTHAN: Where? What! At Humbrecht the butcher's? Lord, and you never said anything. You must know his daughter then, right?

EVCHEN: Only too well, unfortunately.

MRS. MARTHAN: Yeah, really, unfortunately! Sure, one should never judge, but—. There must not have been one drop of good blood in her, else she wouldn't have done what she did! Yesterday with the other washerwomen I heard a longwinded tale about her. If a hussy lets herself be led so far astray that she goes to whorehouses—

EVCHEN: What are you saying! God! Had she been in a whorehouse?

MRS. MARTHAN: Yeah, yeah! She couldn't have said it to your face. With an officer she went there. And her mother with her, that's the best part! The whole city's talking about it. They even told me the name of the house, but I've forgotten it. And so she and the officer gave her mother something to drink that put the old lady right to sleep. *Why* they did it is easy to imagine. And then supposedly the wastrel promised to marry her. But you know how men are! Another town, another girl! So he dumped her and she threw herself in the river. Early yesterday they found her in the Wanzenau.

EVCHEN: Drowned! Ha! If it were only true!

MRS. MARTHAN: Unfortunately, it is. Only too true, as I said. I wish it weren't.

EVCHEN: Why? At least now she's out of her misery.

MRS. MARTHAN: You talk as if . . . well. I don't know what. "Out of her misery"—yeah, and that's that! Just think of the disgrace when they bring her in today or tomorrow. I'll go because of her; she's supposed to be a very pretty girl. Who knows? Who knows? Maybe our gracious magistrate will let her body be dragged about through the city, as an example to others. Like the man who killed his mother, and hanged himself a year or so ago.

EVCHEN: Killed his mother! Are there people who kill their mothers?

MRS. MARTHAN: Are there people who—what a question! You never heard of the fellow, then? Oh, what was his name? Who wanted to slice his mother's throat—

EVCHEN: Yes, yes! I remember now. His mother was a whore, and he a bastard, conceived in a whorehouse. Somebody threw that at him when they were drinking, so he gave his mother the reward she deserved. I remember it very well.

MRS. MARTHAN: God's body, no! You've got it all wrong. He wanted her money.

EVCHEN: Right! Right! He was hungry and thirsty. He wanted to buy himself a roll and a glass of beer. His mother wouldn't give him any, so he tried to tear it out of her body. And then they gave him what for!

MRS. MARTHAN: Are you crazy? Soon I'll be afraid to be alone with you. Better I should tell you what happened. He was a bad lot from childhood on; he squandered most of his mother's money. She was a thoroughly honest woman; I did her wash for ten years until Anne Mey nipped me. How that happened I'll tell you another time. It was a matter of some tattered old muslin neckpiece that swam away from me in the rinsing. Anyway, he joined the imperial troops, and from there—imagine!—to the Prussians. But he deserted them too and came home again, and gave his mother trouble for so long, she finally had to have the magistrate ban him from the house. More than once he had beaten her like a dog. So everything was going well for a few weeks, and then he came around again early one morning, begging to be taken back, promising to be good and upstanding. His mother, who wouldn't let herself dream that anything could be wrong, began to cry bitterly, groped about in her pocket, and gave him a whole little taler. That's a lot of money; I don't earn that much in four days sometimes. Then he sent the maid away—I don't remember now what he used as a pretext—and as soon as he was alone with his mother, he leaped at her throat with a razor. She fought for her life, as you can imagine, as well as possible, screamed as much as she could scream, and got two cuts in her hand and one—but not serious—in the throat. Then all the people in the house ran about and reported the whole thing, which was the least they could do. And you see, what really clinched it for him, was that he had tied the razor with twine so that it wouldn't snap shut. So he was trapped, and he admitted everything, and the verdict was guaranteed, and his fate sealed. But two days before the sentence could be carried out, he let himself be deceived again by Satan—God be with us—and hanged himself in the prison. Then he was dragged through the city, as I said. His cousin, the alderman, a stinking-rich fellow, who lives there on the long street, offered a thousand talers for the body to be brought to him, so he could bury it secretly. Instead he had to watch the show himself, when his cousin was dragged along the road. The head bounced on the cobblestones, so nobody could see. It was horrible, as I said. But that's what such people deserve. Why don't they pray? (*With a very significant look.*) I'm afraid, I'm afraid, it might not go any better with your former mamsell. She killed her mother as much as—

EVCHEN (*who sits as if senseless on the bed during this narrative, only staring at her* CHILD, *sits bolt-upright*): Killed her mother! I killed my mother!

MRS. MARTHAN: You! Who said anything about you? I was talking about your former mistress. Humbrecht's daughter.

EVCHEN: Oh, did she kill her mother, then?

MRS. MARTHAN: Well, she did and she didn't. Of course, she didn't slice her

139

mother's throat, but she might as well have used the knife. If she'd behaved herself from the beginning, her mother wouldn't have died of shame.

EVCHEN: My mother! Dead! And I did it! (*Sinks to her knees, then falls to the ground.* MRS. MARTHAN *rushes to help her.*)

MRS. MARTHAN: Merciful God! What is this? You're scaring me to death. (*Sits her down again on the bed.*) Who said anything about you or your mother? Soon I'll have the pleasure of taking you to the asylum, if you give me a fright like that again. God knows I'm shaking! How often do I have to tell you I'm talking about Humbrecht's daughter and not you? Her mother was buried yesterday, not yours. I don't know your mother or even where you come from. Her father, the butcher, has promised one hundred talers to anyone who brings him news about his daughter. A princely sum! And now the fishermen who found her will get it.

EVCHEN (*stops short, thinks a bit*): Would you like to get the money, Mrs. Marthan? It would help out quite a bit, wouldn't it? A hundred talers! That's rather chintzy. Why not five or six hundred? Now I can contribute something to your welfare, Mrs. Marthan! I still say it's chintzy, though. And I've a right to! I'm no—

MRS. MARTHAN: Again with this "I"?

EVCHEN: Yes! Yes! I! I'm the one who killed her mother, who doesn't have a drop of good blood in her, who wallowed in the whorehouse, who let herself be seduced by a villain, who has here a nursing child that's hardly born and is already fatherless and motherless—for if I were really a mother, I'd be able to feed it, and I can't. I am the . . . the . . . I'm the only daughter of the Humbrechts, the one that you said drowned herself. You see, it's a lie. I wish that all I said was also a lie, but unfortunately it's all too true. What makes me happy is that now I know a way to repay you, at least in part, for all the trouble I've caused you. Go to my father immediately, Mrs. Marthan. Just say that I, Eve, sent you, and that he should pay you the hundred talers. It won't make him very happy, but—go, Mrs. Marthan! Go!

MRS. MARTHAN: Ah, dear God above! No! I don't deserve this from you. So good and so unfortunate—forgive me for all I said. You must have been seduced . . . else you would never have—

EVCHEN: That's me. I was seduced, deceived when I least expected it. You told the tale yourself, except for the part about my drowning. It's all true, everything! But I must tell you that I didn't know we were in that kind of house, and I really didn't know anything about the sleeping powder. These two things that I have just learned from you show me the whole black soul of the villain who brought me so low. I always had at least a shadow of hope. Now that's gone, and everything with it. Now I can't do anything but— (*Stiffens, looks at her* CHILD *compassionately.*)

MRS. MARTHAN: Oh, you can be happy again. Perhaps he'll come back, when you don't suspect it.

EVCHEN: Back! He was supposed to come back! Mrs. Marthan, I'm only a woman, but if he came back and stood before me . . . I'd shove this letter you see here (*Pulls it out of her pocket.*) under his nose with one hand, and with the other I'd shove a knife through his heart. He deserves it! Before, I really didn't understand this (*Indicates the letter and puts it away again.*) at all. You've finally opened my eyes. Now go, Mrs. Marthan, go! I beg you.

MRS. MARTHAN: A hundred talers would of course be a lovely stake—in my whole life I've never had so much at one time—but I'm afraid to leave you alone right now.

EVCHEN: Why, dear? Do I look perhaps a bit overheated, a bit angry? That is only when I am thinking of the faithless cur. But it soon passes. Only a fleeting moment. Now I'm quite calm again . . . just a little weak. Now, go tell my father I'm still alive and that tomorrow he'll hear more from me. If he gives you money, bring me back something for the child. He can hardly cry any more, he's so weak. Go! Go! Every moment is dear to me.

MRS. MARTHAN: Well then, for the child's sake, I'll leave now, but in less than no time at all, I'll be back again and bring him back some sugar.

EVCHEN: Yes, do that, Mrs. Marthan. Come back soon, or it could be too late.

MRS. MARTHAN: Too late?

EVCHEN: It's already getting so dark. (MRS. MARTHAN *leaves*.) I can hardly see! It's already been so long. I was afraid I'd never get her off my back. Yes! Now what did I want? Why did I send her away? I think the poor little bit of reason I have left has had its heart stop. (*The* CHILD *cries again*.) Are you singing? Singing? Singing our swan-song? Sing, little Gröningseck! That's your father's name! (*Picks the* CHILD *up from the bed and cuddles it*.) An evil father! Who doesn't want to be anything to you and me, anything at all! And who so often swore to be everything to me. Ha! He even swore it in the whorehouse! (*To the* CHILD.) Crying? Still crying? Let me cry, *I'm* the whore, the murderess of her mother. You're nothing! A little bastard, nothing else. (*Doggedly*.) But you'll never be what I am, never endure what I have to endure. (*Picks up a pin and stabs the* CHILD *in the head. The* CHILD *cries out dreadfully; to drown it out she sings, at first very loudly, then more and more softly*.)
Hey, my little doll!
Sleep, little baby, sleep!
Sleep for all eternity.
Ha, ha, ha, ha, ha! (*Rocks the* CHILD *in her arms*.)
Your father was an evil man.
He made your mother a whore.
Hey, my little doll!
Sleep, little baby, sleep!
Sleep for all eternity!
Ha, ha, ha, ha, ha!
Are you sleeping, my darling, are you sleeping? How gently! Soon I'll envy you, bastard. Only angels sleep like this! How much my little song can do! I wish someone would sing me to sleep that way. Ha! A drop of blood! I must kiss it away. Another one! That too! (*Kisses the* CHILD *on the wound*.) What is this? Sweet! Very sweet! But a bitter aftertaste. Ha, now I see it. The blood of my own child! And I drink it? (*Throws the* CHILD *on the bed*.) Sleep there, Gröningseck, sleep! Sleep eternally! Soon I'll also sleep. Hardly so peacefully as you sleep, but sleep is sleep all the same. (*Offstage, sound of* PEOPLE *approaching*.) God! Who's coming? (*She covers the* CHILD; *sits next to it; and, as she sees* HUMBRECHT *enter, buries her head in the pillows*.)

HUMBRECHT: Where? Where is she? My Evchen? My daughter, my own

141

daughter? (*Sees her on the bed.*) Ha! Are you there, whore, are you there? Here, old lady! Your money. (*Throws down a sack.* MRS. MARTHAN *picks it up and lays it aside.*) Still hanging your head? You have no cause, Evchen. I forgive you everything. Everything! (*Shakes her.*) Come, I say, come! We'll have a post-ball celebration. I almost feel like making the sign of the cross over such a rotten carcass. If your father quarrels, you run away; if he gives you a good word, you're deaf. (*Shakes her more strongly.*) Are you going to talk? Or do I have to beat your brains out!

MRS. MARTHAN: You act as if you had an ox before you. It would be no wonder if she fell into a fit! Can't you talk properly?

HUMBRECHT: You're right, old woman. Absolutely right! Wait! How is this? (*Kneels before his daughter.*) Dearest, best Evchen! Have pity on your humbled father! Don't insult him again. Be merciful to him! See, he is on his knees before you, pleading with you. You brought your mother to an early grave. Be so good, I beg of you, as to give me the last blow as well. Me, your father—

EVCHEN (*who, during this last speech has been slowly rising, catches sight of her* CHILD, *comes to her senses, and falls face-down on the bed again*): There! There he is!

MRS. MARTHAN (*brings a lighted lamp, sets it on the table, goes to the bed, and uncovers the* CHILD. *Just as quickly, she covers him up again*): Oh, dear God above! What am I seeing! I must go report it at once! Else I'll be lost. I am sorry for her, but— (*She runs off.*)

HUMBRECHT (*leaps up*): There! What is that! A child! Ha! How it smiles! Your child, Evchen? It shall be mine. My bastard, mine alone. Whoever says that he's yours, Evchen, I'll wring his neck.

MASTER (*enters*): I almost couldn't find the house. So, Cousin! This is wonderful! I see you took my advice and forgave your daughter.

HUMBRECHT: I would have done it without you, Cousin! A father is always a father, and often the most so when he seems the least so.

MASTER: Right now I am doubly glad to find you so resolved. You'll soon learn why. But now I must ask my little cousin to listen to me. It concerns her the most.

EVCHEN: Me? In this whole world, nothing concerns me any more, Master. I swear it.

HUMBRECHT: Don't swear, don't swear about anything, my daughter. Look! I swore too, to rip off your arms and legs, and now, swearing or no swearing, I'm very happy that I didn't do it.

MASTER: I think so too. Circumstances can change quite a bit. Now, just listen! You love Gröningseck, little cousin?

EVCHEN: Yes, as I love Satan! I was on guard against them both and let them both lead me on.

MASTER: You loved him once though, else you wouldn't—

EVCHEN: Yes, but I didn't know then he'd turn me into a whore and the murderess of my mother, into—

MASTER: None of that was his intention, let alone his fault.

EVCHEN: So! Are you his advocate now? How long will you be so? Here (*Indicating the child.*) lies mine.

MASTER: I am not alone as his advocate. I mean . . . I mean . . . in your own

142

heart, you will find another. To be brief, Gröningseck loves you as tenderly as before. A nearly fatal illness kept him from returning to you at the appointed time. (*Turns to* HUMBRECHT.) He had no idea, Cousin, of the letter I read you. I showed him the envelope and he recognized it as Lieutenant Hasenpoth's handwriting and seal. He showed me other letters from Hasenpoth, which were filled with untruths about Evchen. He smelled a rat, and set out for here, though barely half-recovered. An hour ago, he stopped by the "Raven," and had me summoned. We saw you run past in the greatest hurry, guessed the cause, and followed you at a distance. Would you like to speak to him yourself?

HUMBRECHT: If he wants to marry her and restore her lost honor, yes! Otherwise, if he's fond of his nose and ears, he'd better not show his face to me.

MASTER: He wants to marry her.

EVCHEN: And if he wanted to ten times, I'd rather face the executioner.

MASTER: But he is innocent! He can prove it to you.

EVCHEN: So much the worse! That means all the blame lies on me. (*Rises from the bed.*) This letter here! (*Throws it into the room.*) The devil wrote it—my own heart's mistrust; fear of you, Father; the thought of having murdered my mother. This, and oh, what else more! It drove me to despair. I wanted to be free from the world, and didn't have the determination to lay a hand upon myself. Now let the hangman do it! My child is dead, killed by me!

MASTER: God! Is it possible? (*Examines the* CHILD.) Truth! Most righteous God! How far your creatures can fall after that first misstep!
(HUMBRECHT *stands with crossed arms, stares at* EVCHEN, *then at the* CHILD. EVCHEN *seems neither to see nor hear.* VON GRÖNINGSECK *bursts in, still in his travelling clothes.*)

EVCHEN: God! That's the one thing I needed!

VON GRÖNINGSECK: How astounded you all look! How pale! What's going on here? What's the matter?

HUMBRECHT: A bit of work for the lout, nothing more. God! I mean, my heart is as heavy as if the whole Muenster tower were pressing on it. Now I can only take rat poison! Here! (*Leads the* LIEUTENANT *to the baby.*) Here! If you have a father's heart! Mine is broken. Adieu! I'll see you again, Eva, in the workhouse. Say your last adieu!

VON GRÖNINGSECK: What! Evchen, gentle Evchen! You couldn't possibly with your own hand . . . your child . . . my child . . .

EVCHEN: Only too possible, sir! But before you reproach me further, read the letter there. Then you may speak.

VON GRÖNINGSECK (*picks up the letter*): Again the hand of Hasenpoth! (*Looks at the signature.*) In my name! (*Glances at it.*) The rest I can imagine. Wait! Blackguard! You'll pay for it with your blood, before another hour passes!
(*He is about to leave, but bangs into the* PROSECUTOR *at the door. The* JAILERS *stand at the door.*)

PROSECUTOR: Not another step, sir! Before the *procès verbal* [25] is set down and signed. (*To the* JAILERS.) Has one of you ordered a *porte-chaise* [26] and

_____

[25] formal statement
[26] transport

143

guard? (*One* JAILER *leaves.*)

VON GRÖNINGSECK (*goes over again to* MASTER HUMBRECHT): The base, cowardly betrayer! Now do you believe, Master, that there are cases where personal vengeance becomes a duty? (MASTER HUMBRECHT *shrugs his shoulders.*) Where is the state, in which such monsters, such Hasenpoths, who destroy whole families under the guise of friendship, are punished as they deserve? Ha! How much good it will do me! With what heart's delight I will dance in his blood!

MASTER: It would be more humane, I believe, if you would try to save this poor girl from the gallows, than to heap crime upon crime.

PROSECUTOR: Yes, that would be some saving! The law that condemns the childmurderer to death is clear and has suffered no exceptions for many years. If the facts here are as clear as they seem to be, you can spare yourself the effort.

VON GRÖNINGSECK: And despite you and all your lawman's lack of feeling, I will set off today for Versailles, to obtain grace for her at the court itself, or—

EVCHEN: Grace for me! Gröningseck! What are you thinking of? I should die ten thousand deaths! Better today than tomorrow!

PROSECUTOR: Not so fiery, Lieutenant! Of course, much depends on circumstances!

(CLERK *and* MAGISTRATES *enter.*)

EVCHEN: Didn't I tell you, Gröningseck? My fate was to be written in blood.

VON GRÖNINGSECK: It wouldn't be, if you had trusted me. If you had given in less to melancholy, and believed somewhat more in honor—or if I had somewhat less.

MASTER (*regards each alternately, sympathetically*): To hide so from me!

HUMBRECHT (*tears his vest open, breaking off the buttons*): The whole world is becoming too narrow for me! (*Takes a deep breath.*) Puuh! (*Claps the* LIEUTENANT *on the shoulder.*) If you need money, sir! Travelling expenses! Do you understand me all right? A thousand, two, three thousand guilders lie ready at my house! And I would give ten thousand if the wretched ball and all its consequences were sent to the devil!

The End

STORM AND STRESS

BY

FRIEDRICH MAXIMILIAN KLINGER

1776

DRAMATIS PERSONAE

WILD
LA FEU
BLASIUS
LORD BERKLEY
JENNY CAROLINE, *his daughter*
LADY CATHERINE, *her aunt*
LOUISA, LADY CATHERINE'*s niece*
SEA CAPTAIN BOYET
LORD BUSHY
A young MOOR
INNKEEPER
BETTY

The play takes place in America.

Act One
Scene One

A room in an inn.
WILD, LA FEU, *and* BLASIUS *enter in travelling clothes.*

WILD: Cheers! In tumult and uproar again, so the senses whirl around like weather vanes in a storm. The wild noise has thundered into me such a feeling of well-being that I really begin to feel a little better. So many hundreds of miles to have ridden to bring you into the obliterating frenzy! Mad heart! You should thank me for it! Ha! Rage and then take it easy! Refresh yourself in confusion! How are you?

BLASIUS: Go to hell! Is my donna here?

LA FEU: Keep up your illusions, fool! I will slurp them from my nails like drops of water. Long live illusion! Hey! Hey! In the magic of my fantasy, I wander in the rose garden, led by Phyllis's hand—

WILD: May Apollo embolden you, foolish boy!

LA FEU: I shall not fail to metamorphose the black house over there, gone up in smoke with the old tower, into a fairy palace. Magic, magic fantasy! (*Listens.*) What lovely, spiritual symphonies strike my ear? By Amor! I want to fall in love with an old crone, live in an old, dilapidated house, bathe my tender carcass in stinking puddles of manure, only to curb my fantasy. Is there no old witch, with whom I can flirt madly? Her wrinkles would become for me undulating lines of beauty, her protruding black teeth marble columns of Diana's temple. Her sagging leather tits would surpass the bosom of Helen. A woman as dried out as I! Hey, my fantastic goddess! I can tell you, Wild, I have conducted myself worthily throughout our travels. I have seen things, felt things, that no mouth tasted, no nose smelled, no eye saw, no mind perceived—

WILD: Especially when I blindfolded you. Ha, ha!

LA FEU: To Hades with you! You raving—! But tell me now once more, where are we right this minute in the real world? In London, right?

WILD: Yeah, sure. Don't you remember that we were on a ship? You were certainly seasick.

LA FEU: I don't know anything about anything. I am not to blame for anything. Is my father still alive? Send news to him then, Wild, and let him say that his son is still alive. I know I came from the Pyrenees mountains out of Frisia. Beyond that, nothing.

WILD: Out of Frisia?

LA FEU: In what quarter of the city are we now?

WILD: In a fairy palace, La Feu! Don't you see the golden skies? The amors and amoretti? The queens and gnomes?

LA FEU: Blindfold my eyes! (WILD *does so*.) Wild! Ass! Wild! Blockhead! Not too tight! (WILD *loosens the blindfold*.) Ha! Blasius, dear, caustic, sick Blasius, where are we?

BLASIUS: How would I know?

WILD: To help you two out of the dream, I'll tell you that I led you out of Russia to Spain, because I believed the king was going to start a war with the Grand

147

Mogul. But the Spanish nation was as lazy as ever, so I packed you up again, and now you're in the middle of the war in America. Ha! Let me feel it to my depths, to stand on American soil, where everything is new, everything is significant. Oh! That I can feel no joy purely!

LA FEU: War and death! Oh, my limbs! Oh, my guardian angel! Give me a fairy tale instead! Woe is me!

BLASIUS: May lightning strike you dead, crazy Wild! What have you done! Is Donna Isabella alive? Hey! Will you speak! My donna!

WILD: Ha, ha, ha! You've finally shown some anger.

BLASIUS: Anger? Finally? You'll pay for this with your life, Wild! What? I am at least a free man. Does friendship go so far that you in your madness can drag people through the world like a pack of dogs? To tie us in the carriage, holding a pistol to our heads, always further and further, clip, clop! Eating and drinking in the carriage, so that people would take us for lunatics. Into war and hurlyburly, away from my passion, the only thing left to me—

WILD: You love no one, Blasius.

BLASIUS: True, I love no one. I have carried it to the point of loving no one: loving everyone for a moment, and the next moment forgetting everyone. I am untrue to all women; therefore, all women are and have been untrue to me. They have pressed me and oppressed me something pitiful! I have assumed all possible poses: I was a dandy, then a madcap, then boorish, then sensitive, then an Englishman. And my greatest conquest I made by being nobody at all. That was Donna Isabella. In order to return once more—your pistols are loaded?

WILD: You're a fool, Blasius, and don't understand a joke.

BLASIUS: Oh, a wonderful joke, this! Take care! As of this moment I am your enemy.

WILD: To duel with you! See here, Blasius, I'd like nothing better in the world than to grapple with someone and give my heart its favorite feast. But with you? Ha, ha! (*Holds the pistol before him.*) Look down the barrel and say whether it doesn't look bigger to you than the Tower of London. Be clever, friend! I need and love you, as you do me. The devil could not have brought together greater fools and prophets of doom than us. Because of that we must stay together and also share the jokes. Our misfortune comes from our own temperaments; the world has contributed but not so much as we.

BLASIUS: Madman! I am eternally on the spit!

LA FEU: They have skinned me alive and pickled me with pepper. The dogs!

WILD: Now we are in the middle of the war here. The only ecstasy I know is to be in the middle of a war. Savor the scenery, do whatever you want.

LA FEU: I'm not one for war.

BLASIUS: I'm not one for anything.

WILD: May God make you even more useless! Again I'm numbed out of my mind. Completely hollow. I want to be stretched over a drum, in order to expand my range. Again and again my heart pains me. Oh, if I could but exist in the barrel of this pistol, until a hand blasted me into the air. Oh, indecision! How far you lead mankind, and how far astray!

BLASIUS: What's going to become of us at the end?

WILD: That you see nothing! I had to flee, to escape the dreadful uneasiness and uncertainty. I thought the earth trembled under me, so uncertain were my steps. My presence tormented all good men who took an interest in me, because they knew they couldn't help me.

BLASIUS: Say instead: didn't want to.

WILD: Yes, they wanted to. But everywhere I had to take to flight. I've been everything. I did odd jobs just to do something. I lived in the Alps, tended goats, lay day and night under the eternal vaults of Heaven, cooled by the wind and burned by an inner fire. Nowhere peace, nowhere repose. The highest noblemen in England wander lost in the world. Ah! And I do not find the magnificent one, the unmatched one who stands there. Look, I am so bursting with power and health, I cannot exhaust myself. I want to join the campaign here as a volunteer. There my soul can distend itself. If they will do me the service of shooting me down, well and good! You'll take my cash and emigrate.

BLASIUS: Well, I'll be damned! No one will shoot you, noble Wild.

LA FEU: Oh, they could do it.

WILD: Could they do me any greater service? Imagine, when we embarked, I saw in the distance the captain on his ship.

BLASIUS: The one who has that mortal hatred of you? I thought you shot him to death in Holland.

WILD: Three times have I faced him in life-and-death situations. Now he will not leave me in peace, though I have never offended the man. I gave him a bullet, and he gave me a stab. It's frightening, how he hates me without cause. And I must confess, I like him. He is an honorable, rough man. Heaven knows what he has against me. Leave me alone an hour.

INNKEEPER: The rooms are ready, milords. Is there anything else I can do for you?

WILD: Where are my people?

INNKEEPER: They've eaten and are sleeping.

WILD: Let them be.

INNKEEPER: And you require nothing else?

WILD: Your strongest punch, innkeeper.

LA FEU: Oh yes, that's just what you need, Wild.

WILD: Is the general here?

INNKEEPER: Yes, milord!

WILD: What visitors are in this house? But I don't really want to know. (*Leaves.*)

BLASIUS: I'm sleepy.

LA FEU: I'm hungry.

BLASIUS: Keep your illusion, fool! A damnable world, away from my Donna. (ALL *leave.*)

Scene Two

LORD BERKLEY's *room*
LORD BERKLEY. MISS CAROLINE.
CAROLINE *sits at a piano in sweet melancholy, fantasizing.*

BERKLEY (*building a house of cards in a childlike, fantastic manner*): To become so completely a child! Everything golden, everything magnificent and good! To dwell in this castle, rooms, hall, cellar, and stable! All of multicolored, muddled, hazy stuff! I find joy in nothing any more. Happy moments of childhood, to return to them! I find joy in nothing more than this house of cards. Symbol of my confused life! A shove, a heavy step, a light breeze will collapse you, but the solid, unflagging courage of a child will build you up again! Ha! So with my whole soul shall I cut myself off, and think and feel nothing more than how marvelous it is to live and move and have my being in you. Lord Bushy! Yes, my soul! I'll set aside a room for you. So unfriendly to me as you were, you shall dwell in Berkley's best room. Ha! It still wells up in me, again and again, obstinate Bushy! Whenever I think back. Driven from hearth and home, merely because Berkley stood fatter than Bushy. It's scandalous. Nonetheless this room, painted with my story, is at your disposal. Who could comprehend that, since my heart is shut up so tight—ha, ha! Lord Berkley! You are fine, now that you have become again a child! Daughter!

CAROLINE: Father!

BERKLEY: Child! You cannot believe how well one can become. Look! I'm building Bushy's room now. How do you like it?

CAROLINE: Very much, milord! Truly I want to be his maid and serve him, for your peace of mind.

BERKLEY: Where he may prowl about. Enemy Bushy! From hearth and home! From wife and property! Bushy, it cannot be! To deprive my sweet child of everything! No, milord, we cannot live together. (*Strikes down the house of cards.*)

CAROLINE: My father!

BERKLEY: What, Miss? You should be ashamed of yourself! Aren't you Berkley's daughter? To serve Bushy? Bushy's maid? Not of any queen. Ha! That could make me fall into a deep sleep and drive me crazy. Bushy's maid, Miss! Wouldn't Miss like to change her mind? Bushy's maid?

CAROLINE: No, milord! Only call me daughter! Oh, that word "Miss" is a bitter sound from Berkley's mouth to Berkley's daughter. (*Kisses his hand.*)

BERKLEY: Hm! Good Jenny! Long live our dominion as lord and miss. But I cannot live together with him. I would truly be tempted to strangle him in his sleep. Oh, give me childish ideas. I find joy in nothing any longer. All my favorite things, my coppers, my paintings, my flowers—it's all the same to me.

CAROLINE: If you would listen to some music . . . perhaps this . . .

BERKLEY: All right! Try it and see.

(CAROLINE *plays for him.*)

BERKLEY: No! No! Oh, I am still the weak, foolish fellow, who can be shaped

150

into anything by a pure tone. It is curious, child, there are tones that through their sound place before my eyes the whole sad picture of my adverse life. And there are others that meet my nerves so happily that when the tone strikes my ear, I see again one of the happy scenes of my life. In one, your mother meets me at the park in Yorkshire, skipping so merrily on the wide boulevard, where on one side a brook meanders and babbles, as you may recall. I can hear it exactly, even to the flies' buzzing about in summer. I was just about to press her to my heart and tell her something pleasant when you played a different chord.

CAROLINE: Dear father! Oh, my mother! (*Rolls her eyes heavenward.*)

BERKLEY: Yes, so, with moist eyes turned heavenward. I know what that is like. She often looked the same way, and her eyes spoke as yours do. Oh, child! When you changed the tones, it was Bushy and Hubert. You see, then, that won't do. I don't know why it is, that there is such strange tautness in me.

CAROLINE: I know what music does, what it gives to the heart. The tones weave a magic spell, and if one looks to see what is there—Him! Him! The sound and echo of all tones—Him! Heart! My heart! (*Frightened, covers her eyes.*)

BERKLEY: Hm! Hm! My heart, my heart! Sit down next to me and help me build my castle again. You see, I have gotten on well, thank God, in destroying and rebuilding Ha, ha! Be merry now! You take the right side and I'll take the left. And when the palace is standing, we'll take the tin soldiers. You command one batallion, and I'll command another. We'll grapple like Bushy and Hubert, then we'll conspire to seize the castle and throw old Berkley out naked, with his little Jenny and good wife. We'll set it on fire. Fire and flames! Eh, Miss?

CAROLINE (*wiping her eyes, kissing his forehead*): Unhappy thought! May heaven trickle calming oblivion on your gray head, old Berkley! Father, we lack for nothing. We're well. What is Bushy, that noble Berkley in his sixtieth year should think of him?

BERKLEY: I don't *think* of him, foolish child! I can't help that it still swells up so bitterly in me. I only *feel* it.

CAROLINE: Exactly.

BERKLEY: I want to proclaim to you how he treated your father. Take your eyes off me! Now then, I wished I had him, he would lay his head calmly and peacefully on my breast. But you would have to stand by me and not move an inch—otherwise, if he stood before me like that—oh, God! You have wondrously formed us, wondrously tautened our nerves, wondrously disposed our hearts!

CAROLINE: Didn't Bushy have a son?

BERKLEY: Of course. I would say a brave, robust, wild lad, if it weren't Bushy's son.

CAROLINE: Wasn't he named Carl? Blue eyes, brown hair, taller than any other boy his age. He was a handsome, wild, red-cheeked youth. He was always my cavalier, and fought for me.

BERKLEY: Bushy! Bushy!

CAROLINE: Father! Oh, my father! Your bad time is upon you again. (*Tries to cuddle against him.*)

BERKLEY: Go away! Didn't I have a son, a brave, stormy, headstrong youth, whom I lost that terrible night? A life for a life, if I catch Carl Bushy in the flesh! If my Harry were here now, I would want his fist to be iron, his heart maddened, his teeth eager. I would have him trot throughout the world until he avenged Berkley on Bushy.

CAROLINE: Milord! Spare your daughter!

BERKLEY (*agitated*): Now then! Let me ponder something for a while . . . yes, something. Do you want to come along, child? Ha, I want to go to the parade. I think the enemy will atttack in a few days, and then we shall march out. Ha, ha! I am a gray old man. Give me only childhood and foolish things! Ha, ha! It is crazy, Miss, and good that hot remains hot and hate remains hate. As becomes a decent man. Age is not so cold; I'll have you feel that. Pack up my castle then, so that nothing more is spoiled. Adieu, Miss, the drums sound. (*Leaves.*)

CAROLINE (*calling after him*): Only good times, dear father!

BERKLEY (*comes back hastily*): God knows, Miss, it was around midnight, pitch-dark, when he fell upon us. And when I in the morning woke up from rigid numbness, I had no wife nor any of my children. I screamed, moaned and groaned in tones . . . in tones . . . hey! And raised my hands to the darkened heavens: give me my children! Make Bushy childless, that he may feel what it is. Childless! Then I found you, wet, cold, and frozen. You hung on my neck, and wrapped your tender arms and legs around me. Miss Berkley! I stood there so saddened and dead in endless pain, in endless joy, at having saved one of my children. And with your trembling hand, you wiped away the cold sweat from my brow. Hey! That was a moment, Miss! (*Embraces her, presses her to his heart, remains silent and fixed. Coming to.*) Yes, Miss! See! It seizes me so! And then a messenger: Your lady is dead! And then a messenger: Your Harry has disappeared! Yes, Miss! And Bushy should have this house! No, by God, no! Adieu, child! Don't cry.

CAROLINE: Not cry? Your child not cry? Lord Berkley, don't go away just now. It's closing in on me here, father! (*Hand on her heart.*)

BERKLEY: No, no! I shall send your aunt and cousin to you. Berkley is a good soldier. When he's had his fun, he's ready and able. Adieu!

CAROLINE (*alone*): What will become of all this? Oh, his sufferings break out in a way that makes me tremble. War then! And my tears and pleas are to no avail. Where then shall I go? I am afraid. Ah, so much sorrow, and still to fear. And eternally this longing in my heart? (*At the piano.*) Take me under your care! You alone understand me; your sound, the echo of my secret feelings, is a solace and a deliverance to me. Ah, each tone! Him! Him! (*Plays a few passages, stops suddenly, starts again.*) Yes, him! (*Sinking into mournful dreaming.*)

Scene Three

CAROLINE. LOUISA.

LOUISA (*enters, dancing and skipping*): Good morning, Miss. Yes, just look, dear cousin. I am in a terrible mood. A day full of vapors. Our aunt and her eternal nagging about the cavaliers! It is not to be endured. "He is courting me, Niece! He said the sweetest things to me!" On and on eternally. If Lady Catherine could only understand that spring is spring, and winter is winter, despite all of our efforts! Has Miss had disturbing dreams? Why are you hanging your head so? What's wrong with you, child?

CAROLINE: Nothing, nothing. My father—

LOUISA: Is he being pigheaded? Is he wild? Yes, what can you say? If only we were out of this hateful country! To London, Cousin! To London! That is the place of glitter and magnificence. (*Looks in the mirror.*) Why am I here? Why are these playful blue eyes here? All London would be talking about them. What use to me are my talents, my lessons, my French and Italian? To capture hearts is our purpose. Here! Oh, I am lost! Believe me, I'll let myself be carried off by the first Englishman who pleases me.

CAROLINE: You're not serious.

LOUISA: Well, not completely, of course. I am certainly kind to you, and I'm kind in general, provided that I have many suitors on whom to practice my powers. But dearest, you must feel yourself that we are not suited to the place. How many suitors do you think I have now, all at the same time?

(CAROLINE *remains lost in thought.*)

LOUISA (*counting them up in her mind, with lively gestures*): I really can't tot up more than six, because I have to leave out the half-serious ones and the ones I scared away. There's Silly, so long and slender, who always keeps his eyes tightly shut when he speaks to me, as if my look has glued his eyes. Once he was stammering to me so, with eyes still closed, and I kept mimicking him. Aunt almost burst, trying to hold back the laughter, so that he wouldn't notice. And there's Boyet, who always and eternally says nothing other than "Miss, I love you." As if there were no other words in the dictionary of gallantries. Never "Miss, I love you tenderly," or "to death," or anything like that. Oh, his language is as short as his finger. Ah well, I could always use him as a dwarf, if a real cavalier someday wanders through here. Now, Toby—

CAROLINE: Wasn't Carl Bushy a dear, good youth?

LOUISA: A brave youth of fiery courage and emotion! I banished Captain Dudley, Miss! I don't know what the fool has in mind. Imagine! A few days ago he said we women have usually far less love, and show far less love than men, because of our feminine nature. What does the solemn fool mean by that?

CAROLINE: I don't know.

LOUISA: Feminine nature! Think of it! Just because I acted somewhat displeased that he said something to you the other day. I don't know what he said, but the way he said it, and the way he looked when he said it—as if he was feeling something which I have noticed in none of my suitors. I am not jealous, Cousin. You are gentle, sensitive, dear, and good. I am beautiful, wild, and ill-tempered. And then there is Stockley, whom I merely tolerate so he doesn't visit Miss Tranch. I can't bear *her* at all. In the end I make fools of them all. I spin them around as lads do with a top, but they enjoy it. One should not know love, Auntie says, until one is twenty-five, and then it has its reasons. And I don't even know what it's supposed to mean: to love.

CAROLINE: You are fortunate, Cousin. I don't know it either, but—

LOUISA: As long as I amuse myself, dispel my boredom, exercise my moods and caprices, it's good enough. But you know what love is—
CAROLINE (*nervous*): What are your suitors' names?
LOUISA: I hear Auntie coughing.

Scene Four

LADY CATHERINE. LOUISA. CAROLINE.

CATHERINE: Oh, how exasperating! Sniffling and coughing on such a wonderful day! Yes, ladies! Come quickly and prepare yourselves. The air in this country will be the death of me. Louisie, pull yourself together. You don't look as much like yourself as you should.
LOUISA: What's the matter, Auntie?
CATHERINE: I felt a premonition of this. Three strangers have arrived.
CAROLINE: Is that all, Aunt?
LOUISA: Isn't that enough?
CATHERINE: Fine people! Oh, a tall, wild lad among them. I could hardly reach his beard. He cursed and looked to heaven as if he felt something very deeply. I perceived it at once. Oh, ladies, it is a good sign when a young man curses. They are Englishmen. Tell me, Louisie, how do I look? They are Englishmen.
LOUISA: And I, Auntie?
CAROLINE: An Englishman! What did he look like, Aunt?
CATHERINE: They will pay us a visit. Yes! Can I wear green with rose-red?
LOUISA: Too young, too old, Auntie. Come, I could never reach a decision in such important matters in less than an hour. We shall seek counsel from Betty. An Englishman! Oh, my Englishman!
CATHERINE: Virtuous and demure, Miss! Don't run so. I'll be out of breath.
LOUISA (*aside*): Because she can't move. Ha, ha! (*Takes her by the arm.*) Come on, Auntie, we young girls shall skip and hop—
CATHERINE: Nasty thing. (*They leave.*)

Act Two
Scene One

BETTY *leads* WILD, BLASIUS, *and* LA FEU *in.*

BETTY: Here, milords, be so kind as to wait. Miladies will soon have the honor. (*Leaves.*)

LA FEU: Good, my pretty Iris! (*Looking around.*) Ah! There's something so endearing, so alluring about first sight. One always feels different in ladies' chambers. My heart flutters so charmingly. Why are you grimacing so, Wild?

WILD: I don't understand myself yet. I feel so good, all things speak to me in this room, and attract me. Yet so terrifyingly wretched, so terrifyingly uncertain. I leap from thought to thought; I can't fix myself on anything. Ah, only when it returns in full purity—the eternal high emotion, where my soul loses itself in reverberations, catching sight of her beautiful face in the magnificent distance, in the evening sun, in the moonlight. Ah! Even if I hurry on the rapid wings of love, it disappears. It's always lost before me. Yes, I am miserable. Living eternally in thought, I am miserable! Ah, me! I thought I would find in this other hemisphere of the world that which was not to be found. But here is like there, and there is like here. Thank God that the imagination sees the distant as marvelous. Once he stands on the point so ardently wished for, how the roaming vagabond flees again, in certain faith that *there* the unquiet spirit will find everything. So it is throughout the world, in magical, insistent fantasy, always the same here and there. Happy spirit! I shall follow you!

BLASIUS: The centaurs trot along again before your imagination. I am again nothing at all, and want to be nothing at all. Wild, it is shameful how you eternally gad about with ghosts.

WILD: I beg of you—I will find them.

LA FEU: The women are taking so long!

WILD: Listen! You know how I am. If the women make a disagreeable impression on me, be ready with some excuse, for I'll be off.

BLASIUS: And then we'll have to explain your boorishness. Go! Do what you want. I am not at all interested in women. Nevertheless, I must seek out their company, for they amount to so little and I to nothing at all. You nauseate me, Wild! It would be kind of you to leave me alone for a while.

WILD: Was it my idea to seek you out?

BLASIUS: I can't stand you. Your power is repugnant to me. You're crushing me to death, and that you're eternally chasing phantoms—I hate you!

WILD: As you wish. You'll love me again.

BLASIUS (*embracing him*): Who can resist you? Lad! Lad! I am more ill at ease than you. I am torn within and cannot pick up the threads of my life again. Let it be! I want to become melancholy. No, I want to become nothing. You saw my noble steed in Madrid pulling carts; I cried from the depths of my soul, and Isabella wiped away my tears. Marvelousness of the world! I can no longer pluck your flowers. Yes, he has lost this feeling, he who has lost thee, undying love, thou who sustainest everything in us.

155

WILD: Blasius, you have more than you believe.

LA FEU: Where are the women keeping themselves? (*Rifling through the books.*) Miladies' books give me great hope that they are given to sweet fantasies. Ah, novels! Ah, fairy tales! Ah, how marvelous all the lies! How happy are they who can lie to themselves!

Scene Two

LADY CATHERINE and LOUISA enter, paying their respects.
Bows and curtsys all around.

LA FEU (*as he catches sight of them*): Heavenly Venus! By the grove of Paphos! (*To* LADY CATHERINE.) Bewitching goddess of this island! Your gaze stirs my heart to tones of love, and my sinews resound with the dearest harmony.

CATHERINE: Milord! (*A curtsy.*) Milord! (*Coquettishly.*) Strangers of your worth make our sad life light and pleasant. I have the honor to address—

LA FEU: You, Blasius, tell her my name. This is my guardian, milady!

BLASIUS: La Feu, milady! (*To* LOUISA.) Miss, I wish that I had not seen you, at least not at this moment. I am so little—

LOUISA: Ha, ha! Milord . . . Blasius, right?

BLASIUS: So they call me.

LOUISA: So, Milord Blasius, I am sorry that my countenance pains you so. Indeed, milord (*A mocking bow.*) Ha, ha! Auntie's presence makes him a sounding instrument. *La vache sonnante!*[1] Ha, ha! Oh, that'll kill me! So, milord, so serious?

BLASIUS: I am not merry. Beautiful and stupid! Woe is me!

WILD: Satan couldn't take this hell. (*Leaves.*)

CATHERINE *and* LOUISA: But why is milord leaving?

LA FEU: I must tell you, milady—Blasius, you certainly know why.

BLASIUS: He has attacks of insanity, miladies, and when he's overcome, it just carries him away.

LA FEU (*indicating* CATHERINE): And the sight of this goddess couldn't stop him?

CATHERINE: Oh, milord! How sorry I am for him—such a handsome man, such a robust, wild appearance.

LA FEU: But a madman. Imagine, he wants to go to war,

CATHERINE: And you?

LA FEU (*kneeling*): Here is my battlefield.

LOUISA (*annoyed*): This is insufferable!

CATHERINE (*solemnly pulling* LA FEU *to his feet*): You may stop kneeling, milord. Presumably—

LA FEU: Ah! You elevate me with such godliness, with such splendor! Surely many a knee has already bent itself sore before milady!

---

[1] The mooing cow!

156

CATHERINE: Oh, milord! Perhaps one doesn't pass through life unnoticed.

LOUISA (*exasperated and indolent*): Where are you, milord? Still in the other hemisphere?

BLASIUS (*annoyed and bored*): Milady, you command—

LOUISA (*mocking his tone*): Milord!! Nothing—

CATHERINE: And you, milord?

LA FEU: Ah, away, away! Caught in love's spell! Happy, blessed fate, that led me on this path! Finally your wrath has abated, wild unlucky star! I feel renewed the thrill in my veins. Entrancing goddess! I wish I had the tiny, tiny eyes of a gnat, that I might scrutinize every detail of your charm and beauty.

CATHERINE: What tone! How pleasantly gay! Has milord been away from London long? Oh, if milord would only tell us something about London!

LOUISA: Oh, from London! (*Aside.*) These people are unendurable!

LA FEU: Yes, milady, from London, but I feel only what is before me. London, milady, is supposed to be a great city. I know little of the world. I was born in London. I come from the Pyrenees. Oh, those are high, high, mountains! Ah, milady, but my love would be even higher, if milady would love me—

CATHERINE and LOUISA: Love? Ha, ha!

LA FEU: Does that strike you as amusing, miladies?

LOUISA: Of course, milord! No, we love nothing.

CATHERINE: Be quiet, Niece! The distinction remains, and it all depends on . . .

LA FEU: Yes, charming lady, on what we have?

LOUISA (*to BLASIUS*): Milord continues to dream. All my gaiety abandons me around you.

BLASIUS: Forgive me, I am so moved—you are beautiful, Miss!

LOUISA: And you are very entertaining.

BLASIUS (*after a long pause*): You are bored. I am sorry that I cannot entertain you better. My misfortune is that of always being nothing when I should be everything. I love so silently, Miss, as you see, that I am really in a case.

LOUISA: Love, milord! What are you trying to say? To love silently! Oh, the boredom! Does Lord Wild also love so? It's not as though I were curious—I don't have to know! If only you were more lively!

BLASIUS: Yes, lively! (*Aside.*) I am absolutely bored to death. My heart is so cold and the girl is so beautiful and cheerful.

LOUISA: I'm having an attack of the vapors. Would milords like to take tea in the garden? Perhaps the room does not agree with you.

BLASIUS: Whatever you like.

LOUISA: Oh, heaven! (*Smacks him with her fan.*) Come to life, already!

BLASIUS: I am still fresh from the sea, and I have . . . I have . . .

CATHERINE (*who throughout this has been quietly talking to* LA FEU): Yes, milord?

LA FEU: Yes, as I was saying, come with me. Oh, my goddess, I have become everything again before your eyes. Who can see so much charm without every fiber of his body being reborn! Yes, my goddess! I want to tell you much, much about the swings of love that drive my fantasy across the sun. And milady (*Kisses her hand.*) I love you.

CATHERINE (*aside*): This is curious! I don't understand him, and yet I like him. (*Aloud.*) Milord, you are—

LA FEU: Oh, you! It seems to me, we are sympathetic.

CATHERINE: What does that mean? Sympathetic?

LA FEU: God have mercy! I don't understand myself enough, milady, to know what the word means.

CATHERINE How spiteful you are, milord!

(ALL *leave.*)

Scene Three

CAROLINE, *alone.*

CAROLINE: Were those the Englishmen? Far, far, eternally far—it's good that they are gone. (*Lost in silent melancholy.*) Yes, just so did he appear, as he came from out of my mind, and placed himself before me. (*Reaches out toward something.*) Oh, so dear to my heart! Why does he stay away so long? Ah! I shall never see Carl Bushy again! I may never see Carl Bushy again! Yet do I not see him? (*Enraptured.*) My eyes see only him, my heart beats only for him; my eyes possess him, my heart possesses him.

Scene Four

WILD *enters without knocking, keeping his hat on throughout the scene. Draws back when he becomes aware of* CAROLINE's *presence.*

CAROLINE (*frightened*): What? Who?

WILD (*regards her fixedly, with his whole soul*): Forgive me, Miss. I have the wrong room.

CAROLINE: Milord. An error that is easy enough in an inn. (*Regards him uneasily.*)

WILD (*confused, impassioned, inquiring, hanging on her words*): Milady, may I? Milady . . . yes, I'm going . . . going right now . . . (*Draws nearer and nearer.*) . . . but, milady . . . I'm staying here . . . and if you are an Englishwoman, as I was told . . . if you . . .

CAROLINE (*trying to compose herself*): Milord, may I inquire as to whom I have the pleasure of addressing? My father will be very happy to see a compatriot.

WILD: Your father? Miss! Do you have a father? Ah! Here! Here! That's so good, so brutally good. Yes, milady, I'm an Englishman . . . an unfortunate one. My name is Wild, and I am—yes, milady, at this moment—

CAROLINE (*suffering*): Wild? Aren't you from Yorkshire? Your face . . . your

158

. . . your . . . yes, milord, surely you must be from Yorkshire.

WILD: From Yorkshire? No! My soul is pounding so—ah, here I find what I have been seeking throughout the whole world. (*Taking her hand.*) You are an angel, milady, a marvelous, sensitive creation. (*Looking towards the heavens.*) You have saved such a moment for me! Let me speak! I feel it so deeply . . . your eyes . . . yes, your eyes full of soul and suffering . . . and this heart . . . torn in two and deeply, deeply unfortunate. I travelled here to let myself be killed in the next battle . . . and . . . and . . . I want to be killed.

CAROLINE: So confused . . . oh, sir, do you suffer?

WILD: Yes, unfortunately! Oh, suffering is so many-sided in man . . . often so wonderful . . . and if I may . . . milady's name?

CAROLINE: My father, milord, is Lord Berkley.

WILD (*starts back*): Lord Berkley! That is . . . the spitting image!

CAROLINE: What's the matter with you? Do you know the unfortunate Lord Berkley?

WILD: Know? No! And you are Jenny Caroline Berkley?

CAROLINE: Yes, sir. (*Looks about herself, in extreme consternation*): Oh, sir! Sir! Who are you?

WILD (*kneeling before her, still grasping her hand*): No, Miss, I am . . . my tongue is so weak, so much is in my heart. I am . . . Miss Berkley . . . (*Leaps up suddenly.*) the happy man who has searched the whole world for you. (*Drawing near the door.*) The unhappy man—

CAROLINE: Carl Bushy! My Carl!

WILD (*at the door*): Ah, here! Here! (*His arms reach out for her.*)

CAROLINE (*hurrying to him*): Carl Bushy, and you would leave me? Is it you? Is it you? Ah, just this word and then let my soul set you free!

WILD (*embracing her*): Yes, I am he! Jenny! I am Carl Bushy! I am the blissful—Jenny! Ah! I've found you!

CAROLINE: Let me gather my thoughts! The joy . . . the anguish . . . you are Carl . . . I believe . . . you are Carl Bushy!

WILD: What are you afraid of? Why do you kill the joy that pulsates through my whole body? I am he who, with your picture in my heart, sought you and your father in every corner of the earth.

CAROLINE: My father! My father! Save yourself! He hates Bushy and his son. Save yourself! Flee! Ah, forsake me! Flee! I haven't seen you.

WILD: I? Jenny! Flee? I am here in your presence, gaze here into your sweet eyes, and the first joy of my life has returned. Flee? Who will tear me away from here? All the wildness of my mind catches hold of me. Who will tear me away from here? Who will tear Carl Bushy from Miss Berkley? Let your father come! Are you not mine? Were you not mine from the first years of our childhood? I grew up with you, our hearts, souls and beings were one. You were engaged to me before you knew the meaning of the word. (*Coldly.*) I'm staying here, Miss! I'm staying here.

CAROLINE: You make me so afraid.

WILD: Should I go? Jenny! Jenny, I have you now.

CAROLINE: Leave me alone for a minute on the balcony.

WILD: Good, Miss! I'll stay here. Nothing will move me from here. Heaven has formed a bond between us that no human hand can sever. Here I'll wait for the enemy of your new fatherland. I'll await my enemy.

CAROLINE (*gently*): But not with this wild, disturbed look! Promise me not to reveal your name.

WILD: As you wish. Oh, Jenny! If you could feel for a moment the anguish that has driven this heart throughout the world! I have worn myself out; I wanted to destoy myself. Ah, this hour! This hour still remaining to me! And still all wretchedness? I wish to feel nothing, to sense nothing more. I have you now and defiance, defiance to the stubborn old mule!

CAROLINE: Why is this doubt, this frightening disturbance, this fury in your haunted eyes?

WILD: Your father! Yes, your father! My father—both ruined! Miss! I shall not leave you. It seizes me so violently! Yes, Jenny, fly away with me! Fly from this land with me! (*Embracing her.*)

CAROLINE: Let me be!

WILD: Is your father setting a trap for me? Oh, how good I feel in the midst of tumult! My darling!

CAROLINE: One moment, Carl! What if my father comes?

WILD: And still hates? Still the vindictive Berkley! My dear, sweet, little Miss! Thank God, who has showered so much of His grace on me in these violent emotions. Yes, Miss! Only love has held this machine together, which through its eternal inner war was so close at every moment to its own destruction.

CAROLINE: Good Carl! You are as always a wild, good youth. So have I imagined you. Oh, the years, the years, that have gone by! Can you really believe I was thirteen years old, and you fifteen, when we were torn apart from each other: I to this other half of the world. I came here; you were there. Yes, you were there, and where was there any spot in the world that you did not occupy?

WILD: And you! What now? How all of this tormented me! You are what I sought and required in the whole world to reconcile my heart. I found you, found you in America; where I sought death, I find peace and blessedness in these sweet eyes. (*Embraces her.*) And so I have you, so I have you, Miss Berkley! And hold you, and what Wild holds—I would strangle your father to possess you. But this is ecstasy, and it is gentle. (*Kisses her.*)

CAROLINE (*breaking free*): Frightening! Wild! Carl! Where is the look that gives me life for that?

WILD: Here, Miss! (*Kisses her.*)

Scene Five

BERKLEY. WILD. CAROLINE.

BERKLEY: Hm! Morning—Eh! What's this? What's going on here?

WILD (*rigid*): I was kissing milady.

BERKLEY: And you, Miss, you let it happen?

160

CAROLINE: Milord!

BERKLEY (*bitterly*): Adieu, Miss!

WILD: Milord, do you mean to insult me? I beg you, Miss, remain. It is not possible for Lord Berkley to insult a man he does not know. I am an Englishman, I am called Wild, and I wished to visit you.

BERKLEY: Well done, sir!

WILD: I have suffered in the world, I have suffered and my senses have become somewhat chaotic. They often seize me violently. A miserable man finds so little sympathy in the world: I found it in Miss, milord, and when one finds that—I kissed Miss and would have done so even if her father had been standing there the whole while.

BERKLEY: So young and yet so miserable? Look at me! At me, milord!

WILD: Yes, milord, so young and yet so miserable, and more miserable that I am lacking in patience, for my emotions are so strong. I have become bitter; only this moment have I felt that there was still joy in the world.

BERKLEY: I could take an interest in you. Please, sir, seat yourself in another light. I cannot bear certain features on your face.

CAROLINE: Oh, Father, milord suffers so much.

BERKLEY: You may leave us alone. I see that one can be honest with milord. All of his turbulent being speaks so sincerely.

CAROLINE: As you wish. (WILD *holds the door for her, nodding.*)

BERKLEY: As I was saying, milord—you must forgive me. I had an enemy, a horrible enemy, who reduced me to the most frightening condition in which an old man can be, and I saw you, milord. If I catch him, wherever it may be, I shall be compelled to torture him, until I see those features, which I criticized in you, disappear from his face. God knows, you seem to be a decent man! It takes all my strength not to fall upon you and press you to my heart as a son. But I also lost a son because of him. And so, milord, you must forgive me.

WILD: As you wish, as you wish.

BERKLEY: Yes, I understand this unease, this doubting tone in which you say that, and looks pass between us that could win one's heart. Have patience! One grows accustomed. If you are miserable and have tasted gall, we are then one.

WILD: That I have, milord—but what does this all mean? Now my supplication to you! Could you allow a man like me to join as a volunteer in the campaign against your enemy?

BERKLEY: With all my heart. Welcome! I shall go at once to the general. Come along!

WILD: I came for this very purpose. The sooner the better.

BERKLEY: Oh, milord! I have long hoped for such a day. I'm never better than when I'm in the midst of cannon fire.

WILD: It will be good for me, I hope.

BERKLEY: What part of England are you from?

WILD: London.

BERKLEY: Well then, you must know Lord Berkley's fate.

WILD: I have heard of it.

BERKLEY: Do not be so cold about it, young man.

161

WILD: I am not cold, milord, only angry at the people who could have made so many things different.

BERKLEY: Are you in your right mind? Man! Have you a heart? I am Lord Berkley, pursued, displaced, ejected, deprived of wife and son. Have you a heart, young man, or has your own misery made you callous? If so, then hold out your arm and bless the world. Do you know Bushy?

WILD: No, milord!

BERKLEY: Have you heard of him? I ask you, how are things with him? Miserable? Wretched?

WILD: Quite happy, milord.

BERKLEY: Fie on you! Happy! Have you seen my daughter? Do you see my gray hair, my crazed eyes? Happy?

WILD: He had to leave his house and property. He fell out of favor with the king and has become invisible.

BERKLEY: A thousand thanks, milord! A thousand thanks! Hey, Bushy! So I have been in part avenged! Is he really miserable? Well, he can't be wretched enough. Right? He has no home to give him shelter, no one to nurse him in his old age?

WILD: He is happy, milord!

BERKLEY: I must ask you to leave my room. You are a friend of him and thus my enemy. You have his way of speech, his bearing—by God! I see Bushy in you. Leave now unless you want to drive an old man into a rage.

WILD: Happy, in the sense that he doesn't care. Happy in his fashion, I mean.

BERKLEY: Well, he shouldn't be. His hair should become as stinging snakes, and the fibers of his heart as scorpions. Sir! He should not be able to sleep, nor wake, nor pray, nor swear. So would I like to see him. Then I would be magnanimous and put a bullet through his brain. What he's earned is eternal torment, but I would be magnanimous, sir, to please my daughter. If you had known my lady, milord, who died from heartache (*Grasps* WILD's *hand;* WILD *pulls it back at the last words.*) I know you would raise your hands with me and curse Bushy and his descendants. Tell me, milord, how goes it with Bushy's son?

WILD: He wanders through the world without rest. Miserable in himself, miserable at the fate of his father.

BERKLEY: That is good, milord! That is good! Do you think he's still alive?

WILD: He's in Spain now.

BERKLEY: But I can hope that his father will never see him again. I can hope that young Bushy will ruin his body through dissipation and rot away in the prime of his youth. He should never see him again, milord, the joy would be too great. To see his son again! Just think, to see his son again! What that must mean to a man! I could go mad. When I see my Harry, my sweet, stubborn son before me in my thoughts, riding on his nag, calling: Father! Father! and cracking his whip—he should never see him again! (WILD *is about to leave.*) Stay a moment, milord! Tell me, did Bushy come away with his wealth? Milord, if someone wanted to tell me eternally of Bushy's misfortune, I would want to do nothing in the world but listen. Has he come away with his wealth?

WILD: Enough, milord, to live contentedly in his calm fashion.

BERKLEY: I'm sorry to hear it. I wish I could see him begging me for a pound. Do you think I'd give it to him?

WILD: Why not, milord? He would give you what he had.

BERKLEY: Do you think so? If my Miss were standing by, perhaps. Perhaps not. Oh, he is a horrible hypocrite, old Bushy. I'm afraid he'd get a pound from me with his hypocritical mien. Isn't he a hypocrite, milord?

WILD: No, truly no!

BERKLEY: What would you know of it? Of course you take his part; you have his nose.

WILD: Milord, I'm going.

BERKLEY: Forgive me. But tell me only, where has the jealous Hubert wound up?

WILD: He accompanies old Bushy.

BERKLEY: Thank you, sir. Miserable?

WILD: There is stuff enough for his raw envy, so he finds himself well in his humour.

BERKLEY: Take care, sir! I won't stand for this! He must suffer as much as Bushy. I beg you, let him suffer! Lie to me! He suffers!

WILD: Now, milord, I must rejoin my friends. You'll see to it, that I am enlisted?

BERKLEY: Yes, milord. Farewell. You have made me very happy. Come back soon. This evening, for dinner. I could almost love you. (WILD *leaves.*) Now I feel well. Ha, ha! Bushy and Hubert, does it weigh heavily on you? Blessed be the king! Go! It gives me a right childish joy. That fellow there is only half to my taste. There is something so fatal and strong in his being, just like Bushy's. The devil knows! I must tell my niece this joy. (*Leaves.*)

Act Three
Scene One

Twilight
Same room as in Act One, Scene One
BLASIUS. LA FEU.

BLASIUS: Wild is so odd, so extraordinarily joyful. Dashes about, reaches toward heaven, as if he wanted to pull it down. I have seen tears shimmering in his eyes. What could be wrong with the man? I can't get him to stay in one place. I'm cold.

LA FEU: Dear, dear Blasius. I'm quite hot.

BLASIUS: You are the eternal fever.

LA FEU: Right, the eternal fever, or else I suffocate. I am again in love. Through my whole body, through veins and limbs, through my whole soul. I am so hot, I'm afraid I may go off like a bomb—if only then it would lift my pure being and lay it down in the bosom of the charming lady!

BLASIUS: The old lady? La Feu!

LA FEU: Old? Old? What is old? Nothing is old, nothing is young. I no longer know any difference. Oh, I am at the point when one begins to be well. Can you believe it, I have forgotten everything, as if I had drunk the waters of Lethe. Nothing bothers me any more. I could take up a crutch and go begging. One must become so at last.

BLASIUS: Oh, if only I were still sitting in the Tower!

LA FEU: Nothing bad can happen to one in the Tower. Oh, do me the pleasure and fling me inside. I want to dream so happily, so blessedly! Man must dream, dear, dear Blasius, if he wants to be happy and not think, not philosophize. In my youth, Blasius, I was a poet, I had ardent, roving fantasies. But they poured ice-water on me until the last spark was extinguished. The dreadful experience, the frightful masks of human faces, when one wants to embrace everyone with love! Here such derision! There Satan! I stood there like an extinct volcano. I travelled through an enchanted kingdom, cold and without receptive emotion. The most beautiful maidens had as little effect on me as the flies that buzz round the Tower. In order to be free from misery, my soul determined to feel differently and to see where it would stay cold. Everything is good now, everything is lovely and beautiful!

BLASIUS: If only I were sitting in the Tower again, where spiders, mice, and rats were my only society!

LA FEU: Were you sitting then in the Tower?

BLASIUS: Of course, of course. In a pretty tower, and looked through a hole that wasn't any larger than an eye. I could see light with only one eye. So I'd peer, first with one eye, and then the other, so as not to become shady. There a man can have sensations, La Feu! There the heart swells, and there the heart withers away—and the man dries up too. I could look at one spot for a whole day . . . and see . . . (*Stiff and distracted.*) Eh, what? In Madrid, La Feu, and in London. (*Bitter.*) Praised be the human race! Eh? They meant well with me. I was the most honest fellow in the world.

LA FEU: That was your failing, dear, dear Blasius.

BLASIUS: In Madrid the Inquisition did it because of my carriage. In London because I shot a fellow who robbed me of my money and wanted to rob me of my honor.

LA FEU: And rightly, Blasius! Dear Blasius! One must not shoot anyone.

BLASIUS: Oh, if only there were an end to mankind's feelings!

LA FEU: How are you getting on with the lady?

BLASIUS: Leave me alone! I have bored myself. She is merry and beautiful and cold as snow and as chaste as Diana's nightgown. She restrains one; I am dead and drowsy. (*Yawning.*) Good night, Donna Isabella! Oh, if I were sitting once again at your feet, most charming one! (*Falls asleep.*)

LA FEU: I must keep watch by the lady's window tonight. She is a quite charming lady, to whom one can say anything, and who understands a man before he speaks. But I want to write a fairy tale some day.

Scene Two

WILD. BLASIUS . LA FEU.

WILD (*enters in uniform*): How are you?

LA FEU: Good! Good, Wild. Blasius is sleeping and I am dreaming. I must send some verses to the lady.

WILD: Dearest La Feu! (*Embraces him.*) Dear Blasius! (*Embraces him.*)

BLASIUS: Hey, what's going on, then? Can't a man have any peace?

WILD: I have become well. Oh, my dear fellows! I have been restored.

BLASIUS: Good for you. I feel awful. (*Goes back to sleep.*)

WILD: May Heaven protect you. I want to pour out my soul into the air. (*Exits.*)

Scene Three

SEA CAPTAIN BOYET. INNKEEPER. LA FEU. BLASIUS. MOOR.

INNKEEPER: What do you wish, milord?

CAPTAIN: Nothing, nothing, except that you leave.

   (LA FEU *sits, writing in ecstasy.*)

CAPTAIN (*to his people*): You all clear off! Little boy, stay here! So, little fellow!

MOOR: Rough captain, what do you want?

CAPTAIN: Would you still let yourself be shot for me?

MOOR: Here I stand, good lord. You have caused me pain, to be sure. By the gods! You are sometimes as mad as a tiger, you lobster! See, on my back lie bruises as large as my fist, harsh lord!

CAPTAIN: Because I like you, little ape!

165

MOOR (*kissing his forehead*): Flay me! Pull my skin over my head, wild lord! I am your boy, your monkey, your Soley, your dog. (*Twisting around him.*) You have given my father life and freedom. (CAPTAIN *pinches him.*) Oh, ouch, why do you pinch me?

CAPTAIN: Because I like you. You want to be a midshipman, boy?

MOOR: Oh, lord, lord! A sword for me, and put yourself behind me when your enemy comes. Good lord! Tiger-fellow! Crazy lord! The blood in my body loves you and throbs under my skin.

CAPTAIN: Sugarcane from a moor-boy! You want some more blows?

MOOR: Do you want to be coaxed? Should I stroke your cheeks?

CAPTAIN: Did you see the ship, the one that sailed by?

MOOR: Yes, lord. Why did you attack?

CAPTAIN: Not to shrink before them. To laugh in their faces, and snatch it from under their noses.

MOOR: Ah, you got a cannon-shot, and the sailers and soldiers dead.

CAPTAIN: Go fill my pipe! Who wants to talk about that? Dead, boy, dead, that's all nothing. Are you afraid of death?

MOOR: While you live, yes. I would want to stay with you.

CAPTAIN: Now we are going to try things here. Death is afraid of me. Ten years I have faced it, and never a wound, except from that scoundrel of a Scot.

MOOR: If all the mothers and fathers you've made childless came together—

CAPTAIN: Gentle boy! You're not fit for the sea. Hold my pipe! Place a stool under my feet! (*Looks about.*) Hey, who's there? Boy, go thin out the people a bit. You are so useless. I tell you, boy, go rap the sleeper there on the nose. I won't have anybody sleep until I'm at rest. And the writer there, so wrapped up in himself—go bother him.

(*The* MOOR *raps* BLASIUS *on the nose. Goes over to* LA FEU *from behind, and snatches his quill, as he's writing.*)

LA FEU: The shimmer of your eyes! Hey, hey!

BLASIUS: Hmph! Hooligans all!

CAPTAIN: Gentlemen, I would like to make your acquaintance. Are you in the army?

BLASIUS: I'm nothing. (*Falls asleep.*)

CAPTAIN: That's a lot. And you?

LA FEU: Everything, everything.

CAPTAIN: That's not much. Come here, Mr. Everything! Let's wrestle a little, to put my joints in order. (*Grabs him.*)

LA FEU: Oh me, you centaur! That is no kind of fantasy! (*Sits down.*) "The shimmer of your eyes." Stupid rhymes! Eyes, dies, lies, buys—"Your body all men would buy!" Terrific!

CAPTAIN: Boy, give no one any peace and don't be afraid. The crazier you act the better. Go wake up the sleeper, boy. (*The* MOOR *does so.*)

BLASIUS: Lout! Ass! Wild! (*Flails about with his fists.*) Wild! If you don't leave me alone—

MOOR: A blow! A blow!

CAPTAIN: Wild! Sir! Where is he? Answer me!

BLASIUS: How should I know?

CAPTAIN: I can say this much to you: either you tell me where Wild is, or you'll

166

take a little walk with me.

BLASIUS: Let me alone, and I'll see if it pleases me.

CAPTAIN: If it pleases—! Sir!

BLASIUS: Yes, if it pleases me! Then you'll hear.

CAPTAIN: I like that. Well, I'll go look up the general. I brought a pretty ship with me. I rely on your word. It will be good to find you, Sir Wild! Come, boy.

MOOR: I follow.

BLASIUS: The dog! How in hell did the fellow wind up here? He's the ship's captain or the devil. I must find Wild. Nobody lets me sleep!

LA FEU: Just let me read this to you.

BLASIUS: Leave me alone!

LA FEU: I want to sing it at her window. You promised miladies a walk.

BLASIUS: Perhaps I'll come.

Scene Four

WILD. PRECEDING.

BLASIUS (*meets* WILD *and the* CAPTAIN *at the door*): I almost trudged off to no purpose. (*Sits silently.*)

(LA FEU *reads through his verses. The* MOOR *plays with toys.*)

CAPTAIN: A stroke of luck, that I find you here.

WILD: Good! Very good!

CAPTAIN: You know of course that I cannot stand you?

WILD: I haven't yet asked about it.

CAPTAIN: So, I shall show you. Eh, Scot! May the thunder strike me down, you shall not share God's air with me. Since the first sight of you, I have borne such a hatred for you that my fist grabs for sword and pistol when I see you from afar. Quick, boy, my weapon!

WILD: You know, Captain, that you are crude and offensive, and that I am guilty of no crime against you. You forced me to shoot you in Holland, and by my soul! It pained me to see you fall for no purpose.

CAPTAIN: Your bullet struck deep, but a bullet that stays in the flesh is no bullet and only inflames the human spirit. Believe me, when you fall I'll have my sailors pipe you a funeral song when the wind is at its wildest.

WILD: Thank you, Captain! As you wish.

CAPTAIN: Because I wish, and must! Because in my eyes you have such a toad-like, fatal appearance. Because when I see you, my sinews twitch as if one of the most hostile sounds bellowed in my ears.

WILD: I can tell you that I can put up with you. But nonetheless, even if I don't much care, I'll do it for a joke. I didn't particularly need to throw my life away today, but you're an honest man, and if we can't live in the same place, and I intend to stay here—

CAPTAIN: That is pretty! Know this, Scot! I must report now to the general, so we shall put our business off until tomorrow.

WILD: That's good too. So I'll see battle first.

CAPTAIN: And I with you. But the devil take you if you let yourself be shot. Take care! (*Leaves.*)

Scene Five

The garden. Moonlight.
LADY CATHERINE *and* LOUISA, *walking.*

LOUISA: The evening air, dear Aunt! You're coughing so dreadfully.

CATHERINE: Coughing! Stupid thing! Coughing! Ha, ha! Now really, child, oh, child! (*Coughing throughout.*)

LOUISA: Well, what then?

CATHERINE: It would be a beautiful gift, if you would tell—

LOUISA: Oh, because I'm bored I'll tell you that never in my life have I seen two more tactless boors than the two strangers. I could say that again.

CATHERINE: Tactless boors? Ha, ha! La Feu! Sweet, English, Milord La Feu! A cherub among men! Ha, ha, Niece! A splendid gift it would be if you would help me praise him. Sit down, let's go through all his endearing traits as the night slips away, and when the sun rises, let's begin again.

LOUISA: Yes, Wild, Auntie! Wild! Have you seen him? I saw him sneaking through the bushes earlier. Wild, Auntie!

CATHERINE: Not Wild! La Feu! Did you see his eyes?

LOUISA: They are, I believe, somewhat dried up, dull, and weak. At least I didn't see any fire or shine within.

CATHERINE: I beg of you, look at those stars! The shimmering, the glittering—his eyes!

LOUISA: Oh, really!

CATHERINE: Aren't you paying attention to what I say? Oh, he speaks! Love makes poets, and poets make such comparisons. The splendor of his eyes, the splendor of the stars—and his hair!

LOUISA: We haven't yet agreed on his eyes. Blasius has killed all my cheerfulness with his stupid boredom. Have I stopped having an effect on men, then?

CATHERINE: His hair, Niece! So blond, so sweetly blond!

LOUISA: He was wearing a wig.

CATHERINE: A wig! Ha, ha! Amor in a wig! How can you be so poorly observant, faced with such beauties? No, your taste is not the best.

LOUISA (*annoyed*): His hair is brick-red.

CATHERINE: Leave me alone, you willful little thing! And you must not keep calling me Aunt when I'm in the throes of love-talk. Say instead: milady.

LOUISA: Where on earth are they? They promised to go walking with us in the moonlight.

CATHERINE: Just wait, La Feu will certainly come.

168

LOUISA: Auntie! Do you know that I spoke with Wild? He came this way and could not and would not get out of the way. I was quite aloof and asked him his name. Then he stammered very confusedly that his name was Wild, as though it were a lie. I have my own ideas about that. He had been alone so long with Miss Berkley. He's in love with her, by all the stars! In love with her! He turned away from me so coldly, and streaked past me like a raw wind.

CATHERINE: Blasius is in love with you.

LOUISA: Oh, him! If we only knew who he was, this Wild.

CATHERINE: La Feu will surely know. We'll ask him.

Scene Six

LA FEU. LOUISA. LADY CATHERINE.

LA FEU (*from some distance*): Do I not find you, my love? Where are you, that I might lay this song at your feet? To sing out to you the hymn of praise to your charms! To wreathe your fragrant hair!

LOUISA: Your Adonis is calling.

CATHERINE: Quiet! Let him speak! Oh, the words of love are more valuable than frankincense.

LA FEU: I've been wandering the garden back and forth searching for you, my love.

LOUISA: Milord.

CATHERINE: Unfriendly girl! But he didn't hear you. Milord!

LA FEU: Ah, this tone inflames my blood. (*Rushes to her.*) Ah, milady! Hours have I wandered about in love-drunk fantasy. I have braided you a wreath, heavenly Venus! Walk now in the woods, bewreathed by love. (*Crowns her.*)

LOUISA: To the madhouse with the fool!

CATHERINE: Oh, milord! How pleasant! How very happy I am!

LA FEU: Happy? Yes, happy! With love, everything is happy; without love, everything is sad. I have established monuments to love that will never decay, even though my heart should decay.

CATHERINE: Oh, milord! Your heart will never decay.

LOUISA: You're coughing more and more, Auntie! Ask him!

CATHERINE: Yes, milord, a question for you. Would you please tell us the real name of your companion Wild?

LA FEU: Wild? Is he still here? Isn't he in the war?

CATHERINE: Not yet, milord. Tomorrow.

LA FEU: Happy journey.

CATHERINE: But he is in love with my niece.

LA FEU (*pointing to* LOUISA): With milady?

LOUISA (*annoyed*): No, milord!

CATHERINE: I implore you, by all the gods of love! Tell me his real name.

169

LA FEU: If I can remember it. Hm! You really want to know this?

CATHERINE: Of course! Now!

LA FEU: I have no memory, milady! I mean, he chased off a servant who betrayed it. I think he's forbidden me to tell.

CATHERINE: No, surely not.

LA FEU: You know? I just can't think of it . . . Carl, I think.

LOUISA: Go *on*, milord.

LA FEU: Bu . . . Bu . . . oh, my memory! Carl . . . Bu . . . Bu . . .

LOUISA: Bushy, milord?

LA FEU: Yes, yes, Bushy! I think so.

LOUISA: Now we've got it! Her Carl! Her Bushy!

CATHERINE: My brother must be told.

LA FEU: Eh, take care. No one but you must know. Come now, let's dance the dance of love in the moonlight. (*Leaps up with her.*)

CATHERINE: Oh, milord!

LOUISA: I shall go along to annoy them. (*They exit down a lane.*)

Scene Seven

WILD enters.

WILD: The night lies so cool, so good about me! The clouds drift by so quietly! Ah, otherwise how cheerless and gloomy everything was! It is good, my heart, that you can again catch this pure feeling of awesomeness; good that the night air sighs around you, and you feel love wafted through the vast stillness of Nature. Shimmer, stars! Ah, we have become friends again! You are carried with almighty love, as is my heart, and you twinkle in pure love, as does my soul. You were so cold to me in the mountains! And when my love spoke to you, and heavy tears gushed forth, you vanished before my wet eyes, as I cried out: "Jenny, my life! Where are you, light of my eyes?" So often have I clung to you, moon, but it went dark around me, as I reached for her, who was so far away. Ah, that everything is so woven together, so bound together by love. It is good that you again understand the rustling of the trees, the gushing of the stream, the babbling of the brook; that all the tongues of Nature are clear to you now. Take me into your lovely coolness, friend of my love! (*Lies under a tree.*)

Scene Eight

CAROLINE. WILD.

CAROLINE (*opening the window*): Night! Still night! Let me entrust it to you. Let me entrust it to you, meadows! Valleys! Hills and forests! Let me entrust it to you, moon and all you stars! No longer to cry over him, no longer to sigh over him. I wander under your light, my former sad friend! No longer in wailing do you answer me, Echo, you that knew no other sound but his name—Carl! Does not that ring sweetly through the night? Carl! Do not my flowers nod to me happily? Do not the winds hurry to carry my call to his ear? You should rejoice with me, lonely little place. I want to entrust it to you, gloomy place. (*She becomes aware of* WILD'*s presence.*) And you who lie there buried in the shadows, darling eavesdropper!

WILD: Life! My life!

CAROLINE: Friend of my heart!

WILD: On the wings of love I come to you. (*Climbs up the tree.*)

CAROLINE: Be careful, my dearest, the branches are bending.

WILD: Let them bend, the swayings of love are strong. (*Reaching for her hand.*) Miss! My Miss!

CAROLINE: Don't be so foolhardy! Don't trust those limbs!

WILD: I hang on your eyes. Let me breathe! Grant me that I may feel, that I may say what it is, this moment. Ah, all you sad nights, how you have disappeared! Heaven, you have wiped them all out, you have brought me here! Miss! Dear Jenny! How are you? Speak to me, my love, why are you hiding your sweet eyes from me?

CAROLINE: Speak! Oh, speak!

WILD: Tears, my love?

CAROLINE: The first tears of joy.

WILD: My best, my love!

CAROLINE: And also tears of grief! Wild! What have you done? Oh, light, retreat! Unhappy man, what have you done?

WILD: Jenny, your knees are shaking. What's wrong with you?

CAROLINE: This coat, tomorrow morning—oh, you and my father! Why do you chase death when you needn't?

WILD: To be worthy of you. Forget this coat! I feel so good in it now. Forget it. This wish also satisfied!

CAROLINE: Alas! Death!

WILD: Death! And love envelops me. Let me wander in the valley of death; love will lead me back.

CAROLINE: And its message leads me to you.

Scene Nine

LA FEU, BLASIUS, LADY CATHERINE, *and* LOUISA *come along the lane.*
CAROLINE. WILD.

LOUISA: What is that on that tree there?

CAROLINE: I hear my cousin, Carl! You must leave!

WILD: Let her come! I'll see you again. (*Springs down. Remains at the window in deep inner thought.*) Tomorrow! Yes, tomorrow! And what now then, if I lie stretched out! This heart has felt all that creation offers, all that a man can feel. Oh, this night! This night! And the coming day! I shall see you again! And your image stays with me and leads me along—I shall see you again. (*Fixedly, to heaven.*) I shall see her again! I'll see you again, as now! So sure as the bond that ties you to me! I shall see her again! Lie here, and my breast swells. (*They come nearer.*)

LOUISA: Did you see that, Aunt? He was there, and so was she! They were together, I say. Did you see him? Did you see her? Do you see him? Oh, I would like to pull away the moonlight, the vile man!

CATHERINE: Does this concern me? Come, to my brother, we want to tell him—

LA FEU: What, milady? You want to go? When the night is becoming more and more fantastic? The music of the spheres sounds more and more charming. (BLASIUS *sits down.*)

LOUISA: Well, milord?

BLASIUS: I am so tired . . . can't move another step. The walk is so wet and cold, I'm going to be sick—

LOUISA: Shame on you, milord. You could at least keep quiet.

BLASIUS: Yes, quiet, quiet . . . fire is fire and tired is tired. (*Rises.*)

LOUISA: Let's walk past him. (*They all walk past* WILD. *He takes no notice.*) What impertinence!

Act Four
Scene One

Night. BERKLEY's *room, as before.*
BERKLEY. SERVANT.

BERKLEY: Tomorrow, battle. Ha, ha, ha! That's really something, a battle. Conduct yourself bravely, old lord! Sleep well tonight! Ha, ha!
SERVANT: Milord, there is a gentleman outside.
BERKLEY: So late. Let him come in. Sir Wild?
SERVANT: No, he said he was a sea captain.
BERKLEY: Treat him with every consideration, if he is the captain who brought along the ship. (SERVANT *leaves.*)

Scene Two

CAPTAIN. MOOR. BERKLEY.

CAPTAIN: Milord! The innkeeper told me that an Englishman lived here. I couldn't go to bed without seeing you.
BERKLEY: Welcome, a thousand times welcome. Good, wild, seaman!
CAPTAIN: Welcome! I paid you a compliment when I arrived. A rich, English ship, milord. By the way, I'm tired. (*The* MOOR *stands behind him and plays with his hair.*)
BERKLEY: Lie down, sit down. As you wish.
CAPTAIN: Thank you. (*Stares at him.*) Yes, milord, I'd like to—if I have arrived at my goal. I traveled the whole world through—
BERKLEY: It's good, sir, that I see you. You do my soul good. I must kiss you, sir!
CAPTAIN: Milord! All my stubborn wildness dissolves in your presence.
BERKLEY: Good! Kind! Spirit of my Harry! Are you staying here? For whom are you looking, sir?
CAPTAIN: An old man. Heaven will swear I have travelled ten years on the sea; I'll be lost until I find him.
BERKLEY: Harry? Is it you? You have his soul, you have his—Harry! I shall call him out of you.
CAPTAIN: Milord, who are you?
BERKLEY: Who am I? God in heaven! In heaven! Harry! Harry! You are—
CAPTAIN: Harry Berkley—
BERKLEY: My son—
CAPTAIN: Father, my father! (*Embraces him.*)
BERKLEY: My Harry! Eh, my boy! Let me hold you then in my arms! Oh, my Harry! I am so happy, my eyes cloud over.

173

CAPTAIN: Oh, my father! I have travelled the world searching for you. I have crawled across every island.

BERKLEY: Yes, indeed, you are he. You have the wildness, the tumult of Berkley. The rolling, threatening eyes, the fixedness, the unshakeableness, the resolution. Hey, Harry! Harry! Let me now truly rejoice! So gallant a seaman, my Harry! To bring us a ship and my Harry!

CAPTAIN: Oh, my father! That I have, ha, ha.

BERKLEY: I am crazy with joy. I must rest a bit. Joy weakens me so, my limbs cannot support me any longer. (*Sits.*)

CAPTAIN (*embraces him*): Unhappy father, what you must have suffered!

BERKLEY: If you only . . . if you only . . . you are here now. I have suffered nothing. No, I can't sit. Caroline! Caroline! Miss! Miss! For God's sake, Miss!

CAPTAIN: My sister!

BERKLEY: Harry! Caroline! You are here! (*To Heaven.*) You have given them back to me! Given them back to this heart! I cannot cry now. There he stands—oh, my Harry!

CAPTAIN: My father, the words do not come. But where is my sister? And my mother?

BERKLEY: Mother! Mother! Harry! Oh, Berkley, your wife—Miss! Miss!

Scene Three

CAROLINE. PRECEDING.

BERKLEY (*to* CAROLINE): Will you cry out? Will you shout and leap up?

CAROLINE: Milord!

BERKLEY: He's there! There! There! There he is!

CAPTAIN (*embraces her*): My sister, my dearest!

CAROLINE: Mine! Mine!

BERKLEY: I can say nothing for tears and joy, Harry! Ah, you cannot speak, it makes you so happy. Ha, ha! What are you seeing, old man? Oh, my children! (*Embraces them.*) Now may heaven give you your son again too, old Bushy!

CAROLINE: Oh, milord! This wish makes your daughter very happy.

MOOR (*kneels before* BERKLEY *and* CAROLINE): Old man, I am your slave. Good Miss, I am your slave.

CAPTAIN: So, boy!

BERKLEY: Stand up, Blackie! Give me your paw!

MOOR: God bless you! I am yours as I stand here. And yours, lady!

CAROLINE: You shall be satisfied with me. Dear brother! Dear Harry! How could you let us cry so long for you?

BERKLEY (*To the* CAPTAIN): Speak! Tell us!

CAPTAIN: My mother, milord! I don't see my mother. I have brought so much for her, and for you, Miss. Where is my mother?

BERKLEY: Only enjoy yourself now!

CAROLINE: Dearest! Best! (*Cries.*)

CAPTAIN: You're crying? Dead! Eh, girl? Out with it! Dead?

BERKLEY: Yes, dead! By heaven! An angel of God! Oh, I could go mad, that my lady doesn't stand here among us, like a shade-giving, refreshing tree, laying her hands on your heads, and blessing you. Dear, gentle woman! Did you look down to see your old lord, lying among thorns, walking the raw path of grief? Look down now! That she is not here among us! Damn Bushy! May he never see his son! Because of him, I've lost her!

CAPTAIN: My mother dead? Dead because of him? Cursed thought of mine, to give him to the sea!

BERKLEY: Gave him to the sea? What?

CAROLINE: Brother! My brother! Speak!

CAPTAIN: Revenge, Father! On Bushy and Hubert. Ha! I was only a boy, but I sensed what they did to us, and avenged you before I found you.

BERKLEY: You did? Sweet child! Harry! Harry! How! How, sweet youth?

CAROLINE: But they're not dead, Brother?

CAPTAIN: Of course they are. Of course.

CAROLINE: That! That! God in heaven! (*Sinks into a chair.*)

CAPTAIN: What's wrong with the child? Eh, Miss?

BERKLEY: I'll wake her up. Hey, Miss! Miss! Bushy, our enemy! He is dead! Are you awake? I would wake from the dead if I heard such news. We are avenged, Miss!

Scene Four

WILD. PRECEDING.

WILD: Milord! You sent for me— (*Catching sight of* CAROLINE.) Miss!

CAPTAIN: Hey, what the hell does the Scot want? Tomorrow we'll be shooting each other.

WILD: Miss . . . Jenny . . . what's going on?

BERKLEY: Eh, milord! So much joy—unfortunate man—so much joy! This is my son, sir!

WILD: The captain? Well, then! That too . . . Miss! Dear Miss!

CAROLINE: Wild! Wild! Please go away!

BERKLEY: Still one joy, milord. Still another joy. Be merry, I forgive you for the way you look. My son here has killed old Bushy. He is dead, milord, my friend! What, no joy? Why are your eyes so fixed? Milord!

CAROLINE: Father!

CAPTAIN: I set him adrift—God knows, in one of the most dreadful storms I have ever experienced at sea—with Hubert in a tiny fishing-boat. It was night and thundering awfully; the winds blew over the sea with such a musical roar that my heart pounded in response. What bothered me was that they didn't move a muscle. If they had prayed and beseeched, then by all the elements, I would perhaps have hanged them, or left them on a desert island, for just then the sea surged so high that I wouldn't have trusted my dog to it. They disappeared from my sight almost the moment they got into the boat. Only when there was lightning could I see them struggling in the distance. It howled so bitterly about me that I could not have the pleasure of seeing them swallowed by the sea, or of hearing their laments. But the storm was no joke.

CAROLINE: It is getting so cold. (*Sinks down dully.*) So dead—

BERKLEY: Hey, then! What are you doing? Truly there's a pounding deep in my heart.

WILD: In you, milord? And what of me? Ha! Awaken in me—you are so stiff! So wooden. Hey, hey, hey! Miss, hey! Awaken with me! Hey, hey, hey! It's really cold!

CAPTAIN: What chills you then, Scot?

WILD (*draws his sword*): Draw your sword! Hey! Draw your sword! Or I'll strangle you in my fever, and tear out your heart with my teeth! And you, old man, eh? Cold! Am I cold? Does my hand tremble? Hey! It reaches for a gun, and will not rest until you lie there and I suck the life from your blood. Am I cold?

CAPTAIN (*draws his sword*): Hey, Scot! If you can't wait any long—

BERKLEY: What? Why are you fighting? What? (*Also draws his sword.*)

CAROLINE: Father! Brother! Wild! (*Sinks into* WILD's *arms.*)

CAPTAIN: What has the girl to do with the Scot? Get away! Don't be surprised, Father. We have fought before. I have sworn eternal hate towards him.

BERKLEY: Eternally, eternally. He so resembles Bushy.

CAPTAIN: Will you wait for morning, to shoot face to face?

WILD: Yes, yes, of course. See only this heart! Only this brain! (*Strikes him on the head.*)

CAPTAIN: Are you mad?

CAROLINE: Father! Must I die here then?

BERKLEY: I want—

Scene Five

LADY CATHERINE. LOUISA. PRECEDING.

CATHERINE: Good evening, Brother! What do all these swords mean? Ay, God! You could frighten a body. It gives me great pleasure to introduce to you Sir Wild Carl Bushy, your daughter's fiancé.

BERKLEY: Carl Bushy?

LOUISA: Yes, yes, Uncle dear! Quite definitely. His friend La Feu told us everything.

CAPTAIN: Wasn't my feeling justified? Wasn't the impression he made on me right? You have lived too long!

WILD: I am he. Cease to be men! See in me your murderer! And this one is

176

mine, old man! (*Takes* CAROLINE *in his arms.*)

BERKLEY: She hates you, now that she knows who you are. Will the Miss soon disappear from before my eyes? Harry! I could never stand him. What shall we do to him? (*Embraces* CAROLINE.) No, I shall do nothing to him, Harry.

CATHERINE: Harry! Harry? What's going on?

BERKLEY: This is my son. Enough joy! Now get out of here!

LOUISA: Fine thing, now that he's here.

CATHERINE: Just remember! Mountains and valleys may not come together, but men can. Good evening, Harry.

BERKLEY: Just go!

CAROLINE (*pleading*): Father! Brother!

BERKLEY: Get her out of here!

(LADY CATHERINE, LOUISA, *and* CAROLINE *leave.*)

WILD: Good night, Miss. We'll see one another again.

CAPTAIN: Oh? Certainly not here.

WILD: So you set him adrift on the sea, the righteous Bushy?

CAPTAIN: On the sea, the righteous Bushy.

WILD: In the middle of a storm?

CAPTAIN: In the middle of a storm, Carl Bushy!

WILD: You didn't do that, Captain!

CAPTAIN: By Satan, I did!

WILD: A weak old man?

CAPTAIN *and* BERKLEY: It was Bushy!

WILD (*jeering*): Oh, let me fall at your feet, Alexander the Great! With only a ship full of men, you were able to overpower two feeble old men. Those are trophies! And they didn't raise a hand against you? Didn't open their mouths? From this I recognize Bushy. Should I now begin to sing your victory song? I shall, by Bushy's blood! I shall, gallant hero! A ship filled with men, and two feeble old men! Ha, ha, ha! Oh, villain! Villain! What a great deed!

CAPTAIN: Villain?

WILD: Of course! Worse! Coward! Old Berkley! You should be very proud of having raised such a son! Be proud of your deeds! By God, they are great! And great deeds deserve great rewards. Hee, hee! Just wait, Captain! I'll sing ballads about it in the streets of London, as soon as the tale of murder reaches its end. Hey, hey!

CAPTAIN: Wild! By all the devils, I'll run you through!

WILD: Hee, hee! But wait till I've put my sword away.

MOOR (*to* WILD): Man! If you didn't look so fierce, I'd want to show you something that I stole from one of the old men. A little picture of a white woman. I tore my kinky hair out over the old man, it hurt me so. The old man was good. Here it is!

CAPTAIN: Boy! (*Approaches him.*)

MOOR: Oh, woe!

WILD: He *was* good, boy! (*Kisses him.*) He was good!

MOOR: He was so kind to me! I was ill, and for a whole week he held me against his bosom, and stroked my hot head, and comforted me, until the captain found him.

177

WILD: All that! Oh, lad! (*Looking at the picture.*) Mother! My mother! Mother most sweet! If there be nothing more of love in me, ignite the last sparks of passion and let them flare up in wrath and thirst for revenge! Hey, my mother! Till another time! I thank you, boy!

MOOR (*secretly*): I have more to say to you.

CAPTAIN: Boy! What are you doing?

MOOR (*at his feet*): Here! (*Laying his hands on his breast.*) I must!

WILD: In the middle of a storm! Why are you sitting there? Do you brood about the cowardly killing? Captain! I will be honorable against you. It was good of you to tell me how vilely you behaved; else I would have knocked you down just now in my inexplicable coldness. I will not attack you unarmed. And so tomorrow. But I cannot sleep until you lie there stretched out! Then shall I fling you into the sea with shouts of joy by Carl Bushy! I shall!

CAPTAIN: I'll be there tomorrow morning!

BERKLEY: First you should come with me to the battle.

WILD: Yes, old man, yes! The battle. (*To the* MOOR.) Good night, boy. If you think of attacking me tonight with some hundred men, feel free—I'll be on guard.

BERKLEY: Won't you stay to dinner?

WILD: Only a cannibal's dinner, milord! I'm hungry for the captain's flesh. (*Leaves.*)

CAPTAIN: Wait till I've gone rotten.

BERKLEY: Come, my son, let's have dinner.

CAPTAIN: I shall not rest until the man is gone from this world. The sight of him oppresses me. I was his enemy from the outset, even before I knew him.

BERKLEY: He is a Bushy! That is enough. But for now let Bushy be Bushy. Come to my heart, you my life!

Scene Six

The garden
BLASIUS. LA FEU. *Both sitting on the edge of the lawn.*

BLASIUS: Are you going to stay here all night, La Feu?

LA FEU: Let me be. Night does me so much good, my heart feels so reborn—

BLASIUS: Oh, under the heavens here, to breathe my last this hour! I feel well, now that I have firm hold of that thought again, and it has turned to feeling and deep emotion. Blessed be thou, Earth, thou that open'st thyself to us so maternally, taking us into thy arms and protecting us! Ah! If the moon wanes, the stars still shimmer above me. I lie lulled to sleep . . . a deep, sweet sleep. I shall still have this feeling. Thou shalt be with me there, I shall be with thee. Let the storm rage, the winds howl about me. Thou givest peace to thy son. Most gracious mother, my pilgrimage is at an end. I have walked through thorns; I have also known joy. Here I am again!

LA FEU: Oh, Blasius, heavenly Blasius! Here, on your bosom, on your heart, with you I imbibe . . .

BLASIUS: Love! Unfortunate ones, all those I have abandoned, don't cry for me! Forget me! I could give you no peace, no help. I had none. Forgive me! How many thousands of times was my heart torn to pieces, how many thousands of times did my soul tremble, when I was so beaten by mankind, so beaten by the wrath of fate? I could not leave here, I could not leave there. I had courage enough to climb mountains, but they soon snapped my power in two. Oh, who here has too much heart, too much feeling! Oh, woe! Lovely air, give me love. La Feu! I feel at this moment no uneasiness. I feel this hour as they must feel who are about to abandon the earth, they whom I always believed to be the most marvelous. My heart trembles so . . . this passing feverish heat . . . ah, the illness of the soul! Good night, Brother! Good night, Brother Wild! And all good souls who sigh here and there! Thank you for this moment! Good night!

LA FEU: Blasius! Blasius!

Scene Seven

WILD *enters, with drawn sword.* PRECEDING.

BLASIUS: Wild! Brother!

LA FEU: What's with you? Oh, dreadful man, don't disturb my soul!

BLASIUS: I beg you, Brother! Leave my heart in peace! You're killing me! What's happened to you?

WILD: What's happened to me? Is everything so different with me? Ha! Everything has withered and died! Father! My father!

BLASIUS: Wild, dear Wild!

WILD: Go away! What do you want from me!

LA FEU: What is the matter with you?

WILD: No answer from me! I am nothing to you or the world until I have revenge! Most terrible revenge! Leave now! And you! Have you power over your tongue? Leave now, if you don't wish to succumb to me!

LA FEU: Brother, I am innocent!

WILD: So go then!

BLASIUS: Now I collapse into myself again, Brother!

WILD: Leave me to the barren insensibility in which you see me! (BLASIUS *and* LA FEU *exit.* WILD *remains, facing* CAROLINE'*s window.*)

179

Act Five
Scene One

BERKLEY's *room*
CAROLINE. BETTY.

CAROLINE: Betty, dear Betty! Is it not yet over then?

BETTY: No, Miss! All my limbs are trembling. I still hear shooting. But not so much now. They say we've won. Oh, God, so many wounded are coming! So many fine people, Miss! There's one with only half a head. It could break your heart.

CAROLINE: I have courage, Betty! Do you not sense that I have courage?

BETTY: Miss! You tremble as much as I. The dear, old lord! And the captain! And the foreign lord!

CAROLINE: Betty!

BETTY: If one of them were killed, I'd tear my hair out.

CAROLINE: Betty!

BETTY: Oh, you're going to faint, yes you are.

CAROLINE: Just leave me alone! Every shot that I heard struck one of them, struck me. Leave me alone, Betty!

BETTY: I'll go see if it's over yet. (*Leaves.*)

CAROLINE (*alone*): Oh, this night, this night! This morning! How have my tender fibers held up? Where did this strength come from? I was about to flee with him! To let him take revenge, and then flee with him! How did this thought come into my soul? How did it fill me so completely? Ah, how he stood before me in torturous, furious pain. His suffering clouded his senses and made him wild. To let him go from me in this torment! And now perhaps his strength is shattered, his heart turned cold—Carl!

Scene Two

MOOR. CAROLINE.

MOOR (*enters, crying*): I can't find any of them. Ah, my lord, to leave me alone! And I can't find the other good lord, whom I had so much to tell. Wretched boy that I am!

CAROLINE: Good boy! Good morning.

MOOR: Yes, Miss. When I woke up, it was truly delightful. I had spent the whole night visiting with my father Zukai and my mother. You don't know them. Oh, you should know him, and how their neighbors love them and their enemies fear them. They didn't want me to leave, and gave me all sorts of things to eat. Now I am sad.

CAROLINE: Poor boy!

MOOR: Good Miss! Where was I? What is all the banging for? Don't you know then where the lord is, with whom my lord and his father are so angry? He was as sad as you, and I wanted to make him happy.

CAROLINE: You? Him?

MOOR: Yes, me. What his name is, I don't know. But it's because of his father. I can't tell you, Miss, even though you are good and would not betray me. I've seen them. Hurrah! The old man embraced me! See, Miss, he kissed me and my cheeks were wet, and my chest was so tight I could not get enough air. He is quite well, the old man.

CAROLINE: *Who* is, boy?

MOOR: Be quiet, Miss! Quiet! You could have almost heard it from me; I was prattling it all out. Your father doesn't like him, and there would be no end of the beating and brawling for me. Listen! Someone's coming. That's good. I want to find my lord.

CAROLINE: Come with me!

MOOR: I can help you cry, Miss. Ah, I often have to cry! You teach us blacks very early how to cry. But then you are laughing. (*Leaves.*)

CAROLINE: You shall not cry, boy, with me.

Scene Three

LA FEU, LADY CATHERINE *enter, both bedecked fantastically with flowers.*

LA FEU: Oh, golden time! Oh, marvelousness! Ah, the eternal, the eternal spring morning in my sick heart! See, my love! I should like to metamorphose my entire future life into a poetic, Arcadian dream, far away from everybody. We would sit by a cool fountain, under the shade of the trees, hand in hand, singing the wonders of the heart and of love. That, milady, would be the only way to forget all my tragic, past situations. We would not complain about men, nor speak of them bitterly, as Blasius does; no, eternal joy should prevail in us, with us, and in everything around us. What men have done to me I forgive as sincerely as I love you. Heaven has given me sensations with which I could never continue to live among men. Of course they have ground me down, but, milady, still a corner of this heart remains uncorrupted. It has now come forward, and may Heaven forgive him who would disturb me and call me perverse.

CATHERINE: I don't understand yet.

LA FEU: Ah, then I shall place my whole feeling in your soul! My Diana! We should dream forever a sweet, gentle dream, ever as sweet as the first kiss of love. But fantastically! A kingdom of flowers!

CATHERINE: You bewitch me!

LA FEU: I am disposed to become a shepherd. That has been my idea for a long time. I lacked only a shepherdess, and that I have found in you, lovely soul!

CATHERINE: Oh, milord! And sheep, a shepherd's hut, a shepherd's crook, and shepherd's clothes—white with red trim! I brought just such a costume from London. I could die from joy at your sweet thoughts.

181

LA FEU: I'll dress as an innocent shepherd. We'll buy a flock. Wild will give us one of his dogs. We shall fantasize our lives away. To live eternally in peace, eternally in love! Oh, the blessedness!

CATHERINE: Milord! Milord! And sheep too?

LA FEU: Yes, milady. And a little hut as well. I am your shepherd!

CATHERINE: And also—ha, milord—to marry?

LA FEU: God forbid! Everything spiritual, everything fantastic. That is the charm of it. Only one thing more. What sort of names should we take to befit our innocent condition?

CATHERINE: Oh, endearing ones, milord!

LA FEU: Oh, of course, very endearing. I'll be Damon, and you Phyllis.

CATHERINE: Yes, milord! I have always loved those names in poetry. I'll be Phyllis. Let's go make the preparations at once.

Scene Four

BLASIUS. LOUISA. PRECEDING.

LOUISA: Oh, Aunt! I have a headache. I'm not well. Blasius is as silent as a fish, and when he speaks he tortures his listener. He keeps speaking of marriage.

CATHERINE: Fie!

BLASIUS: I only said, we're ideally suited to it. Because when we're together, I am bored, and Miss is bored. To have this and to endure this is part of marriage. Our virtuosity consists then in that—

LOUISA: Why do you go on? I must tell you that I am thoroughly tired of you. You have driven me beside myself through your disagreeable conduct. I have started boring myself. Before, I was a creature of genuine cheer, genuine merriment, one day after another, but you have spoiled everything. Now go!

BLASIUS: Miss! Truly, your face is often a bright ray of sunshine to me! Let me look at it sometimes. Just don't talk!

LOUISA: So! If I tried it you'd take a nap in the sunshine!

BLASIUS: Try to understand.

LOUISA: Shame on you!

BLASIUS: Hm! Hm! I'm getting tense again, may God have mercy on me.

LOUISA: Aunt! We want to play. No, dance! Do you dance, milord?

BLASIUS: Oh, agony!

LOUISA: It's so stupid—those men there.

CATHERINE: I have so much to tell you, dear, so much. Just think, we are going to become shepherds. La Feu a shepherd and I a shepherdess.

LOUISA: Ha, ha, ha!

BLASIUS: Good for you. La Feu! Prosperity and good luck!

LA FEU: Yes, Brother! I want to dream until my dying day.

BLASIUS: Be well. I shall become a hermit. I have tracked down a beautiful, overgrown cave. I want to close myself and my remaining feeling off there, and begin anew the life we abandoned on the Alps. Heaven and Earth have become friends with me this night, as well as all of Nature.

LOUISA: Hee, hee! Let us play, and do what you want.

BLASIUS: What are these alarums, drums, and tumult? My senses have fled me.

CATHERINE: They're returning from the war, milord!

LOUISA: The poor people! How bored they must be with shooting!

Scene Five

BERKLEY. CAPTAIN, *limping*. PRECEDING.

BERKLEY: Laugh, youth, laugh! Ha, ha, it was hot. It was fierce!

CAPTAIN: The devil take me, if I ever fight on land again. The water, Father! By all the elements, he who can swim, let him swim and stay away from land. Somebody get this bullet out of my leg! May thunder strike dead the land war! Somebody get this bullet out of my leg, the damned thing is throbbing. I've nearly bled to death, I can hardly stand.

BERKLEY: Is that anything to whimper about? Where is my child? My Jenny?

LA FEU: But how did milord wind up with a bullet in the back of his leg? Were you running away?

CAPTAIN: Go to hell with your questions, Mr. Nosey!

CATHERINE: Not so harsh, Nephew! Come, milord. We want to put our affairs in order.

LA FEU: Yes, dear lady. (*They leave, as do* BLASIUS *and* LOUISA.)

CAPTAIN: I'm glad that they're gone. Oh, Neptune, I'm your sea-dog! They shot devilishly at our wings, Father. Wild must have made a pact with Satan. The damned presence, solidity, and strength in the man--this stupid bullet! Father! Join me on my ship! We will be privateers for the colonies. That damned Wild!

BERKLEY: I can tell you, Harry, I have developed a great respect for Wild, and an even greater hate for Bushy.

Scene Six

CAROLINE. PRECEDING.

BERKLEY: Do you see, Miss? Here we are.

CAPTAIN: Come here, I need you.

CAROLINE: Father! My father!

BERKLEY: Victory!

CAPTAIN: I'd rather have been killed. Bushy had the most honor in it. He did the most devilish things so spontaneously. He made it thunder with bullets! I

183

couldn't shoot him today.

CAROLINE: Poor Brother, a wound! Bushy conducted himself heroically?

CAPTAIN: Oh, shut up. My reputation is gone. I'd like to lose myself in madness.

CAROLINE: Has Wild come back then?

CAPTAIN: What does it matter to you? Of course.

BERKLEY: Don't complain, Harry. You were heroic. Oh, Miss! Take my old head to your bosom. Oh, how marvelous to lie here! It was so foolish of me to go into the fire today. Oh, my children! I cannot bear the joy any longer. I sense that my life has run its course.

Scene Seven

MOOR. PRECEDING.

MOOR (*at the* CAPTAIN's *feet*): Oh, Lord! Lord! Dear Lord! You're bleeding.

CAPTAIN: Take heart, boy! And get this bullet out of my leg. (*Looks at it.*) Why, it's not in back! By God, Berkley! An honorable wound! Kiss your son! Eh, Sister!

BERKLEY: God be praised! You've plagued me no little. (*Kisses him.*)

MOOR: Oh, woe! What a hole!

CAPTAIN: Fool! Grab it! Hey! I was sure, Father, that I had stood fast.

BERKLEY: Let me get the army surgeon then.

CAPTAIN: No! I shall not consider myself wounded!

Scene Eight

WILD. PRECEDING.

WILD: Miss! Dear Miss! Eh, already here, milords! Suppress your emotion, Wild! Good afternoon. So I've come to fetch you, Captain! My wound is deep, and if I'm not to suffocate, I must have revenge.

CAROLINE: Carl! Carl!

WILD: Be still, Miss, and have pity on me. Revenge for Bushy, Captain!

CAPTAIN: I have a bullet here, and can't oblige just now.

WILD: Mount your horse! Hey, coward! If you'd had me on your ship, eh? I'll tear you apart like a wild animal, if you don't come right now.

BERKLEY: Eh, Bushy, stop raving. We are here.

WILD: Good, milord.

CAPTAIN: Have a horse saddled for me. Bullet or no bullet, you shall not trumpet like this for long.

WILD: Marvelous! Miss! Farewell, Miss! Oh, Jenny! Farewell!

CAROLINE: You are going . . . going . . . Carl! I shall not leave you!

WILD: Darling! Dearest! Oh, dearest! (WILD *and* CAROLINE *leave.*)

BERKLEY: Hm! I am so confused! So weak! Hey, Harry! You shouldn't duel with him. With the son of an enemy? Ha! For what? Because you avenged your father? I swear by the shadow of my dear lady, you shall not. Though his father has already robbed me of everything, of well-being and good fortune. I would rather tear out my cried-out eyes! You mustn't! Ha! Come!

CAPTAIN: Get this bullet out of me, and I'll get the life out of him! (*Leaves.*)

Scene Nine

The garden
WILD. CAROLINE.

WILD: Oh, Miss! Miss! This day was good. It did my heart good, but as I come here and as I stand before you in this emotion—Jenny! Why did I have to return? Why was I spared? When I saw so many around me fall? I must have revenge, Miss! On your brother! I feel wrath here, I feel love here. Do you feel it, Jenny, do you see? I stand at the abyss of human beginning, at the end of human emotion. For it is torn here, Miss (*Points to his chest.*) and is born again there! (*Points to the stars.*) And here your image, which I do not want and want more and more passionately. Jenny, all my torture! All my love!

CAROLINE: Is there nothing, then, that saves? Is there nothing, then, that helps? Come here to my arms, dear anguisher! Let me give you peace! Let me give you love! Only not this thirst for blood, this thirst for revenge! Forgive my brother! No, you cannot—Carl! So quiet and dead—and I so wholly wretched without salvation. I would summon up my last bit of strength—but it vanishes. And I! Ah, I had the one, for whom I called and sighed! He was given to me! Carl! And so it ends?

WILD: Hide your tears! Hide your sorrow! Hide your love from me! No, give me love, that I may live and feel until the moment of destruction. I have become so deaf, so benumbed. Only the sympathy of your loving eyes dissolves the stiffness and lets me seize something in the frightening inner turmoil, something to hold onto. Oh, Jenny! How can he be your brother? The murderer! Oh, it is sin, to bring this to your ears. I sense how it must strike your nerves. It will not come from my tongue, it is so deep in my heart, and swells my bosom—hey! You should have it, yearn, yearn! You have taken all my senses prisoner. Miss! Miss! How do you feel?

CAROLINE: Let it now grow darker before my eyes and heavier here. I go to my end, so gladly to my end. You destroy so mightily.

Scene Ten

MOOR: Lord! Lord! Have I found you at last? Ah, I have to tell you, dear lord. But send the Miss away, dear lord!

WILD: Nonsense, boy, Out with it!

MOOR: Oh, lord, lord! I want to tell you about the old man who loves me and whom I love. A gray head, not dead! (*Gently.*) Believe me! By all the gods! I would rather have been thrown with him into the sea. He is not dead!

WILD: Would you lie to me?

MOOR: They are both alive. Be only kind and I shall tell you. Ah! The ship's lieutenant, a good man, protected them. I begged so long at his feet, until he agreed. We lied to the captain that they were in the boat. The boat was set adrift empty. Ha, ha, ha!

WILD: Splendid boy! Miss!

CAROLINE: What, new life! New strength! (*She embraces the* MOOR.)

MOOR: We hid the old men in a tiny, tiny corner and I stole enough biscuits and water for them. But betray none of this to the captain. You too, Miss! He would drive me crazy or beat me to death.

WILD: Godly boy! Where are they?

MOOR: Just be quiet and don't betray me.

WILD (*embraces him, raises him, staring at the heavens*): My father lives!

(CAROLINE *embraces him.*)

MOOR: Oops! Oops! Take care, Lord!

Scene Eleven

LORD BUSHY *enters, with tired, enfeebled steps. As he becomes aware of his* SON, *he summons up his strength, meets him, and without a word, sinks into* WILD's *arms.* WILD *is immobile with joy.*

BUSHY (*after a long pause*): Oh, am I here?

WILD: Father! I am again at your heart!

CAROLINE: Milord, as am I!

BUSHY: I am here! Hold me, Carl! So little breath, so little strength to rejoice!

WILD: I have found you again! (*Embraces* JENNY *and his* FATHER.) My heart! My heart! How well I have become! These silver locks! This look! I have it all again!

BUSHY: All again! All again, your friend and father! Let me just catch my breath a bit.

MOOR (*embraces the old man*): Do you still love me, Father?

BUSHY: Come, dear boy, lie down by me!

MOOR: The captain.

BUSHY: Let him come. I have weapons here. (*Points to his heart.*)

CAROLINE: Milord! Oh, milord! Don't hate me! If you knew me—

BUSHY: I hate no one, my dear. My eyes have become clouded . . . who are you, Miss?

WILD: You allowed me, Father, to seek out in all corners of the earth the one who had my soul. I have found her. Jenny! My Jenny! I have found her and only now do I know what I have found.

BUSHY: Berkley's Jenny! Whom I called daughter before hate divided us, and whom I always loved—come to my arms! Thank you for all the hours that you sweetened with your love, and thank you for this love, Miss! And thank you, good black boy, that you saved me for this hour! Do you know, Carl, what you owe to this boy? He described you to me, your suffering, your anguish. Ah, how easily I recognized you! Did he tell you?

WILD: Everything, Father, everything!

BUSHY: Miss, now and forever my daughter! Love has guided my son well. Where is Berkley? Are you reconciled, Carl? Lead me to him!

CAROLINE: Milord! No!

BUSHY: Does he still hate me?

WILD: Oh, Father! I was just on the brink of—let us flee and speak no further. Since you are here, I forgive the captain and the old man. Jenny! Will you leave us alone?

BUSHY: Be calm. I want to show myself to Berkley. Whatever wrath rises in him at the sight of me, he will surely appease it. I have sought him, and since I have found him—I am here. Stay here, Carl!

WILD: I cannot be there and forgive him.

BUSHY: Why not? Peace and calm have returned to my soul; they shall also return to Berkley's. I have learned nothing else from my errors than this, and I know everything.

Scene Twelve

CAPTAIN. BERKLEY *rushes in.* PRECEDING.

BERKLEY: Harry! Harry! Hey, Harry! You mustn't!

CAPTAIN (*to* WILD): Where have you been keeping yourself? What is here, Miss? (*He becomes aware of* LORD BUSHY.) Is this a dream? Hey, Milord Bushy, are you flesh and blood?

(BERKLEY *composes himself.*)

BUSHY: I am, Captain.

CAPTAIN: Hellfire and damnation! Are you so good a sailor? Father, it's Bushy! Old Bushy!

BERKLEY: So I see. I see. Come with me, Harry. I am becoming so angry—

BUSHY: Lord Berkley.

BERKLEY: Not that voice! I fear that voice! What further blows will you deal

187

me?

BUSHY: Blows of peace and love. (*Tries to grasp* BERKLEY's *hand;* BERKLEY *draws back.*) Repenting my past life, forgetting the wild passions! Milord! I have taken all the sins upon me, and I have ended my pilgrimage here, full of sorrow and suffering. Let me raise here the flag of peace!

BERKLEY: Get out of here! Come, Miss! May I not be led into temptation, for this or that.

BUSHY: Berkley! Are you not yet at the time when one gladly feels serenity?

CAPTAIN: Now, sir! My pistols and horse are ready, my wound forgotten.

WILD: I have forgiven you, Captain, as I have found him again.

CAPTAIN: But I have not forgiven you, sir!

BERKLEY: Come with me, Miss. Why do you stand there with the Bushys?

CAROLINE: Oh, Father!

WILD (*embraces her*): She is mine, milord! You gave her to me when I was a boy. She is mine!

BERKLEY: Shall I curse you, Miss? Come, child!

CAROLINE: Father!

CAPTAIN: Berkley! I am going mad!

WILD (*embraces her*): We shall go far from here, monster! But the Miss goes with us. Here are my pistols and here is death! Take them!

CAPTAIN: Let me kill him, milord!

BERKLEY: Dog! You madman! While he holds Miss so solidly in his arms! She'd be shot as well, and all the charm of the world would lie in the grave. Look at the girl, so beautiful, so good, so hateful in Bushy's arms. Dear Miss! He wants to deceive you! Deceive with love! Won't you come, pretty Miss? Won't you? Come then, dear, virtuous child, to your old father! You alone can ease his nerves, gently and mildly, that I know. Just come, and I'll let the Bushys go quietly.

WILD: Should I end my life here, Miss?

CAROLINE: Forgive! Father, forgive and forget! (*Reaches toward* BERKLEY, *held back by* WILD.)

BERKLEY: Fie, Miss! Shame on you! I beg of you, girl, don't provoke me! Miss, I beg, I beseech you, by my gray hair, by my old head. Give up my enemies and come this instant to me! Come, child! You nursed me and took care of me, now I'll nurse you and take care of you. Eh, Miss! Shall I go mad, Miss? Should I loathe and hate my child? Curse you and the world? I shall become mad, Miss!

CAROLINE: I am your child, lord! Your good, true child!

CAPTAIN: They are playing with us, Father!

BERKLEY: Only this grace, Heaven! That I may forget this child! Leave this mad stress!

BUSHY: Berkley, we once called ourselves brothers. We lived in friendship and love. An evil spirit divided us. The former feeling has at long last returned to me. Could it not happen to you? Brother!

BERKLEY: Be silent! Bushy, be silent! I hated and hate, loved and love!

BUSHY: Your hate fell hard on me. I deserve it no longer. I stand on the edge of the grave. Thoughts of eternal peace have long filled my soul; they give me strength, even as my weakened body becomes feebler. Berkley, at such a time, one does not lie, and thus I do not. Here, where truth is separated from falsehood, I tell you that I am innocent of the devastation of your house, and of your banishment. He who did it has long lain in the valley of death. Peace to his ashes! His name and his motives will never be revealed by this heart.

BERKLEY: You didn't do it? Old hypocrite!

BUSHY: That's harsh, Berkley. My face speaks for me, and my openness, which has cost me much. Our misfortune was a misunderstanding—we sought a goal, our interests clashed. My passions were too hasty, and yours even more fiery. Oh, milord, what we have done! What have we become? Let us make everything good. Let us live in love!

CAROLINE: Oh, Father! It is all so true, what milord says. (*Embraces him.*) Your Jenny! You will relent!

WILD: Noble Berkley!

CAPTAIN: It's disgraceful to get along so well, like womenfolk, at the end.

CAROLINE: Harry! Don't deny your feelings! I see in you that you would like gladly—

CAPTAIN: Oh, stop it. I'm going to my ship.

BUSHY: Berkley, I want to vindicate myself before you. Only know that my heart is pure!

BERKLEY: I can't love you . . . but stay here.

BUSHY (*embraces him*): I recognize you.

BERKLEY: Let me be! I am so confused . . . but stay here.

WILD: Well done, milord! And you, Captain?

CAPTAIN: I don't understand any of this. Come, boy!

BERKLEY: Stay, Harry!

CAPTAIN: It displeases me. I must first become one with myself before I can be one with another. Moor! Moor!

MOOR: Here, dear lord!

CAPTAIN: Come along and amuse me. (*Leaves.*)

MOOR: Yes, I'll cry for joy, if that amuses you. (*Leaves.*)

BERKLEY: Come, Bushy, down the path. I shall make an attempt to tolerate you. I cannot make any promises about my emotions yet. I still hate you and . . . so much comes to mind . . . just come! (*They leave.*)

(WILD *and* CAROLINE *embrace in the full passion of their love.*)

(*The curtain falls.*)

189

JULIUS OF TARENTO

BY

JOHANN ANTON LEISEWITZ

1776

DRAMATIS PERSONAE

CONSTANTINE, *Prince of Tarento*
JULIUS, *his son*
GUIDO, *his son*
ARCHBISHOP *of Tarento, his brother*
COUNTESS CECELIA NIGRETTI, *daughter of his sister*
BLANCA
COUNT ASPERMONTE, JULIUS's *friend*
ABBESS *of St. Justinia's Abbey*
DOCTOR
SECONDARY CHARACTERS

Location: Tarento, Italy
Time: The end of the fifteenth century

Act One
Scene One

A gallery in the palace of PRINCE CONSTANTINE
JULIUS *and* ASPERMONTE, *walking.*

ASPERMONTE: Incredible. And after you had recovered from your love and melancholy, and had been so calm this past month.

JULIUS: Ah my friend, love has avenged itself this month. All the bitter feeling that should have been taken day by day has poured out in this one night. That is why cloudbursts come: because rain did not fall when it should.

ASPERMONTE: I still don't understand at all. Yesterday evening you were so calm. Why this sudden change?

JULIUS: A waking dream, so less than a dream. As I entered my room in the evening, the moon shot forth a few rays, which fell on Blanca's picture. I gazed at it, and it seemed as if the face dissolved into tears; after a moment, bright pearls rolled down her cheeks. It was fantasy, but a fantasy that could make me doubt all reality. Those tears washed away all my steadfastness. I had a night, such a night—believe me, my friend, our souls are simple. If the burden that lay on my soul last night had been pressing on a composite, the parts would have split asunder and the dust returned to dust.

ASPERMONTE: Ah, I know that state all too well.

JULIUS: What would you know of it? Name an emotion and I had it. I was whirled without stop from one extreme of human nature to another: at times I leaped from one emotion to its antithesis, at others I was dragged through every emotion that lay between. All possibilities swirled about me; I must have seen my fate in one of them. In one I had already broken into her convent and led her to my room. But as I neared the bridal bed, I saw my father standing there with an expression of such infinite paternal anguish ... I let her hand fall.

ASPERMONTE: Did you make no use of this? Did not reason come to your aid?

JULIUS: In truth, these dreams seem to have awakened my reason. I cried, "Julius, Julius, be a man!" Yes, I cried, "Julius, Julius," as if steadfastness itself were speaking, but that "Be a man!" dissolved into a sigh of love.

ASPERMONTE: Bare your soul, bare your soul, noble youth. My heart is worthy of your pain.

JULIUS: Her divine image—I see it in a thousand guises, a thousand forms. How she borrows from every age its special charm: the candid innocence of childhood, the attractiveness of youth, and the shyness love gave her with my first kiss. And the holy mien of her present state—that is all it can give her. The flames of religion have purified her whole being. We can approach only up to a certain point. Beyond that men become visionaries, angels do not. Aspermonte, imagine just once the praying Blanca! What, you stand still? Doubtless this is the first time you have had that idea—yet you're not leaping about like a madman?

ASPERMONTE: You surpass me, Your Highness. Never was there a love so strong. You are right, I understand nothing.

JULIUS: And yet you do not know the worst of all. I looked again at her portrait,

193

and thought of what she was doing that very night. How perhaps she was crying over my unfaithfulness. That as the moon was shining through her little window onto her crucifix and breviary, a ray fell somewhere on my picture, and where I had seen tears on hers, she saw my jeers and scorn. Hell came to the aid of her imagination, and the cloister resounded with a hellish, mocking laughter.

ASPERMONTE: Your vision was sent by Hell.

JULIUS: The simple, immortal soul could not bear this vision. For some time I lost all feeling. As I came back to awareness, the first storm of passion was over. The period of plans had already begun. As I staggered around the vestibule, I heard my guard at the door, snoring. I have never envied any man so much as this footman. Even if he loves, I thought, he can still snore. I have a heart and I am a prince. That is my ill luck! How should I still my hunger for feeling? My love has been taken from me. And no prince has ever had a friend. Ah, he who has a true friend, let him not in his good fortune forget the miserable. May he now and then shed a tear for good princes. These thoughts led me to a plan: what is holding you back, I asked myself, from kidnapping her and hiding with her in the far corners of the world? Throw off your purple and leave it for the first man foolish enough to pick it up. I was undecided only about the right time for doing this. Now and then I thought that in order to spare my father grief I should wait a certain amount of time—you understand—but much of the time it seemed to me that even waiting till tomorrow would be too long. The dawn broke even as I was dreaming of this. I went into the garden and was in such sweet dreams, when you came upon me.

ASPERMONTE: Truly I regret now that I disturbed you.

JULIUS: My friend, however giddy I am from love, at least I know that I am giddy. You must guide me, Aspermonte. Tell me your opinion of my plan. Do you truly love me?

ASPERMONTE: The question, and what you said earlier, offend me. Have you forgotten then that I devoted my whole being to you because I knew your heart? I knew how rarely princes have friends, and the thought once crossed my own mind that I perhaps value in you the prince and not the man. Do you no longer remember then, how we then agreed that I should be totally independent? That I would secretly cover my own expenses at the court?

JULIUS (embraces him): Forgive me my disturbed state. Even in the headiness of love, Blanca asked: "Julius, do you love me?"

ASPERMONTE: I shall prove it to you once and for all. If you carry out your plan, and are prince no more, I shall follow you.

JULIUS: So should I do it?

ASPERMONTE: Your Highness, consider a moment. You are the hope of a nation. Consider your responsibility to us all.

JULIUS: Spare me your philosophy! Philosophy for passion, harmony for the deaf.

ASPERMONTE: At least be sure then that your decision is a decision. One dream upset your former plan; a new dream could upset the present one. Wait at least a month.

JULIUS: I shall wait (Embraces him.) but stand by me this month, stand by me!

194

Scene Two

JULIUS. ASPERMONTE. GUIDO.

GUIDO: You've had me looking for you a long time. I have important things to discuss with you.

JULIUS: Forgive me.

GUIDO: Brother, the tone that prevails between us displeases me. I can hate, hate like a man! But there is a certain stifling hate that I detest—the hate of those who cannot admit that they no longer care for one another. They go through the motions again and again, and greet the bodies of dead friendships as if they were still alive, sharing bed and board. Truly these friends are a lovely picture: the eyes full of rancor, the mouth set in such a naturally amiable expression, as if strings were being pulled on a puppet.

JULIUS: Let's change the subject, shall we?

GUIDO: There you meet a new temperament. In conversation they are always afraid to get to the point at hand. They'd rather go a hundred miles around it and talk about strange East Indian animals than about themselves. But I'd rather make a decisive cut through the abscess than let it fester.

JULIUS: If only there were no abscess.

GUIDO: You shall answer me. Good, but let me speak first. You know my right to Blanca. It is not lessened any by the fact that our father, moved by the argument you and I had over her, sent me to fight in the war on Crete for five months, and put her in a convent. Now that I have returned I must tell you afresh that I shall not surrender my right.

JULIUS: Your right—

GUIDO: Let me talk! I offered her my love earlier than you. Before great assemblies, at royal banquets I called her my beloved. Often at tournaments I've heard the women whisper, "Guido of Tarento . . . and her name is Blanca." As I stormed the walls in Crete, I cried out her name, and the whole army echoed it. My honor is at stake; I shall redeem it.

JULIUS: But Blanca herself—

GUIDO: Silence, Brother! Beauty is the natural prize of heroism—and in that women have no say. Do we ask the rose if it wishes to be fragrant for the one who smells it? What have you done to earn her? Believe me, when one sees you wandering through an orange-grove like a lovesick girl, he's more likely to think you're the prize than the soldier.

JULIUS: Brother, you are becoming unbearably offensive.

GUIDO: Fine, just grant me my right to Blanca, and then do whatever you like. Be the plaything of some grown-up girl, come to her like a tame quail when she calls, ward off flies when she sleeps. Be sensitive, pluck violets, be happy when the sun rises and when it sets. Let your Aspermonte meanwhile rule the Tarentines. What concern is it of yours if they're happy or not? It's enough that you know how to love your woman and bid defiance to every sparrow!

JULIUS: Brother, stop and let me speak!

GUIDO: And when you die in her bosom, may your tomb be erected next to the monuments of our heroic ancestor Theodoric. Let the sculptor adorn it with roses and grapevines, and set a pair of billing and cooing doves on them, with a weeping Amor and a sleeping History beneath! And let it be etched above all: "Here lies a Prince of Tarento." That can come in handy, even if your monument is in the middle of our family vault—

JULIUS: Brother, I can see that you want me to go. I'll leave now. (*Leaves.*)

Scene Three

GUIDO. ASPERMONTE.

GUIDO (*scornfully*): He will bear the operation manfully! He can't even bear someone's probing the wound. Not to want to hear the truth! Has the milksop read Plato for this? I praise my plain common sense. Deeds, Aspermonte, make the man. In short, your philosophy is dead—embalmed, I grant, with high maxims, but dead nonetheless. (ASPERMONTE *is about to leave.*) Stay, he gets this love of speculation from you. Even though I have never dueled in your fencing-school of syllogisms, I shall prove to you—yes, *I* shall prove to you—that speculation kills courage. Hm! Did you have something to say?

ASPERMONTE (*coldly*): No.

GUIDO: I am enraged, as no man has been enraged before. What right does that butterfly have to be my rival? How do we know he has the heart? Has he ever seen an army camp? As I said to him: only masculine bravery deserves feminine loveliness! Why else does woman have so deep a sense of her weakness, and man of his strength? In the very nature of woman we thus see determined the merit of a man; and all other merits, results of human institutions, cannot change this law of nature. He is a weakling. Can you find anything to contradict me?

ASPERMONTE (*coldly*): Nothing, sir.

GUIDO: Nothing? Well, I have more to say to you. Julius was the first to introduce weakness into our house, but he will be a Hercules compared to his descendants. Weakness is the only subject in which the pupil surpasses the teacher. It is like men walking on marshy ground: the last one sinks the deepest. And this weakness also will come indirectly from you, Aspermonte! From you! Are you dumb? This coldness you assume annoys me. Don't I deserve that you speak with me?

ASPERMONTE: I can speak, Your Highness. Oh, I can speak, but you cannot hear.

GUIDO: Ha, jester! I feel the full weight of this insult. Satisfaction! (*He draws his sword.*) As sovereign, I am above your insults, but I prefer here to consider myself insulted rather than sovereign. Draw!

ASPERMONTE (*coldly*): I would never duel in your father's palace with his son.

GUIDO: Draw or I'll strike you down!

ASPERMONTE (*draws. They fence,* ASPERMONTE *only to defend himself*): See, Your Highness, how I spare you.

GUIDO: Spare me! Spare me! Horrible! That demands the utmost revenge! (*He *fences more furiously.*)

(*The* ARCHBISHOP *enters and separates the two.*)

ARCHBISHOP: Guido, Guido, do you want to awaken your father on his birthday with this swordclashing? (*To* ASPERMONTE.) And you! You draw against your master's brother?

GUIDO (*to* ASPERMONTE): We must leave off for the time being. But don't forget, only for the time being! (*To the* ARCHBISHOP.) I forced him.

ASPERMONTE: You have seen I am no weakling. But one proof is enough. I will never give him a second. (*Leaves.*)

Scene Four

ARCHBISHOP. GUIDO.

ARCHBISHOP: Guido, Guido, again inflamed?

GUIDO: How could I be otherwise? How could I be otherwise? He pushed me to my limit with his assumed coldness. He uttered scorching insults to me with such a simple face, as if he were too stupid for original sin.

ARCHBISHOP: I know you. You started it.

GUIDO: Who started it: the one who utters a hot word, or the one who drove him to it through a thousand idiocies and silent insults? Who wouldn't explode when he sees the indolent youths on their easy chairs, overflowing with wisdom, where they prattle of immortality and freedom and the highest good—they're more serious than Marcus Porcius Cato with the colic. Yet the only result of the empty talk is the mild exercise it gives the prattlers.

ARCHBISHOP: But Guido, even if that's true, what is it to you?

GUIDO: And they explain everything with examples of great men. By heaven! He who would be a hero cannot be a history scholar. But idle Julius stands there in the temple of fame. He blows the dust from the statue of Alexander, sets a new varnish on Caesar's nose, and gapes at Cicero's mole. He knows so many shining examples! If the seeds of greatness lay in him, he would have become a hero himself—or at least hanged himself. Truly, he can read of lives and deeds all evening long, and then sleep soundly all night.

ARCHBISHOP: Will you never stop, Guido?

GUIDO: But these are the fruits of the much-praised peace in which all bravery rusts! Oh, I feel it myself! Why did my father summon me from the war against the infidels? I sit here now and must gnash my teeth when I hear reports that my friends have become famous and (*Stamps his foot.*) sing the *Te Deum*, when battles are won without me! Don't be angry, Uncle! Let me at least gnaw the bars of my cage!

ARCHBISHOP: Fine, but why do you demand that everyone think as chimerically as you?

GUIDO: If my thoughts were chimeras, I wouldn't give this swordhead for the value of all mankind. But I feel it in here (*Strikes his breast.*) that what I think is real.

197

ARCHBISHOP: Suppose it is. But why should everybody think like you? Why these eternal parallels between you and Julius?

GUIDO: Doesn't he draw these parallels himself? Wherever I am, he is in my path. He prattles where I act, whimpers where I love.

ARCHBISHOP: On that issue, the two of you can at last be at peace: Blanca is a nun.

GUIDO: Uncle, Guido's plans may be thwarted, but never surrendered. I like to wager with fate. If it will bet the execution of my decision, I bet my life—it seems to me the wager is not unfair. Here is my hand; seal the bet in the name of fate!

ARCHBISHOP: Reflect on what you are prattling! Blanca is under the authority and protection of the Church.

GUIDO: I know that is true. I know that compared to a dispute with the Church, a battle is only a fencing-match, but—

ARCHBISHOP: Stop, Guido! I've already heard more than an uncle should. You're about to say things now that an archbishop may not hear. (*Leaves.*)

Scene Five

GUIDO: Hm! (*Pause.*) I am not as calm as I should be after a duel. But it was only half a duel, and besides that they let me stand around there, like a madman who mustn't be antagonized lest he become violent. But what does it matter that others hate my principles? Thank God that I have some, and that I can hold onto them, even against a woman's caresses and a devil's threats! What would Guido be without this constancy? Power, strength, life—just shells that Fate peels off if it likes. My true self is my steadfast resolution—and there Fate's power is broken. Why shouldn't I carry out my plans? Lifeless Nature bows obediently under the hand of a hero, and his plans can be shattered only by those of another hero. Is that the case here? To tear a girl out of the arms of a weakling, whose only strength is my virtue and fraternal bond! They may be holy to me, but by Heaven! I shall redeem my mortgaged honor! Granted, I'll earn precious few laurels in this undertaking, for a victor can take from a victory only the honor that the loser had—and what honor does Julius have? But to hold one's gains is also a victory! Oh, they shall learn what determination is! (*Leaves.*)

Scene Six

PRINCE. ARCHBISHOP.

PRINCE: That sounds all too much like Guido. Honestly, Brother, do you believe that someday I shall be again a happy father?

ARCHBISHOP: I believe it as a fact.

198

PRINCE: At this moment I am not. Oh, how this discord bows me down. If only it is not caused by a true disharmony of their characters!

ARCHBISHOP: I hope not.

PRINCE: So do I, but I have noticed indications earlier. Even when Guido was a boy, he had to be king in all the games. He astonished all his playmates by how recklessly he would clamber up trees and over rocks. They could hardly admire him, their heads reeled so with fear. So I often thought: Heaven help us when the passions of this boy are first aroused! Well, they were aroused. He is so greedy for glory that it displeases him that there are indifferent things that bring neither shame nor honor. If eating doesn't bring him glory, he'd just as soon not eat. He believes what doesn't bring honor, brings shame—that is his misfortune.

ARCHBISHOP: Truly, a wild, dangerous character.

PRINCE: Even more dangerous because he is near Julius. Even as a child, before he knew what love was, Julius had that languishing look. It was always his greatest pleasure to be left alone to dream. Love came early to a heart so ready, and it was as little unexpected as a father in his own home. Now put these temperaments beside one another.

ARCHBISHOP: Brother, what you have described as the special temperaments of your sons is typical of youth. There is no young man of promise who couldn't be likened to one of your sons. Just let the wild fires of youth burn themselves out.

PRINCE: Before that happens, much could be destroyed. As if this fire could burn out so quietly, without consuming something! How I fear the romantic, slow resolve of the one, and the rashness of the other! Ever since I had Blanca put in the convent, Julius has been even more of a problem than before. But didn't I have to do what I did? Wasn't she too far beneath his station? Didn't this obsession strangle every desire in him for what is great and important?

ARCHBISHOP: But no harm has been done.

PRINCE: Are you pleased, then, with the nocturnal wanderings in the garden? With his isolation during the day? Haven't you noticed how he stares at everything, smiles at everybody, and answers like one whose mind is a million miles away?

ARCHBISHOP: If other things weren't as they are, that wouldn't be worth mentioning. What makes it dangerous is that they both love the same girl. But believe me, Brother, Guido's love is no real love. It's merely a child of his ambition, and its every trait reveals its parentage.

PRINCE: You're right—but that doesn't make matters any easier. I know he despises women, and his love in itself may be a very insignificant thing. If it alone were placed against Julius's love, we could sleep soundly: that would be a child matched against a giant, and they would not battle. But therein lies the problem: Guido's honor is colliding with Julius's love. Giant against giant, where neither has a dram less power than the other—that makes for obstinate, dangerous combat.

ARCHBISHOP: What do you think should be done?

PRINCE: My plan is this: Guido loves Blanca only out of jealousy, because she loves Julius. It's only a question, then, of turning Julius to another love. Guido would stop by himself, then.

ARCHBISHOP: And who should this new love be?

PRINCE: Cecelia! That is why I have summoned her here, and I must say, I have not chosen badly. I must wonder that the boy didn't come up with the idea himself. To see such beauty every day . . .

ARCHBISHOP: If he would look! Don't you know that lovers think it perjury to see an alien beauty? If another image appears even in their minds, they believe their hearts are profaned. And take care that he doesn't notice that anybody has such a plan, much less that you have it! You would lose his trust in the matter of love, and once that is lost, it is never regained.

PRINCE: I shall protect myself. Cecelia's virginal modesty is a further guarantee. Do you really believe, Brother, that I shall rediscover fatherly joy through this plan?

ARCHBISHOP: As sure as I am of anything.

PRINCE: And how much it would be increased, if Cecelia becomes my daughter! The domestic joys of an old man come through women; their gentle tone harmonizes so well with his muffled one. Rash boys and men never fit well with his solitude.

ARCHBISHOP: Here comes Cecelia. I shall leave you alone. She will go red enough without me. (*Leaves.*)

Scene Seven

PRINCE. CECELIA.

PRINCE: Good morning, Cecelia. Sit down next to me.

CECELIA: Permit me, dear father and uncle, first to extend to you best wishes on your birthday. (*Kisses his hand.*)

PRINCE: Thank you, dear daughter. Please, be seated. But are you aware that you are wishing me happiness on attaining a new degree of weakness? I sense it, Cecelia, I sense that I am growing old. The rose-colored glow in which you see everything has paled for me. I'm no longer alive. I only breathe, and this mere existence without the delights of life is the only connection between me and the world.

CECELIA: You imagine yourself far weaker than you are.

PRINCE: No, I feel it. Soon I'll feel nothing. Only one channel is left, through which sweetness and bitterness still flow into my heart—my children.

CECELIA: And you said you can feel nothing? Why do the rich so love to present themselves as poor? What more source of pleasure do you need than that which flows from the observation of a fine character? Taken together your children are almost the ideal of manly perfection. The gentleness of your Julius—

PRINCE: Are you serious, Cecelia? But feminine perfection offers me the same pleasure. You are my daughter.

CECELIA: If you aren't joking, you're only showing, in my opinion, that paternal love is often paternal vanity.

PRINCE: If my children are the only channel through which joy can reach me, is it

200

any wonder that I place all my hopes in them? Is not love the greatest delight of life? Not like glory or riches, which are offerings from the often dirty hands of man—no, a gift from Nature, not just loaned for a time but given outright. The love of a couple at the altar is like the love of our first parents in Paradise. See, Cecelia, even on his seventy-sixth birthday, an old man speaks with rapture of love.

CECELIA: A sign that he has loved virtuously.

PRINCE: But I am becoming distracted. The light of love is too strong for my weak heart; only its reflection in my children is for me. My girl, Julius has a heart. It is not revealed by shining deeds, but by his failings.

CECELIA: I know and prize it.

PRINCE: Do you know it? Do you really know it? If only he were happy through love! If only he could give me a daughter! What is dearer to an old man than the womanly care of a daughter! If only Julius had a wife!

CECELIA: She would be my dearest friend.

PRINCE: What value she would give to the rest of my life. At its end I would glide without noticing into the arms of another angel. And you must be this wife, Cecelia!

CECELIA: Uncle, I beg of you!

PRINCE: Declare nothing, my girl! I know what your maidenly modesty requires you to say. But with time . . . but now, declare nothing.

CECELIA: Am I not already your daughter? I shall always remain so. I shall never leave you; I shall do all that I can to please you; always keep watch from afar, and always remain at your side unless it be your pleasure to send me away, but—

PRINCE: Declare nothing! Perhaps you will wish me joy on my next birthday, perhaps in the name of a grandchild, so keep in mind this conversation. Do you hear me, Cecelia? Reflect on this conversation! Come, breakfast is waiting for us . . . your hand. (*He leads her off.*)

Act Two
Scene One

The vestibule in St. Justinia's Abbey
A NUN is present.

JULIUS (*enters*): Summon the abbess! (*The* NUN *leaves.*) I shall see her, even if an angel with a fiery sword stands before her cell. (*The* ABBESS *enters.*) I want to speak to Sister Blanca.

ABBESS: Sir, you know your father's orders.

JULIUS: Reverend Abbess, my father is seventy-six today, and I am his successor.

ABBESS: I understand. But I also know my duty. Under the same circumstances, I would answer your son in the same way.

JULIUS: I shall hold you responsible for it. Nun or no nun! Which is older: the rule of Nature or the rule of Augustine? I shall take her into my bedroom, even if she has become a saint, even if she enters with a halo instead of a bridal wreath, even if the priest, instead of pronouncing the blessing, pronounces anathemas on us down to the thousandth clause! I shall tear off her veil in this room! I swear this to you on my princely honor.

ABBESS: I can only pity you.

JULIUS: As I say, I shall hold you responsible. And if when the time comes I should find the least of her features marked by vexation—I shall easily distinguish that from melancholy—I'll tear apart—note this, Reverend Abbess—I'll tear apart your convent, down to the altar, and your patron saint will smile if she be indeed a saint.

ABBESS: Sir, we are only sheep, but we have a Shepherd.

JULIUS (*paces up and down a few times*): How long have you been in the convent?

ABBESS: Nineteen years.

JULIUS: What cut you off from the world? Devotion or these walls? Have you never loved? Were you always a nun, and never a woman?

ABBESS: Oh, Your Highness, leave me in peace! (*She weeps.*) Nineteen years I have cried, and yet there are still tears.

JULIUS: Isn't it true that *he* cried at this very gate, and is now dead? Isn't it?

ABBESS: Oh, my Ricardo! (*After a pause.*) You shall see Blanca. (*Bolts the outside door and leaves.*)

Scene Two

JULIUS, *then* BLANCA *and the* ABBESS

JULIUS: What cannot love do? A mere memory, the shadow of love, had such an effect on this woman; what will not hope, the soul of love, do with me. Oh,

202

who can endure this month? To lose a principality for you, Blanca, is no sacrifice. It means merely setting myself free. For your sake I would languish for years in the darkest prison, in which only a few rays of light fell, provided there were enough to illuminate your face! To see Blanca! At this moment? This seeing costs me my whole peace. But it is only a wretched rest, and one glance from her would be worth the greatest peace of the wisest man.

(BLANCA *enters, after the* ABBESS. JULIUS *flies to her side.*)

JULIUS: Oh, my Blanca!

BLANCA (*retreats a few steps*): No sacrilege, please!

JULIUS: No perjury, Blanca.

BLANCA: No . . . for I hope to keep the vows I made to Heaven.

JULIUS: Your vows are perjury. Can the second vow, even if sworn to Heaven, nullify the first? What then is sworn fidelity? A locked treasure, to which every thief has the key! But you have consecrated nothing to Heaven. Your vows did not reach that far. The guardian angel of our union still has them in custody, and he will give them back to you as a gift on our wedding day.

BLANCA: Before that altar I renounced you and the world for all eternity. I laid my wreath at the foot of the altar, offering myself and, most of all, my love to Heaven. Ah, it pierced me so deeply! It cut me to the very core of my being. But had I only offered myself and not my love to heaven, I would have given nothing but an utter mockery. This veil became on that solemn day a wall between me and the world. No sigh, no wish dare I cast back. If I am to be happy now, I must think of eternity; if I wish to speak with passion, I must pray. I have a narrow heart: it cannot contain love for you and for Heaven at the same time. I am the bride of Christ . . . and Julius, you more than anyone know that when I love, I love completely.

JULIUS: Yes, I know. And that is why I know you lied to Heaven—in all innocence.

BLANCA: Now I renounce you a second time—this time in your presence. It was only to do so that I accepted your visit.

JULIUS: You would kill me if you weren't speaking untruths. Love has fused us into one simple being. We could be annihilated together, but never separated. Woman, woman, the core of your very soul was love for me!

BLANCA: It was, but I have spent this soul in prayers and sighs. Now I have another soul. (*Draws out a picture of* JULIUS.) Here, take back your portrait—the only thing remaining to me of your love. Take it, I may not keep a picture of a man.

JULIUS: Never! Never! Even if you could give me back my soul and my peace of mind, I wouldn't accept them.

BLANCA (*gives the picture to the* ABBESS): When you look at my picture, do not forget that the original is no longer there, that now another Blanca is crying. Blessings on you for always. I know your heart, Your Highness. Use it soon to gladden another maiden. I shall pray for you and your wife.

JULIUS: Then pray for yourself! Man is born only once and loves only once.

BLANCA: For myself I shall pray for forgetfulness. Take care.

JULIUS (*holds her back*): Blanca, do you remember the innocent days of our youth? Everything that love gave us then: sorrow and joy, reality and fantasy, life and breath? How it made our hardest tasks easy, and the simplest tasks

203

vital? And you can't remember any of this! Such a feeling leaves no memory! In the midst of such happiness, we believed yesterday that our joy could not increase. But are the passions of yesterday dead today? Even a weak memory is still a memory. Oh, Blanca, think of our meeting in the lemon-grove—the tears when we met, the tears when we parted!

BLANCA (*lost in thought*): How wonderful. You too have dreamed of those days? Oh, how I have dreamed of them.

JULIUS: I swear to you, these days shall come again. Either under our lemon trees, or the palms of Asia, or the Nordic pines—I know not where and it does not matter. I want you, even if the path to your cell be more arduous than the path to glory, even if there be tigers growling all about in the bushes, haggard from hunger and thirst. Only my death can prevent this undertaking. But I cannot die, I feel my full power, my limbs are made to last for centuries.

BLANCA: I beg of you, leave me!

JULIUS: There will be a time, when nothing of your current sorrow will remain except a wistful memory. Nothing more than is enough to make an interesting evening chat about past times. With these my arms I shall carry you from this prison. Your emotion shall be the joy of the awakened, who finds that the awful dream was only a dream.

BLANCA: Leave me! Hear, the clock strikes for services.

JULIUS: You must give me a memento of your present being. (*He takes from her the rose wreath at her side.*) Pledge of convent love! How I shall treasure it! I shall never give it up except for your first kiss on our wedding day. Then you can have it back as your finest wedding adornment.

BLANCA: My wedding day has already occurred.

JULIUS: Tear off your veil, Blanca! I shall dare all-out war with Heaven. I know you love me, but I must now hear it from your lips. I implore you by the days of joy that were, and those that shall be—now swear to me, once again. (*He kisses her.*)

BLANCA: Reverend Abbess . . . help me . . . (*She faints.*)

JULIUS: She loves me. You see, Reverend Abbess, there is proof, worthy of our love that she truly loves me. If an angel were to lay his hand on the Book of Fate and swear: "Blanca loves Julius," I could not be surer.

ABBESS: I beg of you, leave us.

JULIUS: Not until I see those divine eyes open again. (BLANCA *opens her eyes.*) That will do. Reverend Abbess, I thank you. You shall not see me so whimpering again.

Scene Three

BLANCA, *completely recovered.* ABBESS.

ABBESS: He's gone.

BLANCA: Ah, if only I hadn't seen him. He has murdered my devotion and poisoned my prayers.

ABBESS: My dear daughter!

BLANCA: I am not your daughter. I'm a coquette in nun's clothing. See, the little seed of hope he has sown has already taken root. Wishes are its blossoms, and doubt its probable fruit. Duty, vows—have you then no strengthening word for poor Blanca? Ah, they are dumb!

ABBESS: Or you are deaf, Blanca.

BLANCA: Not at all. I certainly hear when love merely whispers: "Julius." Didn't he say, Reverend Abbess, the days of joy would return, in some distant corner of the world? He keeps his promises. Yes, I see already the torches in the cloister and hear the steps of the horse and the noise of the sails. Ha! Now we're there, in the farthest corner of the world. The cottage is small, but room enough for an embrace. The little field is narrow, but room enough for pot-herbs and two graves . . . and then Julius . . . for all eternity. Room enough for love!

ABBESS: You're raving. Come away from here, come with me to the garden. Come, Blanca.

BLANCA: Where? Where? Under the Asian palms or the Nordic pines? (*They leave.*)

Scene Four

The gallery in the palace
CECELIA, *very thoughtful throughout the scene.* PORTIA, *a lady-in-waiting.*

CECELIA: The prince is taking a long time.

PORTIA: Don't be impatient. He'll find out soon enough your strange whim to renounce marriage and love forever. (*Pause, while she waits for* CECELIA's *reply.*) Poor girl, do you believe that you can replace the renounced joys of love by having the world marvel at your shining talents and this victory over yourself? Believe me, admiration is a titillating dish, but I assure you, nothing in the world sates folk so readily. Incense is burned forever only before the divine face of a god—or the wooden one of his statue!

CECELIA: I have thought about it. Now I have decided. How often have I said to you: too much reflection or too little, both make for much unhappiness.

PORTIA: Strange! Oh, Cecelia, you do not see the future of love through the eyes of a girl! A rosy future where every hour your cornucopia of joy pours out and is replaced before it is empty! There is no other change except that of gentle joy for lively. It makes life a bed of flowers, charming here with a splendid rose, there with a modest little violet. But you! I watched you at the marriage altar of your brother. There was nothing in your eyes of what I saw in the others—the memories or premonitions of love!

CECELIA: Whoever hears you preach so, good Portia, would swear that you had never been married.

PORTIA: Do you think that you will always be so safe from love? One can put it to sleep for a time, like a troubled conscience, but both awaken eventually—and what is worse, usually too late.

CECELIA: The prince has been keeping me waiting too long. Come with me to my room.

PORTIA: Oh, stubborn people only become more stubborn when you argue with them! (*They leave.*)

Scene Five

JULIUS, ASPERMONTE *enter from opposite sides.*

JULIUS: Ah, Aspermonte, I have seen her . . . spoken to her . . . kissed her.

ASPERMONTE: Blanca? What a step—

JULIUS: The great strides of love! Over a thousand scruples and dangers. Should a man in love limp along for days to go from thought to decision to action, like you reasonable people?

ASPERMONTE: You are too rash! Rashness is not a higher level of speed! No plant ripens in the most burning rays of the sun, which singe the growth. And what did you gain from your visit except one more dagger through your heart?

JULIUS: If you had seen her, you wouldn't ask! Oh, the delightful battle of religion and love in her soul! Both so mixed in her emotions that neither can say to the other: this tear is mine and that one is yours. Only once did I see on her face the smile of love . . . on her nun's face, like a rose that blooms on a grave. She did not open her heart to me until it burst forth on its own accord, and she sealed her confession with a faint, the picture of death, just as she would seal her love with death itself! No lover, Aspermonte, has been so fortunate as I. I have twice seen the cheeks of a girl burn when she did not want to reveal her love, yet did reveal it. Wonderful! The first day of spring twice in one year!

ASPERMONTE: Ha, Your Highness, your ecstasy from earlier today is not yet gone.

JULIUS: Name anything that I wouldn't do for Blanca! The almighty ray of love hatches the most powerful drives and forces in our being; all other rays are too short, and a eunuch might well say: man is weak. Everything in my soul lives and breathes. Do you know the almighty breath of spring, so rich in power that it seems it will shatter the boundaries of creation and bring the dead back to life? Such a breath has penetrated my very being. Not even now do I see all that I am able to do. Only now and then does a resolution show me the whole richness of mankind—shows it to me in a flash, like a bolt of lightning through a subterranean vault lighting up the accumulated gold!

ASPERMONTE: Your fantasy burns at such a level that I fear for you.

JULIUS: Am I not speaking reasonably? Fine, may Heaven and your love forgive you if you speak reasonably in such circumstances!

ASPERMONTE: Is this the tone in which you addressed Blanca? Surely you didn't give any hint of your fanciful plan?

JULIUS: You call fanciful a plan in which no fabulous collection of characters and conditions is necessary in the least, in which I hardly need anyone? My feet carry me over the borders of Tarento. There you see all the wonders.

ASPERMONTE: Wonder enough, that a youth endowed with the power to do everything great chooses to lull that power to sleep with a little love-song. Believe me, Julius, the time will come when you will pine away from hunger for noble deeds.

JULIUS: I say to you, I would hate this glory and this calling if I hadn't seen Blanca. Nothing in the position of a prince befits me, from his holiest duty down to the golden fringe on his clothing. Ah, give me a field for my principality, and a babbling brook for my cheering crowds! A plow for me and a ball for my children! Glory? Let history leave my page in her book blank. May the last sigh of Blanca be also the last breath that any mortal spends on my name.

ASPERMONTE: How artfully you confuse glory and duty! Man does not live by fodder alone, and a man can go to sleep with a sweeter thought than that his stomach is full. There are duties to society. Your life, your education, your upbringing, even this skill of yours of spinning sophistries—all are entered in the account-book of society. What stands there to your credit? A man of honor, Your Highness, pays his debts.

JULIUS: Oh, yes, I owe much to these societal arrangements. They set up a prince and a nun and put a great chasm between them. By God, I owe them a lot!

ASPERMONTE: Colder blood, Your Highness! You should now reflect.

JULIUS: Now I should be more cold-blooded? Do you think that I am a fool? But good, the state only gives shelter and demands in return obedience to its laws. This much I have carried out; the account is settled.

ASPERMONTE: My affirmation wipes away more tears than yours. Lad, lad, your reasoning is specious.

JULIUS: Is Tarento then the terrestrial globe? Outside its walls, nothing? The world is my fatherland and all men are one people. United through a universal language! The universal language of all peoples is tears and sighs; I understand the helpless Hottentots and shall not, by God, be deaf when I am out of Tarento! Can the whole human race only be happy when it is locked up in states, where every man is someone's vassal and no one is free? Each welded to the other end of the chain by which he holds his slaves? Fools can debate whether society poisons man! Both sides admit that the state is the murderer of freedom! See, the conflict is settled! The clay has its own will: that is my most exalted thought of the Creator. I treasure the almighty drive for freedom even in the struggling flies. Only two things do I ask of Heaven: Blanca, and that I gasp for air not a moment longer than for freedom.

ASPERMONTE: How they mill about—Your Highness, your conclusions were produced by the reasoning of love.

JULIUS: Is that a reproach? Hear me, Aspermonte, every man has his own reasoning, as he has his own rainbow! I the reasoning of love, you the reasoning of inertia. If we are never free one moment from passion, and passion rules us, where is the imaginary divine spark? The burning heart gives off finer and weaker particles—they lodge in the brain and are called reason. And that is why we must not argue. Listen rather to the results of my deliberation. I cannot, I cannot endure this frightful month. Tomorrow I shall take Blanca and flee Tarento.

ASPERMONTE: Tomorrow?

JULIUS: Yes, tomorrow! Ha! In Tarento I feel as if the walls were going to close in on me.

ASPERMONTE: Only this morning you were willing to wait a whole month. Now not a day more, and yet you have no more reason now for flight than you had this morning.

JULIUS: No more reason? Didn't I see her cry?

ASPERMONTE: Leave, and leave your father on his deathbed to search in vain for a son? Ah, you do not yet know what a delight it is to kiss a sick father. Leave! You have not yet seen how a son searches every morning for the smile of recovery on his father's face, how angry he becomes at the north wind that howls about the sickroom when the poor man wants to sleep. Leave! Truly, you can never have seen how the father, already beyond speaking, turns his face once more to his child and never turns again. Leave!

JULIUS: Aspermonte, the thought of my father that you have awakened in me has pierced me through the heart! And yet—to give up my plan forever!

ASPERMONTE: Not forever, just until the end of the month. It is only one month.

JULIUS: A month? Ah, do what I will, I am miserable. At the end of the month will I love my father or Blanca any the less?

ASPERMONTE: No, but you will be cooler. That is vital, for in any case you must choose.

JULIUS: Good. So, a month! But that is a terrible space of time. What I shall suffer in that time!

ASPERMONTE: Much. But you shall also distract yourself. However much you wish to remain true to your pain, eventually, when you have clung close to it for a long time, you shall slide to a neighboring position, and from that one to another, and so you shall pass, without even knowing it, over the boundaries of sadness. That is the only true solace of mortals. So can a slave begin with his chains and end with a feast for the gods. I beg of you, Your Highness, submit to distraction.

JULIUS: I shall see.

ASPERMONTE: Compose yourself, Cecelia is coming. She has already asked for you several times today.

JULIUS: Cecelia? What for?

ASPERMONTE: Compose yourself. She's too close to be turned away. (*He leaves.*)

Scene Six

JULIUS. CECELIA.

JULIUS: Your servant. (*Offers her a chair. She sits.*)

CECELIA (*somewhat agitated*): Pardon me, Your Highness, but I have things to say to you for which you must forget that I am a woman. Things only revealed between friends.

JULIUS: You make me extremely curious.

CECELIA: You know how much Blanca and I care for each other. We were born on the same day and created for each other. Even in earliest childhood we swore a bond of unbreakable loyalty, and locked arms in order to go through life together. You have much to thank me for. Through our warm friendship, Blanca's heart ripened for her boundless love. I nurtured this love and tended it from the time that Blanca uttered the words: "The prince is charming," until the time she cried out: "Julius, Julius, embodiment of perfection!"

JULIUS (*leaps up*): Her love imagines me a god. By Heaven, I would not treasure her high praise half so much if it were true!

CECELIA (*agitated*): Let us stop talking about Blanca; I didn't come here to cry. I must only tell you that I hold her love to be a sacred fire, that anyone who dares to profane it will be consumed.

JULIUS: I don't understand.

CECELIA: Bear with me and learn the first secret of my heart. I have renounced love forever: born free, I shall also die free. I cannot bear the thought of being the slave of a man; the word marriage sounds to me like the clanking of chains, and the bridal wreath seems to me the wreath on a sacrificial victim.

JULIUS: Cecelia, I admire you.

CECELIA: Are you trying to remind me by flattery that I am a woman? You will not bind me. I hate my sex, though I wouldn't be a man either!

JULIUS: I don't know what I am supposed to think. You have led me into a labyrinth.

CECELIA (*rising*): Fine, let me lead you out: your father has decided that you and I should be married. (*Quickly leaves.*)

Scene Seven

JULIUS: That I could have expected long ago. Much delight, much perfection! Yet I would not compare all my feeling for her with my least feeling for the least of my friends! Long has she been so near to me, through affinity and intimacy, that one would have thought as soon as my feeling flared up, she would be its first object. Love, you are a chasm! One may understand or feel. Does love perhaps despise everything it hasn't made, even that which is favorable? Or do the basic springs of love belong to those things we shall never know, and that we in our own vexation call chance? Fool, she told me in her speech the reason for my coldness. She is no woman, and so I do not love her; no man, and so she is not my friend. Am I not standing here and pondering why I don't love Cecelia? Did I ever ponder why I love Blanca? There! The name slipped out! I drive myself crazy with these sophistries, in order to distract myself. In vain! Everything in heaven and earth leads to you. Even if I do not think of you, your dominance shows in the way I think of other things.

Act Three
Scene One

The palace
The PRINCE, CECELIA, JULIUS, GUIDO, *the* ARCHBISHOP, COURTIERS *and*
LADIES-IN-WAITING, *among them* ASPERMONTE, *at a gala.* ALL *are present. The*
PRINCE *sits, with covered head, in an armchair. His* SONS
and BROTHER *stand next to him; the* OTHERS *form a semi-circle about him.*

PRINCE (*rises and steps, head now uncovered, into the middle of the assembly*): I
thank you, my friends, I thank you. I am probably celebrating a birthday as
your prince for the last time. (*Pause.*) I am not one of those old men who do
not know that they are old. And even if death does not call me, I intend soon
to pass on the shepherd's staff to my son. My sun has already set, and in the
coolness of twilight I would so gladly survey peacefully the long day's work
once more. I hope my conscience will not show me anything unpleasant.
Indeed, the edge of the grave is the right place for this examination. Every
nation should preserve a history of the last moments of their sovereigns
among the crown jewels. It should always lie open before the throne: that the
ruler may see the trembling of the tyrant who realizes for the first time that he
is only a vassal. But may he see also the calm of the good sovereign, and
bear witness through a good deed that he has seen it. I would have you see
this, my children; you should be present at my deathbed. I hope you will not
be frightened.
AN OLD PEASANT (*with a floral wreath in his hand, presses through the*
COURTIERS): They will not be! Truly, they will not be! Your Highness, I
am a farmer from your village of Ostiola. The common people send you this
wreath as a sign of their love. We can give you nothing better, because we
are so poor we would have starved to death, if you had been like your father.
PRINCE (*gives him his hand*): Oh, that the flowers may stay fresh until I die. I
want it hung over my bed! Their scent would revive a dying man. Take the
wreath, Julius. It also belongs among the crown jewels.
PEASANT (*to* JULIUS): Yes, Your Highness, do as your father did and my son
will someday bring you such a wreath.
JULIUS (*weeps and embraces the* PEASANT): May even your grandson still bring it
to my father, good man.
PEASANT: Your Highness, God protect you and your house.
PRINCE: No, friend, you must not leave without a gift.
PEASANT (*as he leaves*): No, Your Highness, that would make a puppet-show
out of this very serious matter.
PRINCE: My heart is so full. (*Gives a sign; the* COURTIERS *and*
LADIES-IN-WAITING *leave.*) My children, stay here!

Scene Two

PRINCE. JULIUS. GUIDO.

PRINCE: "God protect you and your house." If only a house that is divided among itself could be protected! You do not know a father's pain, my sons; you are not able to know it, but you know nonetheless that it is painful to see the withering of a flower that one oneself has planted and tended. Now imagine in that way the grief of a father who loses his joy in his children.

JULIUS: Father, I hope you are aware that I am not responsible for the dissension.

PRINCE: This joy should requite me for all the sorrow of your upbringing, but now I see ... I believed I sowed pleasure and behold! I reap tears. What may I hope from the future? You already behave in such a manner—what will you do, when love and fear of me no longer hold you back? What emotions do you wish me to feel when I see you at my deathbed? I would bless both of you, but each of you thinks a curse on the other would be a blessing for himself. Oh, Julius! Oh, Guido! The whole world would let these gray hairs rest in peace—only you will not! Only you! I beg of you, dear children, let me die in peace!

JULIUS: I assure you, by all that is holy, I am innocent. You would admire my self-restraint if you heard all the insults he has heaped upon me. Oh, Brother, it tears my heart apart that I must speak so.

GUIDO: And the patience of a martyr could be torn apart if you can speak of insults. No insults, only the truth, which you should hear with restraint. God grant that you could.

PRINCE: Compose yourselves. I know exactly to what degree you are both guilty. But can you deny, Guido, that today you drew your sword against Julius's friend, in an argument over your brother?

GUIDO: I did so, Father, but first my brother and then Aspermonte had wounded my honor so deeply and so cold-bloodedly. I wish you had heard, with what coldness my honor—

PRINCE: Aren't you ashamed to speak of honor against your brother and father? Although this folly drowns out reason, it should nonetheless not stifle the call of blood.

GUIDO: Forgive me, Father. My honor is nothing if it is one thing to one person and another thing to another.

PRINCE: Stop, Guido. I do not like to hear people of your hot-blooded temperament speak of principles. In your impulses you miss the mark as often as others, and you are too much ready to seal each impulsively spoken word with your blood. Now nothing more about it. I shall discuss it with you at a more convenient time ... when you are more good-humored, having returned with glory from a campaign, or having done some other great deed.

GUIDO: May you soon find this opportunity!

PRINCE: I can find it whenever you wish—and you, Julius, can give me a similar one. One of you gives himself airs about his courage, and the other about his philosphy. To overcome your foolish love is an honorable contest for both. Let us see who will be first at the goal. And to think that jealousy can estrange you now. I believed once there was nothing more foolish than your love, but I was wrong: your present passion is still more foolish. It is

211

impossible for either of you to possess Blanca. She is a nun—dead to you both. With no less justification you could love Helen of Troy or Cleopatra. Your love is thus a nullity. And yet you are jealous? Jealousy without love—that means to drink no wine, yet behave with all the foolishness of a drunkard. Or do you believe love finds nothing impossible? Try it, but here you shall find everything that can stop man: vows and religion, bars and walls. Reflect on this, Julius, and stop your mourning.

JULIUS: I have not yet mourned so long as a widower does for his wife—and you did say that Blanca was dead. My sorrow is not the hair-tearing at the coffin, only the tears at the tombstone. Have patience with my weakness, Father.

PRINCE: I have, but if I continue to, my patience will also become a weakness. Awake and be what you can be! You are not a woman; love is not your entire destiny. You are a prince and must sacrifice your desires to those of the Tarentines.

JULIUS: The Tarentines demand too much.

PRINCE: Not too much, my son—nothing more than an even exchange. You give them your desires and they give you their fame. In a century you, the prince, will be the only one of all the Tarentines to be remembered, like a city that disappears with distance, leaving only its towers in sight—nevertheless, every forgotten Tarentine was a part of the state. Without them you could not have been a prince; every one worked for you, added a stone to the pillar of honor on which you finally write your name.

JULIUS: But Father! Suppose I sought only a private life, as eagerly as love does a dark myrtle bush. In that way I would exchange shadows for an actual good.

GUIDO: Brother, you talk like a dreamer.

PRINCE: Julius, Julius, you have sunk low. But I don't want to become angry. I see it is still too early to speak reasonably with you. Reasons are a mighty remedy, but the sickness in you has not yet hit its peak. You're behaving like people who cannot see because they've been staring too long at the same place.

JULIUS: I shall force myself, Father, to fight a battle that will cost me dearly.

PRINCE: Oh, Son, should this gray head have no power over you? Are my wrinkles nothing against your charming features, my tears nothing against your smile, my grave nothing against your bed?

JULIUS: Oh, my father!

PRINCE: Julius, these are not the tears of a woman, these are the tears of a father—and I also shed them for you, Guido. You are going the same way as your brother. Why do you stand there so silently? I beg of you, dear children, make me happy and embrace each other. Even if it's only halfhearted, a play performed on my birthday. I shall deceive myself; a deceived audience still sheds tears of joy at the play. (JULIUS and GUIDO embrace.) I have not had such a great pleasure in a long time. (He embraces them both.) I beg of you, my children, let this gray head go in peace to the grave.

Scene Three

GUIDO. JULIUS.

GUIDO: Julius, can you bear a father's tears? I cannot.

JULIUS: Ah, Brother, how could I?

GUIDO: My whole soul is in turmoil. I could wish for the tumult of battle to become myself again. Can a tear do all that? Ah, what sort of strange wonderful thing is courage? I could almost say it is not strength of soul, merely knowledge of the circumstances. And if that is true, I ask you, what sets a hero disturbed by a tear above a woman who runs from a spider?

JULIUS: Brother, how this tone pleases me!

GUIDO: Not me. How can my weakness please me? I feel that I am not Guido. Truly I tremble—perhaps I have a fever. If so, I shall soon become myself again.

JULIUS: Strange, that a man is ashamed that his temperament is stronger than his principles.

GUIDO: Let us not speak of it further! My present mood could disappear, and I wish to make use of it! One must carry out certain decisions now, lest we regret not having done so later. You know, Brother, that I love Blanca and have pledged my honor to possess her. But these tears make me hesitant.

JULIUS: You fill me with amazement.

GUIDO: I believe my honor will be satisfied if no one else possesses her, if she stays as she is—for who can be jealous of Heaven? But you see that if I give up my claim, you must give up yours, and all your plans of setting her free someday. Let us do so, and be again brothers and sons! How our father shall rejoice when he sees us reach the goal together, when we each return from our contest victorious, and neither conquered. And we must do it *now*, today, on his birthday!

JULIUS: Ah, Guido!

GUIDO: A decisive answer!

JULIUS: I can't.

GUIDO: You can't? Then neither can I. But from now on I am innocent of those paternal tears. I swear it, I am innocent. I too had my share of them, he said so. But here I throw my share on you. Yours is the whole legacy of tears and curses!

JULIUS: You are wrong. Do you believe that a passion is laid aside as easily as a whim, that one can put love on and off like a suit of armor? Whether I want . . . whether I want . . . who loves, wants to love, and nothing else. Love is the mainspring in this machine. Have you ever seen a machine so absurdly made that it drives a wheel to destroy itself and yet remains a machine?

GUIDO: Extraordinarily fine, extraordinarily profound—but our poor father will die!

JULIUS: If that happens, you shall be his murderer. Your jealousy will kill him. You said you could give up your claim if you wanted. Aren't you confessing then that you don't love her and are just persisting out of stubbornness? Your surrender would not have been virtue, but your persistence is a vice!

GUIDO: Bravo! Bravo! That was unexpected.

JULIUS: What do you mean to—

GUIDO: First, I am pleased to see that wisdom is as much a sleek, supple nymph as is justice, equally likely to enter special pleadings for a good friend. I could give up my claim if I wished? If honor wished! That is the spring in my machine! You can do nothing without consulting love, I nothing without consulting honor. We can do nothing for ourselves; that, I believe, renders us equals.

JULIUS: Has something so unfair ever before been spoken? To compare the highest motive of human nature with the whim of a fool!

GUIDO: A fool? You're raving! I scorn you, you stand so far below me! I thought my being disturbed by tears a weakness. But the lowest level of my weakness is higher than your courage ever rose!

JULIUS: It has always been your failing to judge feelings you have never known.

GUIDO: And yours always to blather till doomsday about virtue! Even when you attain your heart's desire and see your father on the bier, instead of resting after your labors, you'll be teaching the pallbearers what virtue is or what it isn't.

JULIUS: How wrong I have been! You are back to your usual tone!

GUIDO: You're hoping he dies! Can you deny it? Do you think that I don't see that you're planning to kidnap the girl from the convent then? It's true that then you'll be Prince of Tarento, and I nothing—but a man. But your tender little brain would burst if it but suspected all the vitality a man is capable of. Thank God that there are swords and that I have an arm. An arm that if worse comes to worst can tear a girl from the fragile grasp of a weakling! You shall not have her in peace: I shall make a compact with the ghost of our father. He shall howl at your bed.

JULIUS: I like no more than our father to hear from you what you will do in passion. (*Leaves.*)

Scene Four

GUIDO: Fine, if you want an eternal war, you can have one. My plan shall stand as it is! I was born to war. Nothing changes except that I shall take Blanca's name as a battlecry! But your plan, Julius, shall be changed; you shall not calmly dally your life away with her! The fear of your rival shall always follow you. I shall place a reminder in your soul that will for all eternity cry out, "Guido!" Yes, cry out, "Guido!" as clearly as the conscience of the murderer of his father cries out "Murder!" I shall brand your every thought with my name, and when you see Blanca you shall not think of her, but of me! In the middle of your embraces suddenly my image will appear in your mind, and your kisses will tremble on your lips like doves over whom an eagle hovers. At night you will see in dreams how I may abduct her from you, and you will start up so frightened that Blanca will fall out of your arms. You shall awaken screaming, "Guido!" (*Leaves.*)

214

Scene Five

ASPERMONTE (*enters*): I must not let him out of my sight for a minute this month. A month is such a short time in which to put together a shattered fantasy! Nonetheless I could barely obtain this much. The best of it is that I know the path I have to follow. His head is no longer an impartial judge. I must appeal to his heart.

JULIUS (*enters hurriedly*): It's good that I find you here, Aspermonte. Get me some trustworthy people and a ship. Hurry, I leave here with Blanca tonight.

ASPERMONTE: Your Highness—

JULIUS: Ha, Aspermonte, no panegyrics to wise princes and worthy rulers! I am tired of them. You could offer me undying glory, glory with no limit, and the stars as my companions! I'm leaving with Blanca—no arguments! My brother is right; I have blathered when I should have acted.

ASPERMONTE: Is the month already gone? And have you no longer a father?

JULIUS: I told you—no matter, I shall once more set aside my resolve not to think about the matter again. I have seen my father cry, and those tears have not caused me to waver in my resolution. Perhaps I was infinitesimally weakened, but the infinitesimal is no matter here! There is no point in waiting out the month. What can happen in my life to weaken my resolution if the tears of my father did not?

ASPERMONTE: I would not be so quick to maintain that.

JULIUS: Hear me out. You should not pass judgment on my individual motives, but on all of them taken together. Guido has provided me a view into my soul that makes me shudder. I shall confess to you, when I gave up the thought of kidnapping Blanca today, I thought merely of waiting until after my father's death, a time I should no more think of than wish for. God, I cannot bear this idea of awaiting my own happiness at my father's death! And when I think of it . . . I . . . you know, I have never harped on this . . . that it was my father who had Blanca put in the convent—I must get away from here, I must, not to dishonor my father.

ASPERMONTE: I love these virtuous motives, but you have not convinced me.

JULIUS: If I don't tear Blanca from her prison, Guido will. He has boasted of it, and we can take him at his word. Aspermonte, I tremble at what may take place—in this hall of my father could run the blood of his sons.

ASPERMONTE: The danger doesn't yet seem so urgent that you still couldn't delay some time.

JULIUS: Can I delay for a longer time, while this perfection decays in the convent, while every day the pain shakes more of her grace and charm from her, like leaves from a tree! Should she still longer sigh over me and try out of high-mindedness to hide it from herself that I am the cause? Oh, the softer these hidden sighs in St. Justinia's Abbey, the louder they ring in the ears of revenge! Brute, I can tell from your coldness you plan to abandon me. What I said was true: princes have no friends! Fine, I'll go alone.

ASPERMONTE: I'm going with you.

JULIUS (*embraces him*): Oh, you have never taken me so tenderly to your heart. I feel already that I have ceased to be a prince.

ASPERMONTE: I shall go now to take care of our business. Do not forget your valuables: they must constitute your future livelihood. But where should we go?

JULIUS: That I leave to you.

ASPERMONTE: I have a friend in a distant corner of Germany who would take us in.

JULIUS: May Germany be the sanctuary of love! Hurry! In the meantime I shall ride and say farewell to my paternal lands.

Scene Six

BLANCA's *cell*
BLANCA sits at a table on which there are books and religious articles.
She reads from a tome.

BLANCA: I cannot go on; my devotions are sinful. Julius! Your face is always in my thoughts! (*Closes the book and rises.*) This change from Matins to Vespers, from longing and regret—is this what they call life? And youth, the springtime of life? God, what will give my soul peace? To unite these feelings that battle each other, and these thoughts that call one another lies? (*Pause.*) Nothing but death! My sweetest thought, after Julius. In the days of joy I thought otherwise . . . thought that death would not alter love. I have never felt my immortality so strongly as in Julius's arms. I felt that my love was eternal, thus I thought that my spirit must also be. But now that I know its agony, my obstinate eyes will not shut. No, no, love dies. (*She reads a few moments, but soon closes the book.*) Ah, I have already felt the delights of devotion; it is with love the first emotion of human nature. Are they not similar, different words to the same tune? I believed myself so strong, feet so firmly on the ground—his face, his face! I sank back fully and saw with astonishment that I had hardly sunk back a step. Poor Blanca! (*Cries.*)

Scene Seven

ABBESS (*enters*): Good evening, Sister. What are you doing?

BLANCA: I'm crying.

ABBESS: Don't be in too much of a hurry. You'll need tears for a long time.

BLANCA: For a long time? But aren't tears against our vows?

ABBESS: I hope not. The weak mortal soul can only promise deeds, not feelings.

BLANCA: Good. I am a woman, and if I am not that, what should I be? I envy no saint. I do not begrudge them their incense, splendor, and palms. Let their images stand always with those of the angels on the altar, or be carried in processions. Let their miracles fill many a book. But rest assured, Reverend Abbess, not one of those women has loved as I have! Else we would have just this one legend of her: she was a martyr to the agony of love.

ABBESS: You are right, a saint is merely a beautiful aberration of Nature.

BLANCA: I may cry then? From today on I am less unfortunate.

ABBESS: But be moderate, child, one can distract oneself.

BLANCA: Distract? My soul was not made for distraction. Even when I was still alive, I had only one thought. What should distract me? In my thoughts that seem to be of devotion, Julius lies hidden. The contemplation of eternity! Eternity is the duration of love. Just see how the moon is shining! You see it as a shining heavenly body. I see it only as the witness to my first kiss. A memento of my love that none can take from me. Welcome, dear moon!

ABBESS: As with my Ricardo. (*She presses* BLANCA's *hand. Pause.*)

BLANCA: How long does a woman in love cry here before the last hope dies, the hope built on the slightest possibility?

ABBESS: Ah, hope never dies. But the woman does.

BLANCA: Can you give me examples? (*Embraces the* ABBESS.) Tell me her name! Before the day breaks I shall honor her grave with roses and daisies and tears.

ABBESS: Save the roses and tears. Soon you will need them for my grave.

BLANCA: No, Reverend Abbess, your tears and roses for me! I shall make a compact with death to think up tortures for me! Such sighs these walls have never heard. Augustine will have to confess his rule was mildness. Saints, reconciled to love through me, shall turn their faces away out of sympathy—and martyrs out of shame!

ABBESS: Daughter, your fantasy is becoming wild!

BLANCA: Roses and tears for me! The nature bent so far will break at last.

ABBESS: Come, it is time for prayers. We are always the last at choir.

BLANCA: Ha! When the soul, free for the first time, flutters over the high cathedral! I would need centuries before I could again feel joy, especially eternal joy. Reverend Abbess, if you bring the promised offerings to my mortal remains, and you hear a gentle whisper, remember, it is saying in earthly language: "Soon, Sister, roses and tears for you."

ABBESS (*as she leaves*): Ah, this vault has heard such cries for centuries!

Act Four
Scene One

The palace

JULIUS: To abandon forever . . . forever! If only I had known that this feeling would be so strong! But I had thought only of my union with Blanca, not of separation from father and fatherland. To abandon a father on the brink of death! How he will suffer until he learns my fate! Yet when he learns it, will he be happier, exchanging uncertain anguish for certain grief? Never again to see you, Tarento! Nowhere else will the sun shine so brightly or the flowers bloom so sweetly! Never again the joy of returning to you after travel! Never to hear the cry of jubilation from the crew when they see the coast of the fatherland! Never again to see the towers of Tarento shining in the evening sun, and to set spurs to my horse! Never again shall I find gathered at one table all whom I love! Never again shall I hear my father say, "God bless you, my children." Some of these bonds I possessed even before I first entered the world; now I tear myself from them all for the sake of a woman! For the sake of a mortal woman! No, not for a mortal woman, for you, Blanca! You are my fatherland, father, mother, brother, and friend!

Scene Two

JULIUS. ASPERMONTE.

JULIUS: How goes it, Aspermonte?

ASPERMONTE: All preparations are complete. The rising sun shall find us already at sea.

JULIUS: What is your plan?

ASPERMONTE: I have twenty men assembled, and plan to divide them into two troops. With one we'll attack the abbey and kidnap Blanca. The other will wait for us with the travel equipment at the garden gate. A ship lies ready and the wind will be excellent.

JULIUS: You have taken pains to assure Blanca's comfort?

ASPERMONTE: As if she were my own beloved.

JULIUS: I thank you, but dear Aspermonte, I have never so deeply felt what fatherland is than at this instant.

ASPERMONTE: Your Highness, there is time! Don't abandon Tarento if you do so unwillingly!

JULIUS: I leave it as a wise man does life: gladly but with involuntary shivers nonetheless—and there is no remedy against those.

ASPERMONTE: Have you taken your farewell ride?

JULIUS: Yes, and these melancholy feelings are its fruit. I fixed deep within me the image of all this region. When I am far away, it will be so pleasant to wander through my paternal lands in thought. They shall be the stuff of my dreamy evenings to come. I swear to you, there is no brook here, no grove, no hillock that does not summon up memories from my childhood or youth. Little events all, but more precious to the man who experiences them than all of world history.

ASPERMONTE: The lemon-grove where you saw Blanca for the first time, and where you so often dreamed—have you forgotten it?

JULIUS: How could I, Aspermonte, how could I? I spent a few more priceless moments there. If I could take anything from this land with me, it would be this grove. At the end, I sought my father's tomb. A true image of the power of sovereigns, I thought, when I saw the silver coffins and the rotted banners! They suffer the same fate as all other men, save for the tinsel that accompanies them everywhere. The handful of dust in this coffin, formerly Theodoric the Great, loved the skull in that one, formerly the beautiful Agnese! They can sleep calmly now, and need no chamberlain in the antechamber whispering, "Hush." Their choking stench is like the stench from a beggar's grave, and no flatterer could say it smells lovely. Theodoric's dog rots just as well as Theodoric, even though the dog's grave bears no rusty scepter. Hm! I thought: I shall likewise moulder, even if in the family crypt.

ASPERMONTE: Your observations are correct, but others may be made about these circumstances that are equally correct. Granted, the position of a prince has its tinsel—it is nonetheless the position for which your great soul was created. You do not despise positions that lack the tinsel, since it is incidental. But it is also incidental for the princes! Julius! You were destined to establish the happiness of many thousands! Should your entire goal now be the pleasure and diversion of just one woman?

JULIUS: You anger me, Aspermonte! But speak on, I am no longer a prince.

ASPERMONTE: I say these things to you to remind you that a prince can have a friend. Consider again the exchange: father and fatherland for a woman!

JULIUS: I am unyielding even on the rack: your arguments can torture me, but not defeat my resolution. You are right, I am sacrificing father and fatherland for her. But is a lesser sacrifice worthy of Blanca? When for her sake I feel the loss of these dear regions, it will seem to me that they have been fused into her. Father and fatherland I shall love through her. I am jealous of my own love; no other objects should divide it in my soul. Everything that can arouse my nature to feeling should be subordinated to her.

ASPERMONTE: One more observation, Your Highness! If you only ceased to work for your subjects' happiness, you could be excused. But you are working towards their unhappiness. By your decision, Guido is their future sovereign.

JULIUS: I am leaving! Perhaps your resolve has weakened?

ASPERMONTE: No, Your Highness, not if yours has not. I follow.

JULIUS: Where shall we meet tonight?

ASPERMONTE: At St. Eleanor's church at eleven o'clock. I'll send a disguise to you shortly.

JULIUS: Still one hard task ahead of me: the farewell to my father. Imagine, to take an eternal farewell from him, without his knowing. See, I am so steadfast in my resolve that I do not fear to look upon him at our meeting—but my whole being will tremble.

ASPERMONTE: Compose yourself; he's coming. I cannot bear to see him. (*Leaves.*)
JULIUS: Heaven, now and in the hour of my death, help me!

Scene Three

PRINCE, JULIUS, *very serious throughout the scene.*

PRINCE: Still this melancholy demeanor, Julius? Can you not find one happy expression for your father on his birthday?—But enough of that. I ask your forgiveness if I spoke to you too harshly before.
JULIUS (*gently taking the old man's hand*): Father—
PRINCE: Oh, my heart melts when I look at you. My days of planning are over, my youth, where one wish led to a thousand more, where in a single seed a whole forest lay dormant. There is no longer a future for me. My only wish is to see you happy and great. (*Pause.*) Julius, do not deprive me of the delightful prospect that someday the blessing of my subjects, which I leave to you, will be passed on even greater from you to your successor. That at the mention of your name the future princes of Tarento will feel their hearts throb, in their desire to emulate you. Doesn't the thought make you drunk with joy: that through emulation of your deeds, others will behave nobly? That inspired by your fame, your children will become famous, as one fire starts another, without itself being extinguished? (*Pause.* JULIUS *stands, deep in thought. The* PRINCE *embraces him.*) Away with this melancholy face, firstborn of my love, who made my wife dearer to me, the first to babble the name "Father" to me. My firstborn, to whom I give my greatest blessing!
JULIUS: Oh, Father, give me now this blessing!
PRINCE (*lays his hand on* JULIUS's *head*): Be wise! (JULIUS *kisses the* PRINCE's *hand warmly and leaves.*)
PRINCE: Oh, my son, why do you flee the face of your father?

Scene Four

PRINCE. ARCHBISHOP.

PRINCE: God! Nonetheless I shall force myself. I have done much, managed much today. I have earned a pleasant evening—if only I could have one! (*The* ARCHBISHOP *enters.*) Brother, I am in a proper mood for a birthday . . . festive-melancholy. Let's open a bottle.
ARCHBISHOP: As you wish.
PRINCE: This is the mood in which wine shows us it is a gift from heaven. It unites the best of sadness and joy. (*During this dialogue, a* SERVANT *brings*

glasses and a bottle of wine.) Ho, Thomas, set the table across from the picture of Anchises and Aeneas. (*They sit.*) Here, Brother, I have spent my most pleasant hours. Do you remember how our father dubbed me knight under this picture?

ARCHBISHOP: As if it were today. I asked him afterwards for a sword, too, but he gave me the book on which you had sworn, and said it was the sword of a cleric.

PRINCE (*who throughout this speech has been staring at the picture*): I was almost like Ascanius then. Now I am like Anchises . . . soon I shall awaken and say: "I dreamt I was the Prince of Tarento." (*Pours the wine.*) If only I don't depart amidst horrors!

ARCHBISHOP: To the health of our house and of our people! (*They drink.*) You worry too much. Look over your day's work now. In evening all that one has planted smells the sweetest. What has the night to do with you?

PRINCE: Ah, my sons!

ARCHBISHOP: Pardon me, Brother, but you have worried too much ever since the time you did look like Ascanius. And now look about you! Isn't your life to be envied?

PRINCE: You're right . . . until now.

ARCHBISHOP: Have you not made your subjects happy? And without fanfare, without revolution? Through a simple life in which almost every day was like the next. Few of your individual deeds could be immortalized, but your life in its entirety could. (*They drink.*)

PRINCE: Don't try to flatter me. I know more than anyone how my deeds pale against my former ambitions.

ARCHBISHOP: Of course a higher beauty lies in our brains than in our deeds, but you can still be content. (*They drink.*) Do you believe our little celebration here is the only one in the land? Every peasant has killed a chicken. I know that at one such meal, the old people talked so much about you that a child finally asked: "What is a prince?" His mother knew how to answer him; she said: "A prince is for many thousands what your father is for you and me."

PRINCE: I thank Heaven that I was given such a small land, that the business of my government is domestic tranquility. Do you think, Brother, that our personal household will ever give me as much joy as the well-being of our people?

ARCHBISHOP: Most certainly.

PRINCE: I want to be truly content tonight. Forget that I am a father . . . by Heaven! I want to be content. If I could only celebrate my next birthday with my children—and Cecelia would be Julius's wife! The woman is my ideal. Brother, the little cleverness I have cost me seventy-six years; take a day off the time, and you take away from the cleverness. But wisdom and beauty both bloomed overnight in this eighteen-year-old girl. Growths from different climates, growing in the same bed so close that their colors mix with each other. And modesty—these dear blossoms shrink from the rays of the sun and exhale their sweetest fragrance in the shade. A young man who has seen her must scorn the women of the court with their shameful combination of cosmetics and joking.

ARCHBISHOP: Brother, you're declaiming! Are you Ascanius or Anchises?

PRINCE: If only Julius sensed her charms! The bottle's not empty yet. Let me propose a toast most seemly for old men: to a glorious end! (*They drink.*)

Scene Five
A street. In the distance, St. Justinia's Abbey.
GUIDO, *a* SERVANT, *both masked*

GUIDO (*removing his mask*): How can you be sure of that?

SERVANT: Quite certainly, Your Highness, they cannot yet be here. Your brother left the palace scarcely five minutes before us.

GUIDO: Oh, that is why the boy paid so little heed to my promise. Should I be nothing to Blanca? Not even a rival, not even a background to show off her beauty? By God! Look, is that his band approaching St. Justinia's?

SERVANT: Yes, Your Highness.

GUIDO: Let us go a bit over to the side, and don't you dare raise a finger. I alone shall scatter them; and no one, from Julius right down to the fellow who carries the torch, should afterward see my face without blushing.

Scene Six

JULIUS, ASPERMONTE *with armed men. All are masked.*

ASPERMONTE: Let us wait here. We could not have asked for a better night. How beautifully shines the moon!

JULIUS: Marvelous. I have never heard the nightingale sing more delicately or the cricket chirp more pleasantly.

ASPERMONTE: You hear it as your wedding-song.

JULIUS: And yet I hear it with some trepidation, more with the uneasy expectation of a bride than the rash lust of a bridegroom.

ASPERMONTE: Compose yourself.

JULIUS: My courage would come back if only there were first some danger and tumult.

ASPERMONTE: Look, the lights are still on in the church. The nuns are at final devotions.

JULIUS: Ah, Blanca has prayed for me. My name in Blanca's voice is heard in heaven! What a thought!

AN ARMED SOLDIER: Look, are those rockets? There over the churchyard wall?

ASPERMONTE: Where? Yes, that means Philip and the others are already at the garden gate! A pistol, Thomas! They may bolt the doors if they see us all here in bright array. I will go ahead alone and take care of the guard.

JULIUS: Do that.

(ASPERMONTE *goes several steps ahead.*)

GUIDO (*leaps, with drawn sword, at* ASPERMONTE): Halt! One does not carry

222

away Guido's beloved so easily!

ASPERMONTE: Is that the voice of a prince or a highwayman?

GUIDO (*tears off his mask*): What! Highwayman?

JULIUS (*who has drawn nearer with the* OTHERS): Calm yourself, Brother! You shall not deter me. Marcellus! Emilius! Restrain him with the halberds!

GUIDO: Restrain me? Guido of Tarento? (*He stabs* JULIUS.)

JULIUS (*as he falls*): Blanca!

ASPERMONTE (*throws himself on the corpse*): Julius, Julius, arise!

GUIDO: Heaven will not deal with me so harshly.

ASPERMONTE (*shouts in the corpse's ear*): Blanca! Blanca! (*Leaps to his feet.*) If he doesn't hear that, he'll never hear again. (*Throws himself again on the corpse.*)

GUIDO: He has just died, for only now the curse of fratricide ran through my limbs! Don't you see the mark of Cain on my forehead, so no one will kill me? Aspermonte, a curse on you and me!

ASPERMONTE (*turns around*): Keep your curses for yourself. I will curse myself enough.

GUIDO: So let the undivided curse be poured over me, and let no thunderstorm wash it away! (*Leaves.*)

ASPERMONTE (*after a pause*): Ah, it was your funeral-song. (*Leaps up and takes* GUIDO's *bloodied dagger.*) Here, Thomas, take this to the old prince. Ask him if it is his and his son's blood. For all that, he is an old man. But I can make myself an old man. (*Draws his sword.*) Marcellus, fetch my horse!

MARCELLUS: Where to, milord?

ASPERMONTE: A fool's question! To Hungary, into the sabres of the infidels!

Act Five
Scene One

The gallery in the palace, dimly lighted. In the background lies JULIUS's *corpse, covered with a shroud, on a bed. A table with a few lamps.*
PRINCE. DOCTOR.

PRINCE: No help! No help! God! Dear doctor, youth is strong, and my seventy-year-old virtue is also strong.
DOCTOR: Oh, Your Highness!
PRINCE: Can nothing help then? Nothing in heaven or on earth? No herb, no balsam, not the life of an old man, nor the blood of a father? Dear doctor, now I believe that sympathy and wonder and all—
DOCTOR: My art is at an end.
PRINCE: Ah, it is difficult to believe ill-fortune. An inner voice still speaks so clearly to the contrary—the voice of conscience as I know it.
DOCTOR: To be sure, it is not easy to be persuaded that a bolt of lightning can destroy in a flash the long-awaited harvest—
PRINCE: And change the soil to stone, for I shall produce no more joy. Good! I am a judge. But . . . nothing can be done, Doctor?
DOCTOR: For the prince, no, but something for you. Come, Your Highness.
PRINCE: For me? You can help me but not my son? Go! Your whole art is a lie! (*Angry.*) Go! (*The* DOCTOR *leaves.*)

Scene Two

PRINCE: I had never dreamed that in the last dregs of my life there would be anything more bitter than death! (*He covers* JULIUS's *face.*) My son! My son! I was so long a father and had to become childless to know what a father is! Here lie my happy plans! Through your children, I thought, I would live on and on; the sweet bond of ancestry would link each generation to the next, connecting me to a distant posterity. Posterity? I shall die childless, unwept! A stranger will close my eyes indifferently, and say at most: "God have mercy on this poor soul, and may he rest in peace." Will the courtier consider it worth the trouble to cry unobserved for the last of a house? Even if I hired mourners and paid for their sighs in advance, they would not bother to keep their word. Shamefully, how shamefully you have fallen! (*He takes the corpse's hand and shakes it.*) But I promise you revenge! Why do you smile, cadaver? Doubt not a father's love! Your murderer is not my son! My wife was an adulteress, and his father a scoundrel. How cold your hand is! Just as coldly shall I sacrifice him to you. His blood will hiss on my hand like boiling water on ice! But is this the tone of a judge? I must compose myself somewhat. A walk under the elms. (*Leaves.*)

Scene Three

BLANCA (*with loosened hair, rushes into the gallery of the palace*): Where, where have they brought you? (*Tears off the shroud and throws herself over the corpse.*) Julius! Julius! Ah, he is really dead. Raise the hue and cry against me! I am his murderess! (*Pause.*) Julius! Julius! Ah, if I could only press all my pain into one cry, he would have to awaken. Why was I born, why was I born? Oh, would that all that is should cease to be! (*Throws herself again over the corpse. Pause. Somewhat more calmly.*) Julius, Julius, when will you ever return my rose-wreath as splendid wedding finery? I too, I too want a memento of your present condition. (*Takes a knife, is about to cut off one of* JULIUS's *locks, but falls again over the corpse.*) Your murderess! Your murderess! (*Pause.*) Compose yourself, Blanca. You have already drained the chalice of sorrow. What you taste now is the dregs. Despair! (*Cuts off a lock and twists it around her finger.*) Here is the engagement-ring I shall give to my grief, pledging not to part from it until death do us part. Is this enough punishment for a murderess? Oh, I shall do what I can. Here I present to you the vow of constant sorrow (*Kisses him.*), here you have all my joy (*Kisses him.*), here you have all my happiness—take it, Julius! His murderess! His murderess! I let the sharp points of these thoughts fall on my soul; death does not understand the gesture.

Scene Four
BLANCA. CECELIA.

CECELIA: You here, Blanca!

BLANCA: Leave me! Leave me! Have you come to steal my pain from me? You will not! You will not! He is now my dearest beloved; now he has no rival.

CECELIA: I have not come to comfort you. I am certainly no messenger from heaven.

BLANCA: (*regards the corpse, meditatively*): His murderess! His murderess!

CECELIA: I beg of you, Blanca, consider what despair is. Come with me. Let your pain stay pain, but I . . . I cannot bear the sight of the corpse.

BLANCA (*who has remained staring at the corpse, in a calm voice*): How can a man so leave the world without a trace, like a smile on the face, or the song of birds in the forest?

CECELIA: Poor unfortunate creature!

BLANCA: See, there he lies in the bosom of the earth. Sun and moon dance their everlasting circles around him; they open and close the fruitful year and he knows not of it! The heart that loved me is dust, capable of nothing more than to be soaked by the rain and dried by the sun—

CECELIA: All of Julius is not dead.

BLANCA: Do you see this lock of hair?

CECELIA: It seems like that of Julius. But, I pray you, why are you rollling your eyes so wildly?

225

BLANCA (*in a lively tone*): Whoever you be, dear girl, rejoice with me! Today, today at last my wedding-day is come! Oh, how dear to me are all my previous torments!

CECELIA: Help, benevolent God, she has gone mad!

BLANCA: But see, it is already midnight. Everything is ready, yet Julius does not come! I ask you, why are the wedding guests so pale? See, how fear makes my hair stand on end so, it pushes off my wedding-wreath. Oh, me, unfortunate bride! There they are bringing Julius's body. (*Points to the corpse.*)

CECELIA (*in anguish*): Don't you know me, Blanca? If the old prince finds her here! Come with me, Blanca!

BLANCA: Mark my words, girl, for I speak the truth. The human race will never die out, but among its thousands, scarcely one will know real love.

CECELIA: Oh, I thought that your repose was a fraud. Love!

BLANCA: Help! Help! The monster that changes its form every moment is devouring me. Into what frightful forms it twists its muscles! A leopard? A tiger? A bear? (*Screams.*) Guido!

CECELIA: I beg you, child, come with me.

BLANCA (*sinking into* CECELIA's *arms*): Dear Cecelia, it is a great misfortune to lose one's mind.

CECELIA: Thank God! I hope this was merely the result of the first shock, without more to follow. But I beg you, come with me!

BLANCA: Ah, I have broken my vow of eternal suffering! Julius appears to me there, the angel with the vial of wrath, whose very aura is death—I have broken my vow of eternal suffering! Pour out your vial! Julius, it is one and the same: destruction or eternal torment! Let none of your palliative tears fall to moderate them!

A NUN (*enters and goes up to* BLANCA): You're here, then, Blanca. We've all been looking for you.

CECELIA: Ah, the unfortunate girl has gone mad. Why did you let her leave the convent?

NUN: Mad! Mad!

CECELIA (*angrily*): Why did you let her leave the convent!

NUN: Truly, we are innocent. She found out the truth at once and wanted to go to him, but we held her back. Then she spent several hours in furious pain. God, I hope never to see anything like that again! Then she became extremely calm. We brought her back to her cell, and so she escaped from us.

BLANCA: Julius, these tremors are unnatural. I see it, I see it, the end of days has come, creation sighs out its breath of life, and all that is dissolves into the elements. Look, Heaven rolls itself up fearfully, like a scroll, and its timid host flees. Night sticks a black banner in the center of the burned-out sun. Julius, Julius, embrace me, so that we may pass away together!

CECELIA: Oh, God! Dear, dear Blanca! Let us leave!

BLANCA (*as she approaches the corpse*): Ha, how calmly he sleeps, the handsome shepherd! Let's make a wreath and set it on the sleeping one's head, so that when he awakens he will search among the shepherdesses for the one who will blush at the sight of him! (*Gently.*) But I am too loud. Ssh! Ssh! Don't wake the handsome shepherd! (*Creeps out with* CECELIA *and the* NUN.)

Scene Five

PRINCE (*thrusting himself into the room, as the* ARCHBISHOP *tries to restrain him*): Let me go! Let me go!

ARCHBISHOP: No, Brother, you may not go into that room. Your pain is too great.

PRINCE: Bring me before a jury of fathers and I shall answer for my pain. But not before a priest! Only a father understands paternal love. Brother, go prattle of books and churches.

ARCHBISHOP: I must not, I must not let you go.

PRINCE: What! This is Tarento, and I am Prince of Tarento! And why need I appeal to that? Is it a right restricted to the sovereign, to tear out his hair at the tomb of his son? Any beggar can do as much.

ARCHBISHOP: I know your heart and shudder at what it now suffers.

PRINCE: Not at all. My pain is indeed quite calm, and here am I at my calmest. I see here on his corpse his calm smile, but he appears far away and with frightful gestures demands of me Blanca and his life.

ARCHBISHOP: Fine, Brother, I shall leave you alone for another half-hour. But then you *will* go, promise me that.

PRINCE: I promise. (*The* ARCHBISHOP *leaves.*) Now I am as I should be. Hey, Thomas! (*A* SERVANT *comes.*) Have you called a priest?

SERVANT: Yes, he's in the antechamber.

PRINCE: Put him in the adjoining room, and call Guido. (*The* SERVANT *leaves.*) Cold, cold, my soul. Let the father not trespass on the office of the judge. That is proper. I will be a judge just a minute, and a father my whole life. (*He removes* GUIDO'*s bloody dagger from under the shroud at* JULIUS'*s feet, and lunges, as if he were stabbing somebody.*) Good, good. The old sinews are stronger than I thought. (*Puts the dagger away again.*)

Scene Six

GUIDO: Here I am, Father. I hate life, but I shall abide by your wishes; you gave it to me. Improve what you have spoiled!

PRINCE: Be quiet. Come closer. (*Meanwhile he uncovers* JULIUS'*s face.*) Do you know the cadaver?

GUIDO: Death to me, Father!

PRINCE: Do you recognize the dead man?

GUIDO: Yes, I know him!

PRINCE (*meanwhile uncovering* GUIDO'*s dagger at* JULIUS'*s feet*): Do you also recognize this?

227

GUIDO: Only in part (*Grabs at it.*) but I shall soon know it thoroughly.

PRINCE (*holds him back*): Heap not sin upon your sin! Cursed be the hour in which I saw my wife for the first time! Cursed be every drop that the wedding guests drank, every round that they danced. Cursed be my wedding bed and its joys!

GUIDO: Don't curse your life! Posterity will utter your name with pride, but if they remember mine, they will have read it on a pillar of shame. Death to me, Father!

PRINCE: Guido, Guido, did I think you would steal two sons from me, when the midwife said to me: "Sir, you have a son," and laid you for the first time in my arms? Ah, Guido, Guido!

GUIDO: Death to me, Father! I am excluded from the temple of glory for all time, and perhaps I am also excluded from the dwelling-place of the saints. Only death can erase my crimes and wash away the mark of sin on my forehead. Death to me, Father!

PRINCE: That I have a father no more! Poor old man! So much unhappiness presses on me, just as much as my brain can bear. Merciful heaven, send down to me a dram more of misfortune! Then I shall see in fantasy my children still united around me. He who is driven insane by a misfortune always sees the opposite happiness. But I am so extraordinarily unfortunate that even that may not happen for me. Yet if I am to spend here one more happy hour, I must needs do it in madness. Right, Guido?

GUIDO (*coldly*): There are more daggers, as well as fire and water, mountains and chasms. (*Is about to leave.*)

PRINCE: You must die! As the father of my subjects I cannot allow innocent blood to stick to the land and summon war and pestilence and all scourges. By my hands, those of your sovereign, you must die. And so that you may be ready, a priest is waiting in the next room for you.

GUIDO: I shall return momentarily. (*Leaves.*)

Scene Seven

PRINCE: Truly, it is day. I thought it would never be bright again. (*He takes the dagger.*) I punish Guido! And who put Blanca in the convent? (*Examines the point of the dagger.*) Ha, I am greedy for you. If you could cut a soul in pieces as easily as you cut the bond between soul and body! But who will guarantee that this story will not return to me a million times in eternal torture? (*Sticks the dagger in his pocket.*) Go, plaything, you are not in the least better than any other comfort in the world! Suicide is a sin! But we can torture you without suicide, Constantine! We can torture you. Even my inclination to melancholy I would like to be able to hate. Inclination itself is a pleasure! How cunning pleasure is! But this one, I think, will chase the others away. I shall always want to see this story, to have it painted, painted often. The first rays of the sun should fall on one painting and the last rays fall on another. They shall awaken me with the name of Julius one day and with the name of Guido the next. I want to write a ballad of all this misery, and Blanca should sing it to me at midnight.

Scene Eight

PRINCE. GUIDO.

PRINCE: So quickly, Guido? Has Heaven forgiven you?

GUIDO: I hope so.

PRINCE (*embracing him*): I forgive you as well! Bring Julius this kiss of peace.

GUIDO (*throws himself over the corpse*): Only now may I approach you. Linger, linger, martyr. If you are not yet in the dwelling of the saints, hide me, a sinner, in your radiance, that I may pass in with you!

PRINCE: Embrace me once more, my son! (*Embraces him with one arm and stabs him with the other hand.*) My son! My son!

GUIDO (*falls over the corpse and grips its hand*): Reconciliation, my brother! (*Extends the other hand wordlessly to his* FATHER.)

PRINCE (*falls over the dead* GUIDO, *lies over him for some time, then rises and paces despairingly back and forth.*) Yes! Yes! I'm still alive! (*Again paces back and forth.*)

Scene Nine

PRINCE. ARCHBISHOP.

ARCHBISHOP: Brother! What have you done!

PRINCE: Administered my supreme judicial office for the last time. Now give the Carthusians a mandate to take me in. You assume control of the government for now, and let the King of Naples know that he may have my principality.

ARCHBISHOP: Consider your age and what the Carthusians are.

PRINCE: My house has fallen. The young orange-trees with blossoms and fruit are cut down. It would be a shameful sight if I, a withered old trunk, stood there alone. Pain already has devoted me to the Carthusians. *Memento mori.*

ARCHBISHOP: I beseech you, consider your responsibility to the land, and the harshness of the Neapolitan regime!

PRINCE: *Memento mori.*

ARCHBISHOP (*embraces him*): My brother, my brother!

229

The texts of the plays in this translation were taken from *Sturm und Drang. Dramatische Schriften*, ed. Erich Loewenthal. 3rd. ed. 2 vols. Heidelberg: Lambert Schneider, 1972.